Social History of Canada

Allan Greer and Craig Heron, general editors

Making Law, Order, and Authority in British Columbia, 1821–1871

In 1821 British Columbia was the exclusive domain of an independent Native population and the Hudson's Bay Company. By the time it entered Confederation some fifty years later, a British colonial government was firmly in place. In this book Tina Loo recounts the shaping of the new regime.

The history of pre-Confederation British Columbia is a spirited one, rich in lore and tales of adventure surrounding the fur trade, conflict between settlers and the Hudson's Bay Company, and, above all, the gold rush. Loo takes the familiar themes as a starting-point for fresh investigation. Her inquiry moves from the disciplinary practices of the Hudson's Bay Company, through the establishment of courts in the gold fields, to conflicts over the role of juries and the nature of property. By detailing specific incidents and then drawing from a wide historical field to sketch in new background, she has revised established history.

Loo structures her analysis of events around the discourse of laissez-faire liberalism and shows how this discourse styled the law and order of the period. She writes with wit and elegance, bringing life to even the most technical aspects of her investigation. This is the first comprehensive legal history of British Columbia before Confederation.

Tina Loo is a member of the Department of History, Simon Fraser University.

TINA LOO

Making Law, Order, and Authority in British Columbia, 1821–1871

UNIVERSITY OF TORONTO PRESS
Toronto Buffalo London

© University of Toronto Press Incorporated 1994
Toronto Buffalo London
Printed in Canada

ISBN 0-8020-2961-2 (cloth)
ISBN 0-8020-7784-6 (paper)

∞

Printed on acid-free paper

Canadian Cataloguing in Publication Data

Loo, Tina Merrill, 1962–
  Making law, order, and authority in British
Columbia, 1821–1871

(The Social history of Canada ; 50)
Includes bibliographical references and index.
ISBN 0-8020-2961-2 (bound) ISBN 0-8020-7784-6 (pbk.)

1. Law – British Columbia – History – 19th century. 2. Sociological
jurisprudence – History – 19th century. I. Title. II. Series.

KEB165.L66 1994   3409.11590971109034
KF345.L66 1994   C94-930571-5

Social History of Canada 50

University of Toronto Press acknowledges the financial assistance to its publishing program of the Canada Council and the Ontario Arts Council.

This book has been published with the help of a grant from the Social Science Federation of Canada, using funds provided by the Social Sciences and Humanities Research Council of Canada.

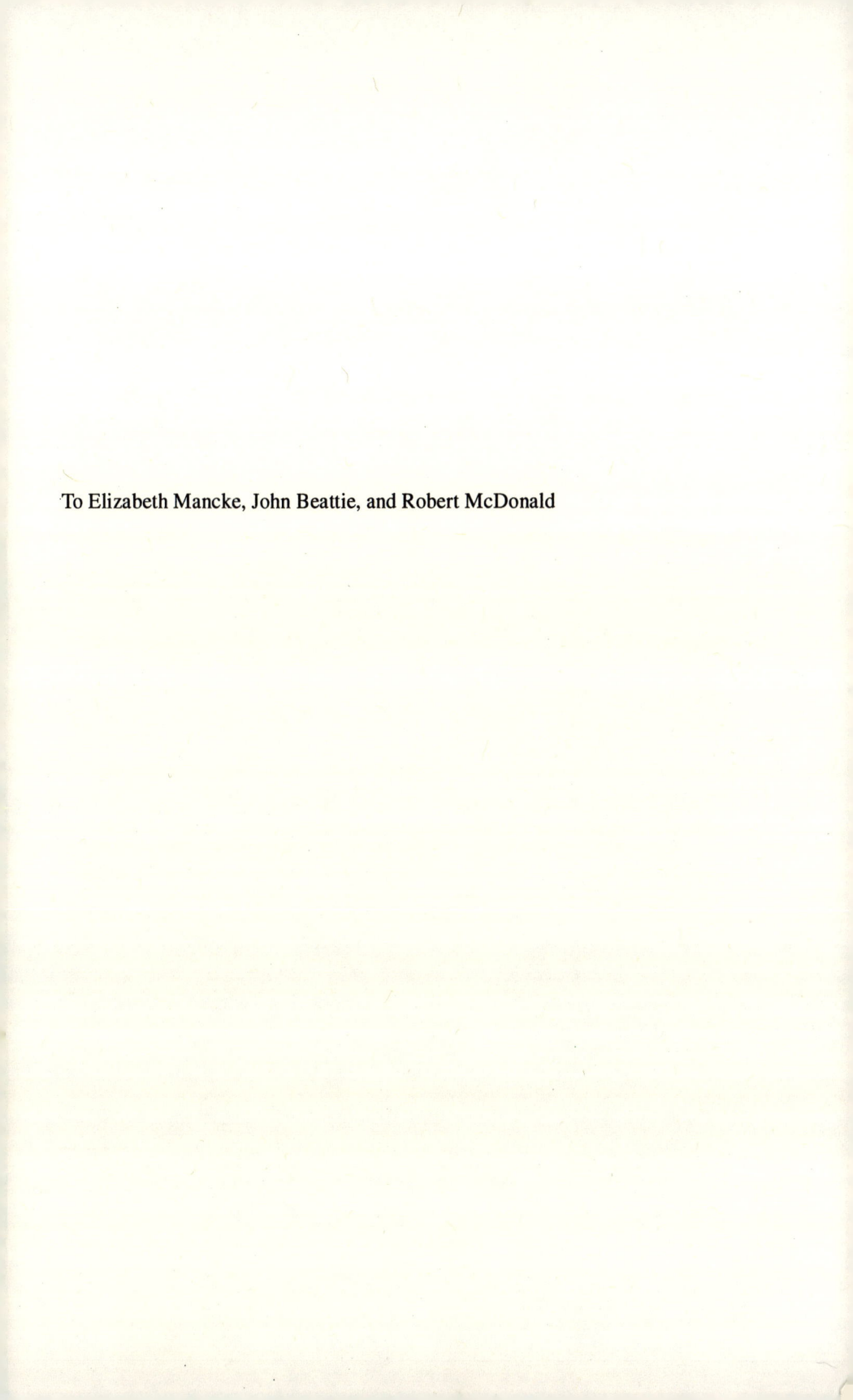

To Elizabeth Mancke, John Beattie, and Robert McDonald

Contents

TABLES AND FIGURE ix

ACKNOWLEDGMENTS xi

Introduction: Rethinking Law, Order, and Authority 3

1
'Club Law' and Order in British Columbia's Fur Trade 18

2
'A Squatocracy of Skin Traders': Law and Authority on Vancouver Island 34

3
Property, Geography, and British Columbia's Courts 54

4
'A California Phase': Civil Litigation, Economy, and Society in British Columbia 73

5
Cranford v. Wright: Law and Authority in British Columbia 93

6
The Meaning of Law and the Limits of Authority on Grouse Creek 113

7
Bute Inlet Stories: Law, Crime, and Colonial Identity 134

Conclusion: Law and the Limits of Liberalism 157

APPENDIX 163

NOTES 165

BIBLIOGRAPHY 215

INDEX 235

PHOTO CREDITS 240

Tables and Figure

Table 1   Anti- and pro-Cameron petitioners, 1854   50

Table 2   County Court actions, 1858–71   79

Table 3   Richfield Mining Court actions, 1864–71   81

Table 4   Value of County Court actions, 1858–71   83

Table 5   Cost of County Court actions, 1858–71   84

Table 6   County Court decisions, 1858–71   86

Table 7   Richfield Mining Court decisions, 1864–71   87

Figure 1   Gold production and civil suits in British Columbia, 1858–71   78

Acknowledgments

Though the act of writing is usually a solitary enterprise, finishing a manuscript is the product of a collective effort. In the course of writing this book I have benefited from the advice, support, good humour, and distraction of, and the occasional dressing down from, a number of people and institutions whose efforts it is a pleasure to acknowledge. As the first incarnation of this manuscript was a dissertation, I would like to thank my committee, Peter Ward, Robert McDonald, and Jim Winter, as well as the other members of the examining board, Alan C. Cairns, David H. Flaherty, and Allan Smith, for their sometimes relentless but always careful questions and valuable insights.

Transforming the thesis into a book was made easier because of the efforts of my editor, Laura Macleod, and the comments provided by Allan Greer, editor of the Social History of Canada series, and two anonymous reviewers.

I would also like to acknowledge the kind assistance of the staff at the British Columbia Archives and Records Service, particularly Indiana Matters and Brent McBride; the University of British Columbia's Government Publications and Special Collections Divisions of the Main Library; and the National Archives of Canada.

The Social Sciences and Humanities Research Council of Canada, the Native Daughters of British Columbia, the Faculty of Graduate Studies at the University of British Columbia, the President's Office at Simon Fraser University, and the Social Science Federation of Canada all provided financial support at various stages of this project. My colleagues in the History Department at Simon Fraser University generously allowed me time away from teaching to complete this manuscript, and the Centre of Criminology at the University of Toronto provided me with a conducive atmosphere in which to do so.

As important as those formal networks were, I also benefited considerably from the care and interest of a number of other people who have allowed me to bend their ears and otherwise helped along the way: Lois Kelly, Susan Lewthwaite, Derek Loo, Mary Loo, Katherine Ridout, Louise Robert, Clifford Shearing, Erwin Sui, and Alan Tully all have my thanks and appreciation.

In what follows, much will be made about the process of 'making' law, order, and authority. Given this, it seems only appropriate to recognize three friends who have been particularly important in the 'making' of this historian. Elizabeth Mancke, John Beattie, and Robert McDonald have each, in different ways, shown me what it means to be a scholar and an academic. For that I am grateful.

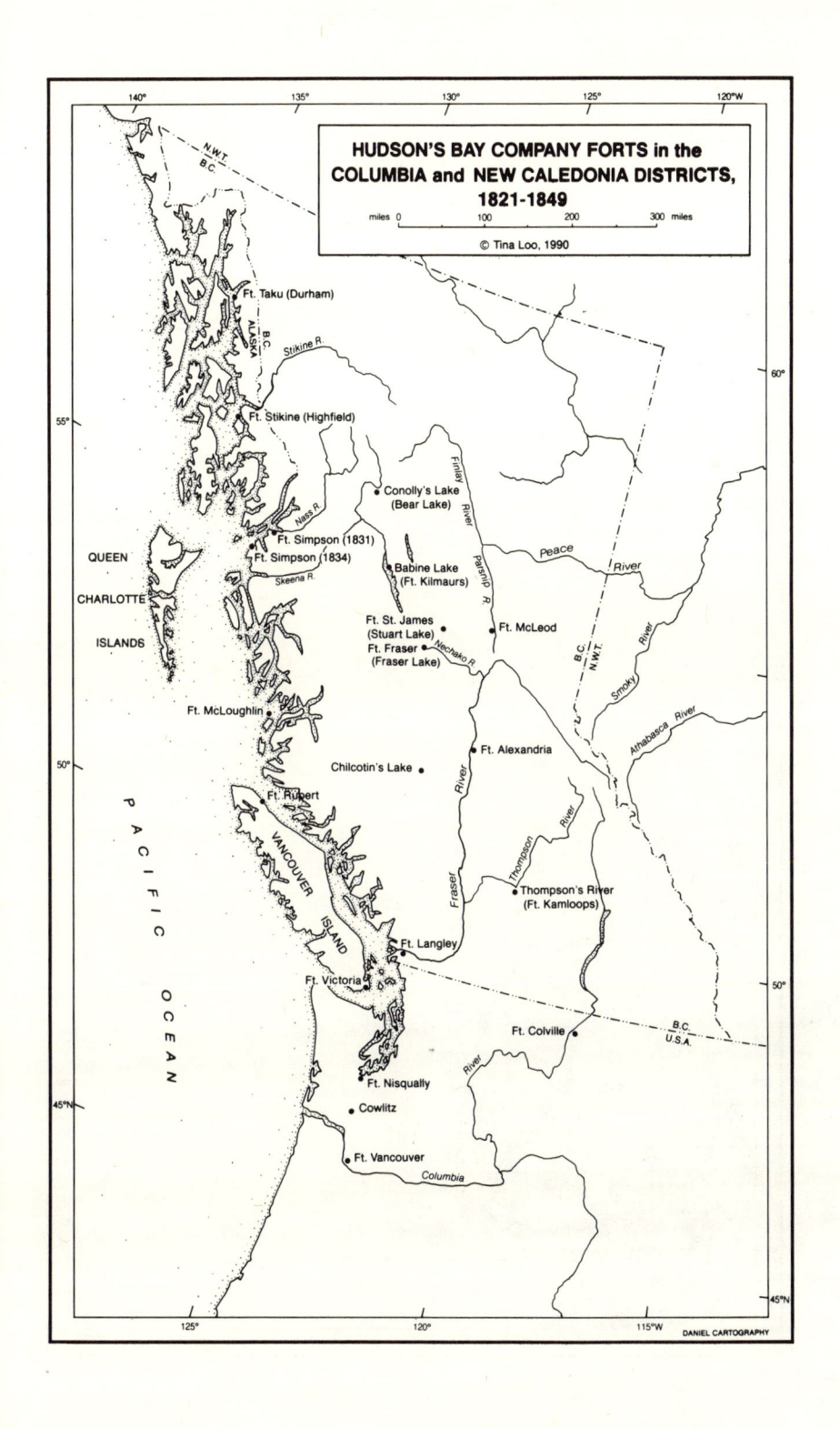

HUDSON'S BAY COMPANY FORTS in the COLUMBIA and NEW CALEDONIA DISTRICTS, 1821-1849

© Tina Loo, 1990

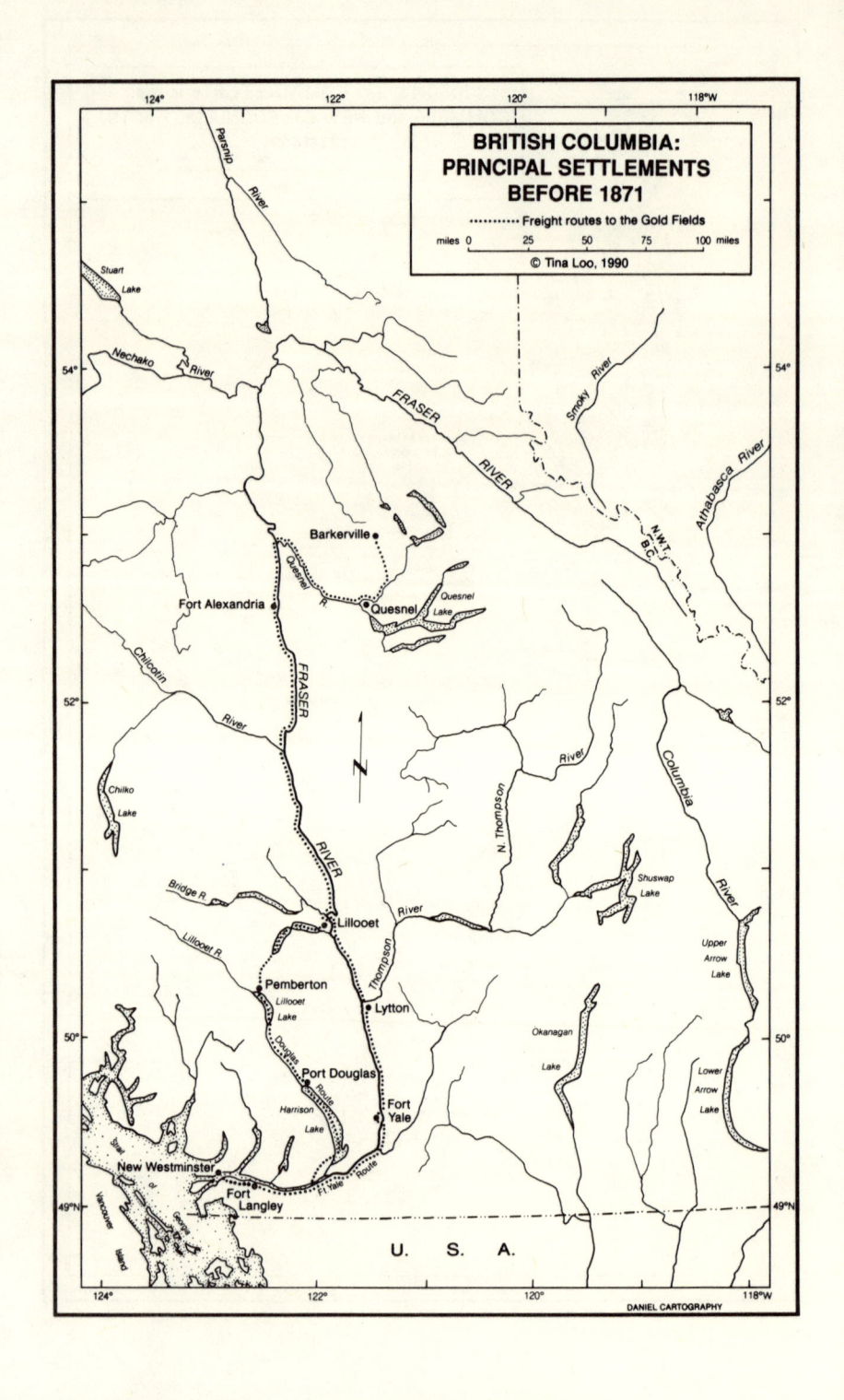

BRITISH COLUMBIA: PRINCIPAL SETTLEMENTS BEFORE 1871

.... Freight routes to the Gold Fields

© Tina Loo, 1990

DANIEL CARTOGRAPHY

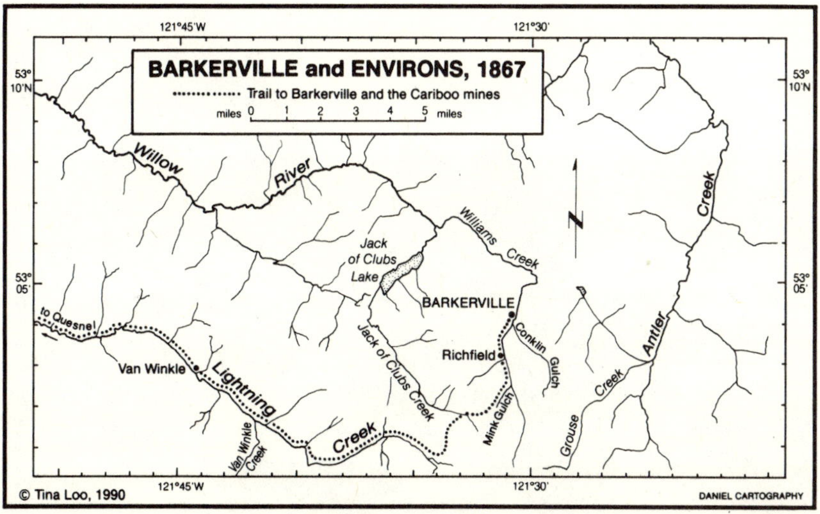
BARKERVILLE and ENVIRONS, 1867
Trail to Barkerville and the Cariboo mines
miles 0 1 2 3 4 5 miles
121°45'W
121°30'
53° 10'N
53° 05'
Willow River
Williams Creek
Jack of Clubs Lake
BARKERVILLE
Richfield
Conklin Gulch
Jack of Clubs Creek
Mink Gulch
to Quesnel
Van Winkle
Lightning Creek
Van Winkle Creek
Antler Creek
Grouse Creek
N
© Tina Loo, 1990
DANIEL CARTOGRAPHY

British Columbia's road to prosperity: the Cariboo Road, which was opened in 1860

Of the many get-rich-quick schemes to be born in the gold fields of British Columbia, the Cariboo Camel was one of the most whimsical. The rocky terrain of their new environment proved too hard on the animals' sensitive feet. Camels are characteristically bad-tempered; when used as pack animals, they grew even worse. Photo, 1880–90

The lively town of Barkerville, pictured here before the fire, was the social and service centre of the Cariboo gold rush.

The (in)famous Canadian Company on their claim, 1867 or 1868

There may have been 'Mucho Oro' (above) in the Cariboo, but miners who thought they would 'Never Sweat' (right) getting it were sadly mistaken. Though some gold was found in the sand banks of the Cariboo's creeks and was best suitable for placer mining, most was embedded in hard rock and was accessible only from deep shafts. Once the hard rock was removed, it was crushed and the gold separated by a hydraulic process – hence the need for a waterwheel at the Mucho Oro claim. Photos, 1867 or 1868

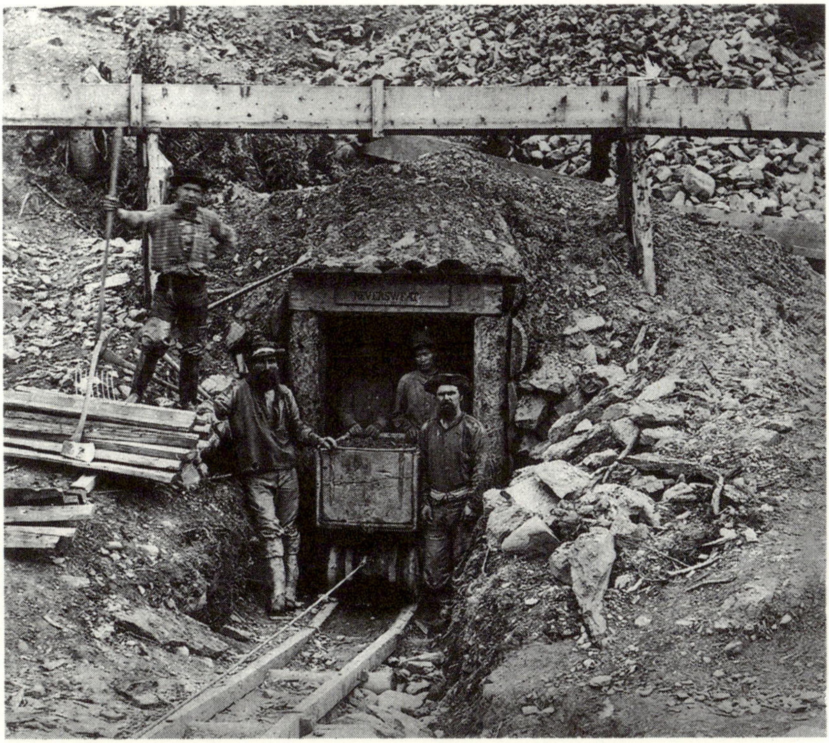

The Grouse Creek Expedition, 1867: Supreme Court Judge Matthew Baillie Begbie (second from left), Governor Frederick Seymour (centre, with gun over his knees), and Colonial Administrator Arthur Nonus Birch (second from right)

Supreme Court Judge Matthew Baillie Begbie, the 'Hanging Judge,' resplendent

Alfred Waddington's folly: the Bute Inlet Route, captured by the *Illustrated London News*, September 1868

MAKING LAW, ORDER, AND AUTHORITY IN
BRITISH COLUMBIA, 1821–1871

INTRODUCTION
Rethinking Law, Order, and Authority

'Everything,' recalled Judge Henry Crease of British Columbia in 1874, 'which affected the condition of the law in this country reverberated through every fibre of the body politic.'[1] Crease's observation was based on his earlier tenure as the colony's attorney-general, a position that placed him at the centre of the many controversies over the administration of the law that characterized British Columbia in the years before Confederation. As both the judge's experience and this study reveal, the Europeans who inhabited the area that became British Columbia took an active and critical interest in the law, seeing it as central to their identity and to securing their future in Britain's far western possession. But in spite of their geographic isolation, a potentially hostile and numerically larger Native population, and American expansionist interest, European British Columbians were concerned less with countering the possibility of violence and crime with English law and its institutions than they were about structuring a particular kind of social, political, and economic order and privileging a particular set of values through both the civil and criminal law.

That order is best described not simply as the absence of 'lawless misrule,' to use the contemporary phrase, but as a positively liberal and individualistic one. For European British Columbians, law was central to the making of a liberal order, but both it and the courts were also constructed through a discourse of classical or laissez-faire liberalism which delineated their role, the ambit of their power, and the basis of their authority. European British Columbians were concerned first and foremost with their economic futures – that, after all, was their raison d'être, as well as the colony's – and with the colony's economic development, and they saw the law as a means to secure both. Their notions of the law's role in doing so and, by extension, the role of government, as well as their understanding of authority, were shaped by the discourse of laissez-faire, which was ascendant in Britain at the colony's creation in 1858. To European

British Columbians, a strong central state and the intervention of the law and the courts were necessary to aid the pursuit of individual gain. Both the law and its institutions were supposed to create an arena of economic exchange in which all transactions and the resolution of any disputes that arose from them would be guided by a set of standardized, rational, and predictable rules. Standardization, uniformity, certainty, and above all rationality also became the basis of the law's authority and, ultimately, the chief constituents of justice in a liberal order.

If this was what European British Columbians wanted of the law, it was also what they got. But the process of creating the desired liberal economic order was by no means a foregone conclusion. There was nothing natural or automatic about the creation of law and order, and the chapters in this book are largely concerned with delineating the conflict and negotiation that accompanied the making of it. A number of tensions were woven into the debate over the law and its administration, tensions that pitted paternalism against individualism, customary law against formal and especially statute law, the periphery against the centre, and, most broadly, a concern for social relations against a concern for economic ones. It was because the law and the debate surrounding its administration stood for all of these things that Henry Crease made the observation I began with. The construction of the colonial legal system and its administration proved to be a site of struggle among a number of norms, and it is through those conflicts that the values which the law reflected and created become visible and the limits of the liberal order it made in creating the justice British Columbians sought are revealed.

Law, order, and authority are familiar subjects for Canadians because they define what Canadians believe themselves to be: a society committed to law and order and notable for its deference to authority.[2] Canada, the popular argument goes, was and continues to be the most lawful and orderly inhabitant of the continent. Canadians committed fewer crimes, did not engage in the same active policy of cultural genocide towards the indigenous population, and were generally more accepting of state authority than were their neighbours immediately to the south. The differences between Canada and the United States in this respect are perhaps best summed up and represented in the contrasting images of law and order north and south of the forty-ninth parallel: the Canadian Mountie and the American gunfighter.[3]

Symbols are one thing, but explanations for them are another. Canada's orderliness is commonly attributed to two factors: first, to an inherited political culture (variously called 'loyalist,' 'liberal,' 'liberal with a tory touch,' or 'court') that imbued Canadians with a suspicion of republicanism and local government and a trust of strong central authority; and, second, to the circumstances of its settlement.[4] Unlike the United States, the peopling of Canada occurred largely in the wake of corporate and state enterprises like the Hudson's Bay Company, the North West Mounted Police and, the Canadian Pacific Railway.[5] As a result, Canadian settlement was structured in such a way as to preclude the need for individuals to develop institutions of local government and their dangerous corollary: a tradition of localism and vigilantism that could – as was the case in the United States – be at odds with the policies of the central authority.[6]

Given this explanation, there appears to be very little left to say about law, order, and authority in the Canadian context. However, this is only the case if we accept the two assumptions that underlie this body of literature: that Canada is orderly, and that order is most meaningfully defined as the absence of violence. And there are a large number of historians who do not define it thus. Rather than take Canada's orderliness as a given, some historians have made it the subject of investigation. Eschewing the Upper Canadian and élite-centred focus that characterized the political and cultural histories described above, these historians demonstrated that Canada was not nearly as lawful or orderly as we have been led to believe. Crime and violence were part of the frontier and settlement experience, albeit, it appears, on a much more limited scale than in the United States. Moreover, Canadians did not act as humanely towards Native peoples as they would like to think. Canada's past may not have been characterized by Indian wars of the American kind, but it was marked by violence as well as a perhaps less than honourable treaty process and the passage of the Indian Act, both of which are considered acts of judicial genocide by many. Even the Mounties, those icons of order, did not escape the revisionist gaze: while their importance in western settlement has been confirmed, their role was revealed to be one of aiding in the subjugation of Canada's indigenous population and in controlling labour unrest.[7]

If Canada was not orderly, there was also more to order than simply the absence of violence. As the Mounties' involvement in western settlement and regulating labour suggests, the criminal law was used to uphold a particular kind of order, and it is the nature of that order – the values as well as the social and institutional practices that maintained them – that are more properly and fruitfully the focus of study.[8] If Canada's criminal law and its enforcement held up a particular social, economic, and political order, so too did its civil law, particularly that dealing with marriage, divorce, child custody, labour, immigration, property, and contracts.[9] Canada's legal system as a whole was and continues to be implicated in the production and reproduction of a racist, classist, and sexist system of domination, privileging the rights of the few over the many. The most recent formulations of the 'law-is-biased' school attempt to look at the complex interplay of race, class, gender, and sexuality rather than to use a single 'master category' of analysis, and to balance the law's oppression with human agency, recognizing that the power was more ambiguous and the domination it perpetuated more uneven than they might initially appear to be.[10] However, few scholars locate the biases they identify in a context that would lend coherence and a larger significance to what is now a somewhat fragmentary literature. How, for instance, is the classist labour legislation of the nineteenth century related to the racist Indian Act, or to the sexist Married Women's Property Act? Do these disparate laws contribute to and uphold a single identifiable order?

Answering questions like these requires one to explore how order is constituted as well as to delineate its normative nature. It was with this in mind that I approached British Columbia's legal history as the *making* of law, order, and authority. I argue that the order that characterized the colony and that was created and reflected by and through the law was itself constituted through a particular discourse; specifically, through the discourse of liberalism. Indeed, the right by which the law commanded – its authority – was also derived from the same discourse. Because 'discourse' and 'liberalism' are such commonplace terms in historical and other academic writing, it might be useful to explain what I mean when I use them.

Discourse and discourse analysis are part of a trend in contemporary cultural theory known as post-structuralism.[11] Emergent in the 1960s, post-structuralism rejects the possibility of scientific objectivity and comprehensive understanding, and instead focuses on the instability, uncertainty, partiality (in both senses: incomplete and biased), and plurality of meaning and knowledge – and hence of reality. 'Reality,' according to the post-structuralists, does not exist outside our own social, cultural, and perhaps individual constructions of it, nor do those constructions – the multiplicity of realities – fit into a single, unified, independent whole.

Those constructions of reality are given voice and form and gain currency through a particular language. Language is central to the way in which we conceive of the world. We use it to organize our own experiences and to convey them to others. According to the post-structuralists, language is not just a vehicle of communication. Words do not simply describe things; they are value-laden. So when we use words we are both describing the world and making certain implicit judgments about it, judgments that will influence how we subsequently act. Some examples might clarify this theoretical position. Consider these two sets of words: king/queen and bachelor/spinster. Both 'king' and 'queen' suggest royalty and power, but they are not equal. Whereas queens may be the consorts of kings, the reverse does not hold true. Moreover, 'queen' has other less regal connotations, for it is also the term used to describe flamboyant male homosexuals. Similarly, though both 'bachelor' and 'spinster' describe the marital status of men and women, each summons up rather different images: 'bachelor' signifies a lifestyle of freedom, adventure, and, above all, choice, while 'spinster' suggests something very different: male rejection, orthopaedic shoes, and a retiring life of prudence and caution. This line of thinking gives power even to the unassuming pronoun. When we use 'he' and 'his' to describe hypothetical situations we are implying that the masculine experience is either universal (that men and women experience things in the same way) or that women's point of view or experience is unimportant. These examples show that single words act as a shorthand for a whole set of values; they are like individual clouds within larger formations of meaning. Like cloud formations, however, the meaning embodied in language can shift, evoking different sentiments which, in turn, can provoke a particular range of actions from us. When we use language, then, we not only communicate meaning but we create it as well, and the assumptions implicit in the world we create through language will, as a result, influence how we act and interact. Because language is shared, when we use it we create a community – a community built around the shared understanding – and (as the Quebec experience has shown) a culture.[12]

All of this brings us to 'discourse.' Though 'language' and 'discourse' are often used interchangeably, the latter is preferable when referring to the constitutive and performative role of language; that is, when we talk about what we actually *do* with language. Whereas 'language' can refer simply to a method of communication and connotes a certain neutrality, unity, and fixity of meaning, 'discourse' refers to the more open-ended, cultural, and 'ideological work' of language, which consists of creating a way of seeing the world and a range of options for acting in it.[13] There is more to discourse, however, than the multiple meanings and actions it can provoke. Indeed, what gives a discourse its power is its coherence and self-referentiality; its ability to explain the world in terms and through ideas of its own making. Thus, a discourse is also 'a coherent body of statements that produces a self-confirming account of reality by defining an object of attention and generating concepts with which to analyze it.'[14]

Consider the discourse of the law, for instance. Most people would agree that the law is a discourse: it is characterized by a particular language and a way of seeing and explaining the world. The 'person' is the law's 'object of attention': it defines what and who a person is or may be, and it delineates the rights and obligations that frame a person's actions and interactions, setting out sanctions for their violation. Despite the apparent inclusivity and comprehensiveness suggested by the law's ambit of interest, not all people are persons under the law. Though legal language is inclusive, legal discourse is exclusive. We are not, despite Ronald Dworkin's assertion to the contrary, all citizens of 'law's empire.'[15] Though we may all fall within the boundaries of its realm, we are not all citizens, nor are we all equal. The law itself makes distinctions, both benign and invidious, between categories of persons, and assigns different rights and duties to them. Women, children, and those deemed to be of diminished mental capacity are only the most obvious examples; less obvious, but no less powerful, were the distinctions the law made between people of different religious, ethnic, or national backgrounds and different sexual preferences.

The partiality and power of legal discourse suggested by its capacity to define personhood is given real effect through the procedures and standards it sets out for adjudicating disputes between people. In dealing with conflict, the law defines what the issue in dispute is and what facts are relevant to it, and then assigns those facts value and meaning by referring to its own rules of evidence as well as to other laws, both statute and common, and finally reaches a decision based on its own construction of the 'truth.' The law's reliance on statutory interpretation, precedent, and a complex body of rules of evidence first to determine the 'truth' and then to impose a sanction or remedy thus comprises a self-referential system of knowledge.[16]

Legal discourse, then, is not simply a language or a 'coherent body of statements.' As its capacity for and means of truth-finding suggest, the language of the law was embedded in a set of concrete institutional practices – a 'legal method' – which produces a 'self-confirming account of reality.'[17] Discourse analysis thus consists of both an attention to language and the culture and order it reflects and creates and an exploration of how that language and, more particularly, the assumptions contained in it are embodied in tangible forms – or, to use the practitioner's terms, 'embedded' in 'discursive formations,' which further act to buttress and reproduce that order.

Like the law, laissez-faire liberalism is a discourse. Both liberalism and laissez-faire have many faces and a complex genealogy, and while I cannot do service to their complexity as well as their multiple and tangled lines of descent, it might be useful to outline what I mean when I use that phrase.[18] Liberalism is a political philosophy whose emergence in the eighteenth century not only paralleled the growth of capitalism, but shaped and was shaped by it. Like all political philosophies, liberalism consists of a body of ideas about the way societies should be organized. Implicit in liberalism's theory of social organization is a vision of the good society – of what justice, equality, and freedom within the social order should be and mean. Hence liberalism is prescriptive and not simply descriptive; moreover, it is unabashedly ideological and normative. That many of us forget this is testimony to the hegemony of liberal discourse in passing off what is cultural, and hence a product of human artifice, as natural.[19]

If society is the object of liberalism's attention, a particular understanding of human nature is fundamental to its analysis of it. Liberalism postulates that all individuals are inherently rational. Though people may exhibit rationality in varying degrees, their actions are all, at root, motivated by the pursuit of their own self-interest, of individual gain. Though liberalism's definition of rationality or reason is anchored by the notion of self-interest, it recognizes that rationality includes an ability to calculate what one's self-interest is as well as the best way to achieve it. Despite the multiplicity of interests and the diversity of the people who hold them, liberalism considers them secondary to the more fundamental fact of the universality of human nature. All individuals are essentially the same: to liberals, then, human nature transcends the differences created by gender, culture, space, and time.

Having argued that rational human behaviour consists of the calculated pursuit of self-interest, liberals consider that the greatest happiness and the wealth of nations will result from allowing individuals to engage in that pursuit, from promoting the fundamental urge of human nature for gain instead of denying it. Thus, in addition to being universalist, liberalism is also 'meliorist': liberals believe that the world can be made better by human effort.[20]

In addition to having a theory of human nature, liberalism delineates the role of the state. In a liberal order, the role of the state consists of creating conditions conducive to the pursuit of self-interest and the realization of individual will. Chief among them is certainty or security: the state is charged with creating standardized and uniformly administered rules and institutions to guide the pursuit of self-interest and to manage the inevitable and natural conflict that results from that pursuit. By creating such rules and enforcing them consistently, the state not only creates an arena of interaction that provides a degree of certainty in social relations, but also creates a degree of predictability in them that benefits the calculating individual.

As should be apparent, law and the courts can play a significant and fairly active role in constructing the security that is central to a liberal order. However, the activist role of the law and its institutions seems to be at odds with the non-interventionist state implied by 'laissez-faire.' In fact, the two are not as contradictory as they may appear: but let me begin my explanation by clarifying what I mean by 'laissez-faire.' Like many historians, I use the term as a shorthand reference to a particular nineteenth-century variety of liberalism which others have called 'classical.' Though laissez-faire or classical liberalism was marked by an especially strong commitment to economic individualism as the basis of social organization, none of its proponents – not even Adam Smith – believed in a complete absence of intervention in the marketplace; rather, they argued for a minimalist state, recognizing that a degree of interference was a necessary evil.[21] Indeed, a large degree of intervention might be necessary initially to order the marketplace in a manner that would maximize the pursuit of self-interest, and a small degree subsequently as a kind of fine-tuning to guarantee the most efficient exchange. Intervention was thus a matter of degree rather than an absolute.

As a final illustration that laissez-faire doctrine and state intervention were not inconsistent, Arthur Taylor argues that we should make a distinction between theory and practice: though administrative practice did not always bear out laissez-faire theory, that theory certainly animated governmental policy debates and framed public discussion in England, and a belief in its prescriptive powers remained unshaken until the last quarter of the nineteenth century.[22]

There is hardly a discipline in the humanities or the social sciences that has not taken the linguistic leap, or, as one of its critics would say, a 'descent into discourse,' over the last decade.[23] Anthropology, sociology, literature, political science, geography, criminology, and law have all, to varying degrees, recognized and approached their subject-matter as 'texts' whose meaning is not fixed but constituted and reconstituted by the reader and the writer or the audience and the teller. Thus for instance, the anthropologists James Clifford and George Marcus can analyse the way in which ethnographers 'write culture,' the lawyer and classicist James Boyd White can discuss the 'rhetoric and poetics of the law,' and the geographer Sharon Zukin can 'read landscapes.'[24] History has not escaped the textual turn. Indeed, Michel Foucault's work on the emergence of the penitentiary in the late eighteenth century (1975) and the history of sexuality (1978) can in many ways be considered to mark the beginnings of the kind of discourse analysis that is now a part of many disciplines.

In this respect, Canadian history remains somewhat apart. It has been, relatively speaking, an island of empiricism separated by a gulf of discourse from the larger sea of social theory. As one historian has observed, 'Canadian historians have been committed empiricists. Admittedly, they have come a long way from the days when a passion for biography marked the field's highest aspiration, but they remain reluctant to ground their work in the fertile soil of theoretical reasoning.'[25] However, there have, been two recent and notable departures from this trend: Kay J. Anderson's *Vancouver's Chinatown: Racial Discourse in Canada, 1875–1980* (1991) and Mariana Valverde's *The Age of Light, Soap, and Water: Moral Reform in English Canada, 1885–1925* (1991).Though they may be harbingers of Canadian history's 'descent into discourse,' it is notable that neither of these scholars is, strictly speaking, a historian: Anderson is a geographer by training and Valverde a sociologist.

In writing this study, I have attempted to do what both those authors have done: to build a bridge – or, in true British Columbian fashion, a road – between two scholarly traditions: the empirical and the theoretical. For in addition to delineating the character of law, order, and authority in colonial British Columbia, I hope that this study will also show how discourse operates – how the discourse of laissez-faire liberalism informed, shaped, and limited the debate over the legal system and was embedded in it – and, in that sense, I hope to provide a more general sense of how one might look at the Canadian past.

I cannot leave this discussion of post-structuralism without acknowledging the controversy it has generated among historians and the intellectual community in general. Though historians have on the whole been wary of using social theory, post-structuralism seems to have generated a particularly vocal and occasionally virulent response.[26] The title of Bryan Palmer's recent book – *Descent into Discourse: the Reification of Language and the Writing of Social History* – encapsulates what for many historians is the problem with post-structuralist theory. To those who practice one of the most contextually oriented of all disciplines, the reification of language and the erasure of the social, political, and – particularly for Palmer – material context in which it is generated and used is ahistorical and perhaps anti-historical. While this can be the case, it is not always or necessarily so: a close attention to language should not be conflated or confused with a reification of it. Though discourse occupies a central place in my history of colonial British Columbia, the fundamental question that animates it is one of the most basic: why these developments at this time and in this place? Why, in other words, the concern over the construction of the courts and the legal administration of the colony? Why were the concerns and criticisms framed in the way they were? And what does this tell us about the kind of social order European British Columbians wanted and the authority that underpinned it?

In articulating answers to these questions, a post-structuralist approach has led me to view the legal order that came to characterize British Columbia as something that was constructed through a particular discourse (the discourse of liberalism), rather than something that was natural, inevitable, or self-evident, and that emerged without conflict or negotiation. While I argue that liberal notions regarding human nature shaped what European British Columbians expected of the law and their legal institutions, liberal discourse did not in any simple or causal way *determine* action, nor was it the *only* factor that shaped responses. Certainly the geographical, historical, and material contexts in which European British Columbians found themselves were also important in shaping their expectations of law and authority, and these, I hope, are acknowledged in the chapters that follow.

More broadly, the 'descent into discourse' signals for many a descent into the kind of moral relativism Cynthia Ozick was witness to at a party when she overheard some one say, 'For me, the Holocaust and a corncob are the same.'[27] If post-structuralists are taken at their word, then all experience is socially constructed, and therefore all experience is equal: the Holocaust and a corncob are the same thing. Again, this is not necessarily the case. In arguing that we should acknowledge the artifice and interest inherent in social, political, and economic life and make the categories and assumptions we use to see the world explicit, relational, and unstable, post-structuralism can be the first step toward greater social justice and liberation. By freeing ourselves from the shackles of 'nature,' new cultural futures become thinkable and possible.[28]

It is impossible to understand nineteenth-century British Columbia, its legal system, and the ensuing conflicts over the system without first understanding the fur trade period, for it was during this time that the initial links between law and economy were forged – links that would be elaborated on in the colonial period. Chapter 1 examines the kinds of disputes that characterized the fur-trade period and how the Hudson's Bay Company dealt with them. HBC 'law' was generated in large part by the social and economic context in which it was administered. Concerned almost exclusively with regulating behaviour that threatened the company's economic well-being, HBC law was administered informally, and relied on the paternal authority of its chief factors and chief traders for effect. Though its dynamics are interesting in themselves, HBC law was central to the political debate that followed in the newly formed colony of Vancouver Island.

As far as the administration of the law was concerned, little changed when Vancouver Island achieved colonial status in 1849. As a proprietary colony of the Hudson's Bay Company, Vancouver Island continued to be governed in the same manner as it had been when it was previously a fur-trade preserve under private control. As it turned out, this was a problem. The colony's independent settlers (independent, that is, of the company) rejected company rule and labelled its paternalism and its status as both colonial proprietor and monopolistic business enterprise anachronistic and illegitimate. Private enterprises could not be expected to act in the public interest, and the independents demanded change. In doing so, they framed their criticisms in the language of laissez-faire liberalism. The colony's land laws and legal system proved to be the focal point of these calls for reform. Chapter 2 explores the conflict between the independents and the company over the constitution of a legitimate political order on Vancouver Island through an examination of *R. v. Robert Staines*, a case that polarized the colony's small European population.

The 1858 gold rush diverted the colonial government's attention from the internal political wrangling on Vancouver Island to the banks of the Fraser River on the mainland, where the sudden influx of miners led to the formation of the separate colony of British Columbia. One of the first concerns of the new colonial government was to establish British law and legal institutions in the gold fields to preclude the development of a strong and potentially disruptive tradition of localism. However, the government also acted in response to a series of demands on the part of British Columbians for the rapid establishment of a system of law and courts that would aid them in their pursuit of economic gain. As chapter 3 shows, British Columbians constructed the law as central to economic development, and the liberal discourse with which the colonists framed their demands was quickly embedded in a number of institutions and practices. While the kinds of courts the colonists wanted were shaped by the discourse of laissez-faire, however, their operation was also influenced by British Columbia's geography, which had the effect of placing more power and discretion in the hands of the colony's magistrates.

Just as economic concerns had animated the courts' construction, they subsequently filled their calendars. As chapter 4 reveals, British Columbia's lower courts were occupied almost entirely with civil matters, and particularly with cases for debt incurred as a result of mining activity. A quantitative analysis of the actions initiated and their disposal sheds light on the nature of the colonial economy and on the the courts' role in regulating economic transactions. British Columbia's legal institutions proved to be a reliable means for those seeking to secure their debts: they ruled overwhelmingly in favour of plaintiffs. Litigation (and particularly the extent to which the court had to intervene to resolve cases) also suggests much about the nature of social relations and attitudes towards state intervention in the gold fields. Though litigation has been viewed as pathological and indicative of social breakdown, that was not wholly the case in British Columbia. While the bonds of community were not sufficiently developed in a new society like British Columbia (and one characterized by transience) to allow for the informal settlement of disputes, British Columbians actively sought the application of law and the construction and intervention of the courts (chapter 3). They did not see recourse to the courts as unnatural or as a sign of social breakdown, but as a natural outgrowth of human nature and the conflict that accompanied the pursuit of self-interest. Moreover, going to court was in keeping with the demands of laissez-faire liberalism for predictable, certain, and rule-bound mechanisms of dispute resolution. In short, liberalism constructed conflict and the particular form of conflict resolution British Columbians availed themselves of as natural.

If capitalism created an institutional legal structure that both supported and furthered its needs, it also constructed an ethical system that did the same thing. The language and logic of laissez-faire liberalism defined a set of standards for assessing the law's authority or the right by which it commanded obedience. As chapter 5 shows, those standards were revealed in *Cranford*, a rather prosaic suit for debt that was appealed to the British Columbia Supreme Court in 1862 and that precipitated a storm of controversy about the administration of justice in the colony. The conflict surrounding the case had little to do with the substantive issues of fact or law, and much to do with the larger question of how authoritative legal decisions are reached. *Cranford* pitted Supreme Court Judge Matthew Begbie, who insisted that character assessment must override legal convention and documentary evidence, against the Cranfords' lawyers, who argued their clients' case from that evidence and from legal doctrine, and who took great exception to the judge's actions. Public sentiment was very much on the side of the lawyers, and the public discourse surrounding the case revealed, first, that legal authority was written, rooted in texts and in the experts who could interpret them, and, second, that justice or fairness was a matter of simply applying the simple application of rules. Unlike paternal authority, which was based on personal discretion, textual authority and expertise conferred the certainty and predictability that was the necessary precondition of success in the marketplace.

Liberalism may have constructed the law as a central support of a particular economic and social order, and authority as arising from the uniform application of a system of predictable and rational rules, but events on Grouse Creek in 1867 delineated the limits of that discourse in meeting some British Columbians' demands for justice. Chapter 6 centres on three mining disputes, all involving Matthew Begbie and all controversial. As in *Cranford*, Begbie's behaviour in the first two cases was deemed arbitrary and tyrannical, and as a result he, or rather his court, was prevented by an amendment to the Gold Fields Act from hearing mining appeals. Popular will and popular notions of law and authority appeared to have triumphed. However, when the judge did exactly what British Columbians wanted him to do – abide by the letter of the law – and refused to hear the *Grouse Creek* appeal, a near riot broke out in the gold fields. The conflict and controversy surrounding the 'Grouse Creek War' revealed other standards by which legal authority was measured, standards that derived from local sensibilities that contradicted those expressed in *Cranford*, and that adumbrated the limits of justice under the rule of law.

If the events on Grouse Creek revealed the limits of the law – the danger of ignoring the social context in which disputes occurred and the injustice that could result from doing so – the incident at Bute Inlet suggested the possibilities for justice under the rule of law. In 1864 eighteen road construction workers were killed, allegedly by the Chilcotin Indians, in an incident that became known as the 'Bute Inlet Massacre.' As chapter 7 shows, the discourse of liberalism provided a large part of the framework in which European British Columbians understood the killings and acted in response to them. Liberalism has an understanding of human nature that defines natural and rational behaviour as universal and consisting of the pursuit of individual self-interest. Deviance, by extension, is defined by a failure to act in this way: to conduct oneself in a manner designed to maximize economic gain. Within this context, British Columbians labelled the Bute Inlet killings as senseless. The Chilcotin, they observed, had been gainfully employed by the roadmen as packers, and had, like all Indians of the colony, been the beneficiaries of the generous 'bread and treacle' policy of James Douglas. With their material needs looked after, the Chilcotin had little to complain about. Moreover, European British Columbians argued, the road crew was neither well equipped with tools nor lavishly supplied with food; there was little of value to pillage, and little reason for an attack. But to understand white reaction to the killings, we need to take note of the symbolism of Bute Inlet: the eighteen labourers who lost their lives at the hands of the Chilcotin were working on a road – and not just any road, but one that led to the gold fields. In a sense, the Bute Inlet Massacre stood for the clash of civilization and savagery, of progress and backwardness, of culture and nature.

Though many European British Columbians felt that the savage perpetrators of the massacre deserved savage treatment, the actual response was not as straightforward. The two military expeditions that were sent to track down the Chilcotin 'assassins' were placed in a rather curious position: they were ordered to hunt down the perpetrators, not to kill them but to bring them to the colonial capital to stand trial. Though the discourse of liberalism and its concept of human nature shaped European British Columbians' understanding of the Bute Inlet Massacre and its perpetrators, it also demanded that the Chilcotin be treated equally before the law. Thus, Bute Inlet and its aftermath suggest both the limits and the possibilities for justice in a liberal order.

'The West beyond the West': the title of Jean Barman's recent text encapsulates the way in which she and many other historians of British Columbia and Canada see the region beyond the Rocky Mountains: as a place beyond the pale, of extremes and unknowns, and above all, as a place separate and distinct.[29] In many ways, they are right: British Columbia does not fit easily into the frameworks that Canadian historians commonly use to make sense of the country.[30] Though the Montreal merchants had established posts in the far west in the early nineteenth century, the North Westers proved to be a transient presence. British Columbia was not a meaningful part of Donald Creighton's 'Empire of the St. Lawrence.' Nor, according to Barry Gough, was its frontier really a Turnerian one – that is, one characterized by individualism and democracy, peopled by the kind of 'New Man' that Crèvecoeur and later Tocqueville observed inhabiting the United States. Instead, British Columbia was an 'imperial frontier' an extension of metropolitan and British authority.[31] It was a frontier only in the geographic sense, not a cultural one. The European settlement of British Columbia also proved unconventional. For one thing, settlement occurred from west to east, defying not only a national but a continental pattern, and it occurred relatively late: it was not until the mid-eighteenth century that British Columbia entered the ambit of the European world, and a century later that significant non-Native settlement began. Even with settlement, its geography prevented integration with Canada, and favoured – at least in the realm of economics – north/south rather than east/west links.

Ties like these, both intellectual and sentimental, are neither missed nor sought by most historians of the region or by many British Columbians, who emphasize and celebrate their distinctiveness. Nor is the province's absence something historians of 'Canada' are concerned about. In Canada and the west, but not of them, British Columbia is often overlooked in general treatments of the country's history.

While the absence of British Columbia, whether by intent or indifference, may be testimony to its distinctiveness, it may just as easily be a result of the shortcomings of the national and continental frames of reference that historians have used to make sense of the Canadian past. Geography and economy were important determinants in understanding the colony's past, but British Columbia's experience is better understood not in terms of the frontier or Laurentian theses but as occurring within the particular discursive space provided by liberalism, and as part of the larger process of state formation in the nineteenth century. This space and the process that occurred within it were not bounded by nation or continent, but transcended them.

The extension of state power over a vast and largely unknown land involved the gathering of knowledge – as simple as ascertaining where people were and what were they doing – and with it the imposition of a set of rules and procedures that would govern their relationships with each other and with the state. In so doing, the state managed to create the certainty and security that was the source of its ongoing power. Though establishing dominion over a region was a political and economic process – that is to say, one that had ideological and material aspects – it was at heart a social one: it involved socializing people to a particular kind of authority, namely, the rule of a standardized and text-based law. To a great extent, the cultural hegemony of this particular form of authority had already been established among the Europeans who came to the region. Many were conversant in the law and had fairly well-defined expectations of it; they called for the establishment of courts and criticized their administration. Though in many ways, the state did not have to impose the law at all because of

Introduction   17

European British Columbians' propensity for self-regulation, state formation did not occur without conflict and negotiation. In addition to delineating the particulars of the British Columbian case, this book also outlines the tensions attendant in the process of creating a 'colonial leviathan' and the unevenness of its development.[32]

1

'Club Law' and Order in British Columbia's Fur Trade

Though claims that the Hudson's Bay Company's initials stood for 'Here Before Christ' did not hold true in British Columbia (the company had been preceded in the area by the American John Jacob Astor's Pacific Fur Company, the Russian-American Company, and the Montreal-based Nor'westers, not to mention a sizable Native population), the company did have the largest, most enduring, and – in terms of understanding the legal history of Britain's westernmost North American colonies – the most significant presence there. With their employees and supplies spread over an immense geographic area and a volatile international market for a staple resource like furs to contend with, the Hudson's Bay Company found itself confronted with several sizable obstacles to its simple long-term viability and prosperity. Given these, the company, like any other business, attempted to limit as much uncertainty as it could. While the 1670 Charter that granted it an economic monopoly went a fair distance towards accomplishing that end, the HBC also concerned itself with regulating the conduct of its employees: this was the realm of HBC 'law,' and is the subject of this chapter.

The conventional wisdom about law and order in the fur trade is that the former was absent and therefore the latter was violent. The two imperial statutes that regulated the conduct of those in HBC territory, about which I will have more to say, were largely unenforceable and played little part in ordering fur-trade society. Instead, as the aptly named Fort Vancouver chaplain Herbert Beaver pointed out, Hudson's Bay Company 'law' consisted of 'the use of the lash and cutlass, supported by the presence of the pistol.'[1] Beaver's sentiments were echoed by the governor of the Hudson's Bay Company, George Simpson, who described the regulation that characterized the fur trade west of the Rockies as a system of 'Club Law.'[2] Disputes between HBC men and between traders and Indians threatened the company's operations and were settled with violent and sometimes deadly informality, rather than through the formal legal process outlined in the imperial statutes that theoretically governed the territory.

Though the conventional wisdom appears to be sustained by the evidence, which points to the existence and operation of a system of corporal punishment in the area that became British Columbia, its significance remains largely unexplored. There was much more to the system of law that characterized the fur trade, to say nothing of the order and authority it upheld and was a part of. 'Club Law' was wielded in the name of a particular kind of order. As the contracts signed by company employees reveal, that order was designed to ensure the HBC's economic viability and profits. In regulating economic behaviour in its own favour, however, the company came up against its employees' demands that their welfare be considered. A balance between the company's economic interests and its workers' welfare was achieved by striking another one: in return for the deference and obedience of its servants, the HBC, through its officers, took responsibility for all aspects of their social and economic welfare. Thus, in addition to paying its employees their wages, the company also provided them with food and clothing and attempted to regulate their relations with Indian women and their family life. The disputes that came to characterize the fur trade arose when one side perceived that the terms of their reciprocal relationship had been breached.

This reciprocity suggests that though club law was dispensed in the economic interests of the HBC, it also reflected and upheld a particular set of paternal social relations. Within a paternal order, inequality and mutuality are the keys to social stability. Though society is composed of a variety of unequal parts, each is equally necessary and the cooperation of all is essential for the integrity and well-being of the whole. One's place in the social hierarchy determines one's duties. Those who possess power and authority do so by virtue of their elevated status; but with that status comes a responsibility for the welfare of those with less power, whose primary duty is obedience. If either the powerful or the powerless fail to meet their responsibilities, the entire social order is threatened with disruption.

In the fur trade, the mutuality and hierarchy that were the linchpins of paternalism were given structure and symbolized by the HBC's corporate organization and the rituals of everyday life, which went a fair distance to ordering its workers well before they felt the blows of the lash or cutlass. Indeed, corporal punishment was a simply the most visible outgrowth of the company's paternalism, and the significance and effectiveness of the HBC's club law as well as the authority of those who wielded it can be fully understood and appreciated only within the context of the larger web of regulation that enveloped its workers.

Important in itself, Hudson's Bay Company law, its authority, and the social system it was a part of also stand as a useful counterpoint to developments in the colonies of Vancouver Island and British Columbia before Confederation. Thus, the exploration of the making of law, order, and authority begins, necessarily, in the fur trade.

From 1821 to 1859 two imperial statutes, the Canada Jurisdiction Act (1803) and the Act for regulating the Fur Trade (1821) provided for the legal administration of the politically unorganized 'Indian territories' under the control of the Hudson's Bay Company.[3] The Indian territories referred to included all of British Columbia, parts of the Northwest Territories, Saskatchewan, and northern Alberta, and were distinct from Rupert's Land, whose government was derived from Charles II's charter of grant (1670) to the Hudson's Bay Company. The 1803 act was an attempt on the part of the imperial government to deal with the violent clashes among the various Montreal trading concerns (especially the old North West and XY Companies) that merged in 1804 to form the North West Company, the HBC's chief rival. It extended the jurisdiction of the courts of Upper and Lower Canada over the Indian territories and empowered the governor of Lower Canada to appoint territorial justices who could commit offenders for trial in the Canadian courts. Violence also spawned the 1821 act. Its provisions limited the violent clashes between the two companies by granting one of them – the Hudson's Bay Company – a monopoly in trade over the Indian territories for twenty-one years.[4] It also extended the provisions of the 1803 act to cover all the territories under HBC control and further empowered the Upper Canadian courts to take cognizance of all suits originating in the Indian territories, with the exception of those involving land title, which were to be determined by the laws of England rather than Canada.[5]

No territorial justices were ever appointed under the 1803 or 1821 acts, and though a number of cases were tried in the Canadas pursuant to the 1803 act between 1810 and 1818, there was only one known instance in which offenders and witnesses were conveyed to Lower Canada for trial after 1821.[6] Given the great distances and great expense involved, the two acts were unworkable, and disputes were settled locally, within the confines of the company, rather than by statutory authority. In any case, the HBC was concerned with checking the commercial conduct of its workers rather than their violent tendencies.[7]

Although formal procedural justice as stipulated in the acts of 1803 and 1821 may indeed have been 'theoretical,' the absence of its machinery did not mean that the Hudson's Bay Company lacked the means to regulate economic behaviour.[8] Company servants signed contracts that imposed stringent terms of service and obligations on them. Their dependence was not given unconditionally, however. Rather, as the labour disputes that characterized the fur-trade period suggest, it was offered in return for the maintenance of a certain standard of living at the posts. If that standard was not met, servants protested by laying down their tools or, in the most extreme cases, by deserting. Given the precarious position of many of the HBC posts, situated as they were deep in 'Indian country,' and the constant shortage of able-bodied labourers that plagued the Columbia and New Caledonia districts (parts of both would become British Columbia), such actions were of serious consequence to company operations. Despite their subservient position, HBC servants and officers were truly mutually dependent.

Throughout the fur-trade period, the Hudson's Bay Company used a standard-form contract to engage its servants.[9] The most notable characteristic of the document was its extensive protection of the company's monopoly and property and the lack of similar protection for those who signed it. Not only was a servant of the 'Honourable Company' expected to 'devote the whole of his time and labour in their service and for their sole benefit,' but he was also expected to 'defend the property of the said Company and their Factories and settlements; and will not absent himself from the said service, nor engage, or be concerned with any trade or employment whatsoever, except for the benefit of the said Company and according to their orders.'[10] In addition, 'all goods obtained by barter with the Indians or otherwise, which shall come to the hands or possession of the said [servant] shall be held by him for the said Company only, and shall be duly delivered up to the said Governors or other of their Officers or Agents ... without any waste, spoil or injury thereto.'[11]

By protecting their monopoly, the company criminalized the one activity – barter – that could have given its servants a certain degree of independence, for the contracts closely circumscribed their movements within the service. The independent mobility of servants was not allowed; however, the company took care to engage servants for 'the Department *generally*,' so 'that they be subject to the inconvenience, or have the benefit of being moved about or transferred from one part of the country to the other at pleasure.'[12] The terms of release from the company's service further regulated the fur trade labour force: servants were required to give notice 'one year or upwards before the expiration of the said term ... of his intention to quit the service,' and upon doing so were required to leave the company's territories.[13] In this way the company assured itself a predictable labour supply and rid itself of potential competition from its former employees. Moreover, the HBC retained the right to dismiss any of its employees from their service and imposed a penalty amounting to a year's wages for desertion, neglect, or any failure to discharge the proper duty. From this penalty, the contract stipulated, 'there shall be no relief either in law or in equity.'[14]

Despite the extreme dependence suggested by the terms of their engagement, company servants managed to establish a looser working relationship with their employers, which gave them a certain amount of latitude in the day-to-day conduct of the trade and their lives at the post. They were aided in part by the harsh realities of service in the west, which created a constant labour shortage. Hudson's Bay Company work was gruelling and difficult at the best of times, but conditions in British Columbia made engagements there particularly demanding. New Caledonia (mainland British Columbia) was particularly despised for its 'misery and privation'[15] and 'poverty of fare.'[16] Chief Factor John Tod recalled that in HBC Governor George Simpson's day (1820–1860) the district was 'looked on in the light of another Botany Bay Australia; the men were in dread of being sent there.'[17] So loath were the company's men to serve in the region that in 1827 the stingy Simpson proposed to raise the district's wages by two pounds to compensate its New Caledonia servants for the extra work they would have to do because of the loss of labour precipitated by the retirement of a great number of that district's men.[18] The sheer isolation and ruggedness of the New Caledonian posts contributed greatly to the district's poor reputation. Simpson described the McLeod's Lake post in 1829 as simply 'the most wretched place in the Indian Country,'[19] perhaps because of the 'surround[ing] mountains which almost exclude the light of day,' and snow storms 'so violent and long continued as to bury the establishment.'[20] The coastal location of Fort McLoughlin did little to ameliorate service there, as Charles Ross's letter to his sister revealed:

Than our way of life in this dreary wilderness nothing can be more dark and insipid. The posts we occupy, though many, are far between, and seldom have any intercourse with each other, oftener than once a year and then for the most part is for the purposes of exchanging cargoes for furs. There is no society – that is the person in charge must divert himself the best way he can with his own thoughts.[21]

In addition to the isolation and rugged geography, conditions in New Caledonia were made more difficult by the periodic failures of the salmon fishery, which led to famine for both HBC men and Indians. In 1827 the fishery failed in the Chilcotin, effectively preventing the establishment of a post.[22] Two years later Simpson reported another salmon shortfall in the area of McLeod's Lake. Upon reaching the fort in the course of his tour of inspection, Simpson found its complement of men 'starving, having nothing to eat for several weeks but berries.' Their faces, he noted, 'were so pale & emaciated that it was with difficulty I recognized them.'[23] Generalized famine also led to theft and to increased confrontations between fur traders and Indians.

Even under better conditions traders viewed the Native population with suspicion and hostility. The company's sentiments were not without some basis, as the murders of its servants and officers demonstrated. In 1823 the complement of men at Fort St John were 'massacred' and the fort abandoned.[24] Farther south at Fort George two HBC workmen were 'done to death by two Fraser Lake Indians' in the same year.[25] In 1828 a company interpreter was killed by two Babine Indians,[26] and in 1848 a refractory HBC servant, Alexis Belanger, was murdered.[27] Garnering particular notice were the murders of HBC officers and clerks: Chief Factor Samuel Black in 1841,[28] postmaster William Morwick at Fort Babine in 1843,[29] and clerk John McIntosh of Fort Chilcotin in 1844.[30]

Company servants liked the Columbia district better, but it too posed peculiar dangers and discomforts to the HBC's servants. Initially celebrated for the 'salubrity of its climate and the excellence of its soil,' the Columbia quickly fell into disfavour because of the dangers posed by navigating the 'tortuous channels' of its rivers, its hostile Indian population, and the malaria or influenza that struck the district with regularity in the 1830s and 1840s.[31] At least some of the dangers that characterized the district were thought to be due to the unruly American population, some of whom were 'people of the worst character, runaways from jails and outcasts from Society, who take all their bad qualities along with them.' 'This motley crew,' wrote Simpson, 'acknowledge no master, [and] will conform to no rules or regulations.'[32]

With such miserable working conditions, it was not surprising that many of the HBC's servants tried to improve their situations by engaging in some private trading with the Indians to fill their stomachs or, as Chief Trader James Murray Yale put it, by entering into the exchange of 'more smutty commodities.'[33] Such activities could and often did result in violent conflict. Even if they did not, however, they could still bring the censure of the company because of the threat they posed to the company's monopoly and the security of its supply of furs and provisions. Officially, anyone trading on his own account was immediately dismissed and forced to forfeit three times the value of the goods traded for, a quarter of which would be rewarded to the person who discovered and reported the illicit exchange.[34]

Unofficially, however, the company dealt with transgressors far more informally, and did not always punish its wayward workers as harshly as it could have. Contracts were not enforced to their London letter. The company's officers found it easier to 'wink at' transgressions or deal with them in a more direct manner. For instance, in 1826 at Fort Kilmaurs, clerk William Brown attempted to drive down the Indians' price for salmon. Unfortunately, his men 'were in every corner endeavouring to trade one or two from them,' rendering Brown's efforts 'to appear to dispise [sic] their salmon,' and thus drive down the price, ineffective.

24 Making Law, Order, and Authority in British Columbia

This [the illicit trade] I for some time winked at until I saw it was going too far, then caught Gilbeau who was coming out of one of the Lodges with a Parcel he had traded, for which I gave him a severe scolding and made him go throw them in the River. At this same time I gave the whole party to understand that the first I saw enter a lodge or have any communication with the Indians I would split his head with my sword – this proceeding put an end to their traffic.[35]

A French-Canadian cook's plan to trade with the neighbouring Tsimshian in 1853 proved to be doubly threatening to the company's interests. 'Léon' not only engaged in private trading, but also offered the Tsimshian a particularly dangerous item in return for their furs: how to turn the large quantities of potatoes raised by the Tsimshian, Haida, and Bella Bella into 'whisky.'[36] In doing so Léon violated the conditions of his contract and endangered the post's food and fur supply and its general safety. Indian potatoes were both an indigenous staple as well as an item of trade. HBC posts were provisioned by the potatoes, and Léon's plan to diversify the Indians' economy by teaching them how to manufacture home brew was not appreciated by the company's authorities and its employees, who were often faced with food shortages. Liquor also created disorder, and, as the Bishop of Columbia noted, the HBC did not use liquor as a trade item because it 'ministered to the wild incentives of their [the Indians'] nature.'[37] 'In consideration of his previous good behaviour' and probably because of the shortage of labour, Léon was offered 'another situation in the company's employ, provided he would make a full confession and tell how far the scheme had progressed. Otherwise he should be dismissed immediately.' Léon did confess, but he made his escape the next day. He was captured shortly after, 'bound hand and foot' and sent to Victoria and out of the district.[38]

Isolation also led company employees to seek out relations with Indian women, much to the dismay of its officers and the governor and council. 'Improper familiarity with their [Indian] Women' was singled out by George Simpson as one of the causes of 'serious differences ... between the Natives and the people of our Establishments' in 'nine cases out of ten.'[39] At New Year's celebrations in 1829, Archibald McDonald of Fort Langley discovered 'the drunken sot Dilenais had contrived to haul up an Indian woman by one of the Portholes.' After confirming the servant's guilt, McDonald called him in and told him 'that had there been *Irons* he should have felt the weight of them, for three months to come.' Instead, Dilenais was fined half his wages – 11 pounds – for his 'unpardinable [sic] crime,' and told 'to taste no liquor ... during the present year of our Lord.'[40] Two years later at Fort Vancouver, Francis Ermatinger, a clerk, 'got into disgrace' when he instructed the post's interpreter to cut off the tip of the ear of an Indian who had had 'an intrigue with his woman.'[41] Chief Factor John McLoughlin excused his clerk's actions, noting that 'though in a civilized world such an act will appear harsh ... if the Indian had not been punished it would have lowered the Whites in their estimation, as among themselves they never allow such an offence to pass unpunished.'[42]

Many of the relationships company men formed with Native women were of a more permanent and loving nature.[43] Family life was often the only consolation traders had in a country with, as Charles Ross said, very little 'society.' Though Simpson and the London Committee considered these alliances uneconomical, there was little they could do about them, though they tried.[44] When William Brown's term of service expired in 1837 he was not allowed to retire, but was ordered to go back to Fort Langley. Brown took his complaint to Fort Vancouver's chaplain, Herbert Beaver, telling him he 'had a child of eight months old, the mother being dead, and that he was unwilling to remain unless he should receive £20 per annum instead of the £17 his former wages.' Before Beaver could intercede, a boat arrived to convey Brown and others to Fort Langley. Brown refused to board and was flogged until he did.[45] In other cases, however, the company found it more beneficial to capitulate to the demands of family affairs. Finan McDonald, a 'very careful and economical trader but not bright,'[46] expressed some 'anxiety about his Family' and was allowed to retire because, as Simpson explained, 'no one should ... be pressed to remain in the Columbia of a discontented turn of mind as the feeling spreads like contagion.' 'Family affairs,' he continued, 'are a source from whence much of this evil arises.'[47]

Though HBC officers granted their servants a certain amount of latitude within the bounds of their contracts, company servants were also possessed of a strong sense of the duties and obligations owed them. Though subservient, they did not accept poor working conditions or harsh treatment at the hands of their superiors without question or action.

Wages and provisions were a regular cause of dissension between the HBC and its employees. Following the economic restructuring precipitated by the HBC's merger with the North West Company, George Simpson wrote to the governor and committee in London, informing them that it was impossible to reduce servants' wages and deny them certain supplies 'without running very serious risks of mutiny.' 'Generally speaking,' he wrote, 'they are dissatisfied with the new order of things.'[48] Much to Chief Factor John McLoughlin's chagrin, the high price of company goods caused several of Peter Skene Ogden's men to desert Fort Vancouver in 1827. '[A]s we had only a precarious tenure of the Country,' he wrote, 'we ought therefore to have allowed the trappers have their supplies at as low a price as possible so as to get while in our power all the furs we could.'[49] Herbert Beaver considered the company's 'inferior servants' 'ill-treated, especially in the article of food,' and from the number of complaints received, he was likely correct.[50] In 1830 eight apprentices complained that 'they had not a sufficiency of Bread,' but company authorities felt their allowance of '4 lbs. Biscuit 2 lbs. flour p. Week' and potatoes in the winter or 'fresh provisions' in the summer was adequate.[51] To 'prevent a general strike and desertion' James Douglas gave Fort Victoria's European servants '2 ozs. Tea and 1 lb. of Brown sugar weekly' in 1850.[52] Such 'luxuries' were in limited supply and, according to the economic historian Harold Innis, smuggling was commonplace.[53] Even the water served to the company's servants did not escape complaint in 1851. A fresh supply was ordered, but the company's servants refused to get it until 'an extra glass of 'grog' [was given] to *all* hands.' Douglas then sentenced fifteen workers to twelve weeks' imprisonment for their part in this 'conspiracy.'[54]

HBC servants also railed against the company's efforts to economize in the post-merger period by refusing to provide for their Indian wives and mixed-blood children and prohibiting unattached employees from marrying Native women à la façon du pays unless they agreed to take full responsibility for their wives and any children they fathered, both during their term of service with the company and afterwards.[55] In their opinion, the company had as much responsibility to their dependants as it did to them, and, as an 1822 petition to Simpson noted, the change in policy was 'repugnant to former usage & held to be unfair.'[56]

Thus, whether they traded in salmon or more smutty commodities, lay down their tools, or deserted the service entirely, HBC servants showed that their obedience to company authority was conditional. Though no fundamental challenge to the legitimacy of company power underlay actions like these, HBC servants expected their employer to look out for their welfare by winking at minor transgressions such as trading small items on their own account and by providing a certain standard of living for them and their dependants at the posts. Within the world of the Company of Adventurers trading into Hudson's Bay not only were blankets exchanged for beaver pelts, but deference and obedience were traded for corporate responsibility. It was this kind of reciprocity between officer and servant, which was premised on face-to-face relations, that was the undercarriage of authority in fur-trade British Columbia.

The hierarchy and mutuality characteristic of paternalism and suggested by the disputes described above were manifested and symbolized by the Hudson's Bay Company's corporate organization and the rituals and routines of post life. Both ordered the lives of fur-trade workers and provide the larger context in which to understand the effectiveness of club law and the authority of those who dispensed it.

Centralization and hierarchy were the two chief characteristics of the organization after its merger with the North West Company. While ultimate control remained in London with the governor, deputy governor, and committee of seven directors, the company's North American field structure became increasingly centralized, particularly under the administration of George Simpson, governor in Chief of all the HBC territories in North America.[57] The company's territories were organized into four departments, the affairs of which were overseen by the governor and the company's chief factors at the annual meeting of the Council of the Northern Department.

The potential for regulation offered by the centralization of the fur trade under Simpson was reinforced by the company's occupational structure, which reflected its belief in the stabilizing and ordering powers of hierarchy.[58] Employees were of three types: commissioned officers, clerks, and servants. Servants comprised the bulk of the company's employees, and included, in order of the 'degrees which were implicitly recognized,' interpreters, mechanics, guides, steersmen, bowsmen or boutes, fishermen, middlemen ['common boatmen'] and apprentices.[59] For this group 'promotion was naturally out of order, each man pursuing the vocation his abilities or training fitted him for.'[60] Clerks, like servants, were engaged by the company for a fixed number of years (usually five), but differed from servants primarily in their education.[61] They were, as their occupation suggests, literate, and were employed in letter-writing and accounting. At the end of their five-year apprenticeship they were eligible to be given charge of the less important and smaller posts, and could eventually be promoted to the ranks of the officer class.[62] Despite the often similar social and economic circumstances from which the clerks and servants came, 'the lines between the different classes in the service were strictly drawn': 'The clerks, even when in a subordinate position in an important establishment, sat at the officers' mess and, as a rule, had rooms in the same house. They were called gentlemen, and in letters were addressed as "Mr."'[63]

The commissioned officers – the chief factors and chief traders – formed what the historian Adrien-Gabriel Morice called 'a veritable oligarchy.'[64] Although they too were engaged for a fixed period, officers held shares in the company, valued at an average £350 each (chief factors held two and chief traders one), and were thus tied even more directly to the company's economic fortunes.[65] This practice ensured the fiscal accountability of its officers. As a further check, the HBC held each officer responsible for all goods sent to his post and for the wages of the men in his charge.[66] Every year each post turned in accounts for every man in the company's employ and took an inventory. The records were used as a guide for apportioning provisions and goods for the following season; a mistake or a lack of productivity by the officer in charge could have immediate and long-term implications for the profitability of his post and the size of his own purse.[67]

In addition to the wages and greater responsibilities of the officer class, a variety of symbols and ritual displays also served to delineate in a tangible way the company's social and occupational hierarchy. Dress was an important means of distinction, as clerk and, eventually, chief trader J.W. McKay's description of a chief factor illustrates:

This exalted functionary was lord paramount; his word was law; he was necessarily surrounded by a halo of dignity, and his person was sacred, so to speak. He was dressed every day in a suit of black or dark blue, white shirt, collars to his ears, frock coat, velvet stock and straps to the bottom of his trousers. When he went out of doors he wore a black beaver hat worth forty shillings. When travelling in a canoe or boat, he was lifted in and out of the craft by the crew; he still wore his beaver hat, but it was protected by an oiled silk cover, and over his black frock he wore a long cloak made of Royal Stuart tartan lined with scarlet or dark blue bath coating. The cloak had a soft Genoa velvet collar, which was fastened across by mosaic gold clasps and chains. He also had voluminous capes.[68]

Such sartorial splendour was impossible for the company's servants, who were issued '2 striped cotton shirts and two yards of common cloth.'[69] In fact, dress was considered so effective in eliciting respect and maintaining order that in 1825 Governor Simpson wrote to the governor and committee in London requesting 'permission to introduce a uniform to be worn by every person coming under the denomination of Gentlemen both in the Honble Coys Sea and-Land Service.' 'The object for suggesting this uniform [sic] that it will add to the respectability of the Service in a certain degree in the estimation of our Servants the Natives & Strangers, That it will tend to introduce a certain Esprit du [sic] Corps which is much required.'[70]

The physical space of the company's posts was also apportioned in a manner that reflected the social distance between the different classes of employees. The most significant building at HBC posts was the officers' residence. Usually the largest building on the site, the officers' residence, or 'Big House,' as it was called at Fort Langley, dominated the landscape; its whitewash, trim, twelve windows, wide sills and hipped roof set it apart from the post's other unpainted and unadorned buildings. At Fort Langley the Big House was situated at 'the back of the fort on an upward incline from the river [the Fraser] provid[ing] a view of the river and McMillan Island directly in front of the fort.' Its importance was further accentuated because visitors had 'to walk the length of the fort square before reaching the Big House.'[71] Servants, by contrast, lived communally in barracks. The exteriors of their dwellings were almost indistinguishable from the warehouses and barns that comprised the rest of the post's structures.[72]

The interior social space of the officers' residence was divided into private quarters for the use of the chief factor and his subsidiary officers and a communal ceremonial space used for dining. Dinner was an occasion to display status publicly, as Thomas Jefferson Farnham's 1839 description of the dining-hall at Fort Vancouver demonstrates:

The dining room is a spacious room on the second floor, ceiled with pine above and at the sides. In the south-west corder [sic] is a large close stove, giving out sufficient caloric to make it comfortable.

At the end of a table twenty feet in length stands Governor McLaughlin [sic, McLoughlin], directing guests and gentlemen from neighbouring posts to their places, at distances from the Governor according to their rank in the service. Thanks are given to God, and all are seated. Roast beef and port, boiled mutton, baked salmon, boiled ham; beets, carrots, turnips, cabbage and potatoes, and wheaten bread, are tastefully distributed over the table among a dinner-set of elegant queen's ware, burnished with glittering glasses and decanters of various coloured Italian wines. Course after course goes round, and the Governor fills to his guests and friends; and each gentleman in turn vies with him in diffusing around the board a most generous allowance of viands, wines, and warm fellow-feeling. The cloth and wines are removed together, cigars are lighted, and a strolling smoke about the premises, enlivened by a courteous discussion of some mooted point of natural history or politics, closes the ceremonies of the dinner hour at Fort Vancouver.[73]

The arrivals and departures of chief factors and other persons of importance were also occasions for ritual display. McKay recalled that 'salutes were fired on his departure from the fort and his return,' while Archibald McDonald described the rather more elaborate ceremony surrounding George Simpson's arrival at Fort St James in 1828.

The day as yet being fine, the flag was put up; the piper in full Highland costume; and every arrangement was made to arrive at FORT ST. JAMES in the most imposing manner we could, for the sake of the Indians. Accordingly, when we came within about a thousand yards of the establishment, descending a gentle hill, a gun was fired, the bugle sounded, and soon after, the piper commenced the celebrated march of the clans, "Si coma leum cogadh na shea," (Peace: or War, if you will otherwise.) The guide, with the British ensign, led the van, followed by the band; then the Governor, on horseback, supported by Doctor Hamlyn and myself on our chargers, two deep; twenty men, with their burdens, next formed the line; then one loaded horse, and lately Mr. McGillivray (with his wife and light infantry) closed on the rear. During the discharge of small arms and wall pieces from the Fort, Mr. Douglas met us a short distance in advance, and in this order we made our entree into the Capital of Western Caledonia.[74]

But as McKay noted, while 'all this ceremony was considered necessary; it had a good effect on the Indians; it added to his [the chief factor's] dignity in the eyes of his subordinates,' it 'sometimes spoiled the chief factor.'[75] The ceremony also created tensions between and among the different classes of employees, and led Governor Simpson to report in 1822 that 'a considerable degree of reserve approaching to coolness appears to exist between the Chief Factors and the Chief Traders, arising, in my opinion, from the circumstances of the former being desirous to make a wider distinction in the rank than is either necessary or proper.'[76]

Provisions also reflected distinctions between the company's employees. The officers' 'roast beef and port, boiled mutton, baked salmon, and boiled ham' contrasted markedly with the servants' allowance of '3 lb. of Salt fish and 2 lb of potatoes,' which was the prescribed 'dietary of the Country for the company's establishments west of the Mountains.'[77]

These examples convey important messages about the nature of everyday life in the fur trade. The ordered and hierarchical nature of post society was part of the regulation of the labour force. It reinforced the authority of company officers by emphasizing the proper place of labouring men, as Farnham's and McKay's descriptions showed. Farnham reported that 'guests and gentlemen' were seated 'at distances from the Governor according to their rank.' McKay described Simpson, on horseback, preceded only by a piper and the British ensign, leading a group of mounted and provisioned attendants who were arranged in an orderly fashion. As well, costume served to segregate the company's officers. It was a direct badge of importance for McKay's chief factor, and in Simpson's case, 'the piper in full Highland costume' set him off from others in his party. Horses were also important bracketing devices. From the lofty height of a company charger, HBC officers commanded a wider view of the landscape – commensurate, perhaps, with their status in the company, which integrated them more intimately into the larger trans-Atlantic world of the fur trade. Mounted, the company's field officers gazed down, both actually and symbolically, at their inferiors. McLoughlin's position at the head of the Fort Vancouver dining-table was also revealing. It underscored his position as the head of an economic establishment as well as the paternal role he occupied with respect to his men. The HBC's officers wielded authority in the social and economic spheres of their servants' lives, acting as parents and providers and meting out punishment.

Corporal punishment, the most direct means used to regulate the labour force, was in many ways a natural outgrowth of both the paternal relationship between HBC officers and servants and the isolated location in which disputes occurred, something that encouraged local and immediate solutions to problems. The company's treatment of its workers was also informed by general attitudes towards the labouring classes and by ethnic prejudices, both of which were consistent with an organic and hierarchical view of society in which identity, power, and authority flowed from status as well as individual ability.

Though rough treatment at the hands of HBC officers was the subject of much complaint, it was explained and justified by the rhetoric and rationale of paternalism. While 'the most unpleasant of our duties is the inforcement [sic] of order,' Chief Trader James Douglas admitted in 1838, the use of 'strong measures in repressing insolence and arresting the dangerous progress of insubordination' was justified because the company had to deal with 'a class of men with whom obedience is the result, neither of upright principle, nor the dread of legal penalties; but in almost every case ... from a high degree of respect for their officers.'[78] Other contemporaries ascribed the 'hard usage' of the company's servants to the 'autocratic' nature of HBC officers and their tendency to make status distinctions.[79] For instance, the 'irascible' William Thew of Fraser Lake 'was too prone to believe a gentleman against a plebian,' and often beat his servants cruelly when they complained.[80]

These status distinctions were based on the company's assumptions about the nature of their workforce. Labouring men had to be taught how to work and, in Governor George Simpson's estimation, needed to be 'managed' and 'moulded' into industriousness.[81] Ethnic stereotypes also crept into the language of labour regulation. The HBC considered Orkneymen 'a close, prudent, quiet people, strictly faithful to their employers,' 'avaricious,' and likely to act with great 'propriety' around the Native population. French Canadians were 'a volatile and inconsiderate race of people, but active, capable of undergoing great hardship and easily managed.' Red River Métis were a cheap source of labour, but were effective only if they were introduced into the service 'at a sufficiently early period in life.' Otherwise, they tended to be of 'changeable disposition and unsteady habits.' Such attitudes were encapsulated in Simpson's remarks about the company's methods of disciplining its workers. Whereas European labourers were 'not accustomed to receive corporal chastisement and we would not consider it would be proper to introduce it,' he noted, 'with Canadians it is different; they stand more in awe of a blow than a fine.'[82]

Despite these sentiments, in an 1853 letter to Donald Manson, the chief factor in charge of New Caledonia, Simpson made his disapproval of such attitudes clear. Charges of ill treatment continued to surface, providing him with 'ample evidence' of 'a system of "club law."'

We duly appreciate the necessity of maintaining discipline and enforcing obedience; that end is not to be attained by the display of violent passion and the infliction of severe and arbitrary punishment in hot blood. When a servant is refractory or disobeys orders he should be allowed a full hearing, his case examined fairly and deliberately, and if guilty, either taken out to the depot, put on short rations or under arrest – in fact, almost any punishment rather than knocking about or flogging.[83]

As should be apparent by the examples scattered in this chapter, there was little evidence to show that Simpson's call for the fair and deliberate examination of misconduct was heeded. Dispute resolution in the fur-trade period continued to be characterized by 'knocking about or flogging,' practices that stemmed from local conditions and that were sanctioned by a system of paternal authority that placed great discretion in the hands of those who ruled by virtue of their social status.

Though the HBC had several formal instruments at its disposal to regulate its employees' behaviour, company law was far more informal, uneven, and discretionary. Company authority was paternal and reinforced by its corporate organization and the routines of everyday life at the posts, which emphasized social distance, hierarchy, and order. Although HBC employees were subservient and accepted that position, their obedience was not unconditional. Club law may have been wielded in the economic interests of the company and its shareholders, but those interests were necessarily tempered by social responsibility. Social and economic relations between officers and servants were mediated by a system of mutual obligation in which deference and obedience to company strictures was procured in exchange for corporate responsibility for their welfare.

The degree of control afforded the company was, however, much less than one might expect from a system of law and authority that did not draw distinctions between the social and economic spheres of its servants' lives, but attempted to regulate both. Though they were possessed of few formal rights, HBC servants enjoyed a certain amount of latitude in their behaviour precisely because of the informality and unevenness of their relationship with the company's officers. There was more diversity in social relations and a greater tolerance for it than would characterize the colonial period.

In both Vancouver Island and British Columbia, the arrival of immigrants independent of the Hudson's Bay Company disrupted its system of informal law and corporate paternalism. To these people, club law was illegitimate not because they felt it irrational and uncivilized, but because it represented private interests – because it represented the interests of what they considered a 'club.' Excluded from the system of mutual obligations that bound employers and employees, rulers and ruled, they pushed for the formalization of relations between the state and its citizens.

2

'A Squatocracy of Skin Traders': Law and Authority on Vancouver Island

In 1865 the English adventurer and journalist Charles Aubrey Angelo recalled his introduction to Vancouver Island during the Fraser River gold rush in 1859 with a bitterness suggestive of deeper tensions in the young colony.

In my unsophisticated innocence, I foolishly imagined that I was entering a Colony governed by British Institutions, but I was quickly undeceived: it was far worse than a Venetian oligarchy, – a squatocracy of skin traders, ruled by men whose life had been spent in the wilderness in social communion with Indian savages; their present daily occupation being the sale of tea, sugar, whisky, and the usual et ceteras of a grocery, which (taking advantage of an increased population) they sold at the small advance of five hundred per cent ... I found these 'small fry' claiming under some antediluvian grant, not only Vancouver Island, but a tract of country extending from the Pacific to the Atlantic Ocean! The onward march of civilization was checked ... And a country which might now be teeming with a hardy, industrious population, was crushed and blasted, by a set of unprincipled autocrats, whose selfish interests, idle caprices, and unscrupulous conduct, sought to gratify their petty ambition by trampling on the dearest rights of their fellow man.[1]

Angelo's sentiments were symptomatic of the bitter debate over the constitution of legitimate authority in Vancouver Island following its creation in 1849 as a proprietary colony of the Hudson's Bay Company.[2] At a time when laissez-faire principles informed much of British policy and suffused public sentiment, the HBC's position as a monopolistic business enterprise and a colonial proprietor rested on insecure foundations.[3]

For five years, from 1849 to 1854, Vancouver Island's independent settlers (independent, that is, from the HBC) voiced their opposition to the company's attempts to turn its economic monopoly into a political and social one. Of particular concern to the independent settlers was the HBC's use of the law and the courts to buttress its position. To the independents, the colony's land laws not only were detrimental to its settlement and economic development, but also had the effect of extending the HBC's rigid occupation-based social hierarchy over the island and, because of the land-based franchise, of concentrating political power in company hands. In framing the colony's courts, the HBC drew on its fur-trade experience. Equating law with the regulation of its work force, the company appointed men who had experience in managing the large numbers of labourers as justices of the peace: its farm bailiffs. These appointments did not attract much attention, but when Fort Victoria Chief Factor and Vancouver Island Governor James Douglas named his brother-in-law and the manager of the company's coal mines chief justice of the Supreme Court in 1853 the independents took action and petitioned the Colonial Office and the Queen for relief.

What was happening on Vancouver Island was the redefinition of the relationship between rulers and ruled, between the colonial state and its citizens. Unlike company servants, the colony's independent settlers were excluded from and untutored in the informal, unarticulated customs of corporate paternalism, and were insensitive to the mutuality that underlay that system of authority. In their eyes, the company's attempts to control the island's political and legal institutions smacked of arbitrary rule. Rather than submitting to the uneven and discretionary practices of paternal rule that stemmed from the company's economic and social organization, the independents demanded what amounted to a formalization of their relationship with the colonial state. They wanted access to the political process and political office through land law reform and an elected assembly. As well, they demanded regular courts of law manned by properly trained and reasonably neutral judges. Both the company's land policy and the appointment of David Cameron to the Supreme Court compromised the idea that the law was above the capricious dictates and prejudices of men and served some loosely defined human good. But overlaid on the independent settlers' concerns for the rule of law and their rejection of the paternal authority of the HBC government on this basis was a rejection of economic monopoly. The independents considered company authority illegitimate not only because its actions and policies contravened the rule of law, but also because of the growing illegitimacy of economic monopoly in the Anglo-North American world of the mid-nineteenth century. As in the fur-trade period, law and economy were still closely associated, but the intersection of these two discourses – rule of law and free market, rather than moral, economics – suggests the outlines of a new configuration of authority in the colonial world.

From the colony's beginnings, tensions existed between the island's de jure civil authority and the de facto authority of the Hudson's Bay Company. Despite the arrival in March 1850 of a colonial governor unconnected with the HBC, effective control of Vancouver Island remained in the hands of the company. Richard Blanshard found himself both superfluous and unwanted from the moment he arrived. Like a poor relation, the inexperienced barrister found that he was completely dependent upon the company's generosity. Food he received; but shelter proved a contentious issue throughout his short tenure.[4] When Blanshard arrived, he was forced to live aboard HMS *Driver* because the construction of a governor's residence was unfinished. Though he was given a room at the fort, Blanshard grew increasingly annoyed at his lack of appropriate lodging, interpreting it as a sign of his insignificance. By June the governor was positively cranky, and informed Chief Factor James Douglas that he considered 'the labour of a single man [on his 'Cottage'] ... a mere mockery.'[5] Blanshard's problems ran deeper than his petty exchanges with the HBC indicated. Although the Crown's representative of British authority in the colony, Blanshard was a ruler without subjects. Though the new governor had jurisdiction in 'the administration of civil government and military affairs,'[6] he complained that 'there [was] little indeed to do except settle disputes between representatives of the Company and their employees.'[7] Even in this capacity Blanshard was ineffectual. As the events at Fort Rupert in 1850 showed, the Hudson's Bay Company was a state within a state. With two parallel authorities in the colony, financing the construction of his cottage was to prove the least of his problems.

In 1850 the 'miserable affair' at Fort Rupert illustrated the degree to which company control and civil government were indistinguishable.[8] Located on the northeast coast of Vancouver Island, Fort Rupert was a coal-mining and fur-trade post. Like its other servants, Fort Rupert's miners were contracted by the Hudson's Bay Company; however, because they were skilled workers, the Ayrshire miners' contracts stipulated that their labour was to be confined to the diggings.[9] Unlike the company's other servants, they were not subject to performing whatever task their employers might order. When the fort's officers tried to make the miners do so, they promptly struck. Fearing a breakdown of authority in an area populated heavily by apparently hostile natives, Blanshard commissioned John Sebastian Helmcken, the company surgeon, as justice of the peace for Fort Rupert and sent him north.[10] Shortly after Helmcken arrived, the bodies of three British seamen, deserters from the British barque *England*, were discovered near the fort – murdered, it was presumed, by the neighbouring Newitty Indians. Unable to secure the cooperation of the servants at the fort, who charged the company with instigating the murders,[11] or of its officers, who 'asserted that [they] owed no obedience except to the Hudson's Bay Company,'[12] Helmcken submitted his resignation.[13] The episode, which ended relatively peacefully for the Europeans,[14] convinced Blanshard of 'the impropriety of making appointments among the company's servants,' who 'even after retiring from the service ... are in a great measure subject to the same influence as they receive certain allowances which may be forfeited if they act in any manner that is considered as prejudicial to the company.'[15] Blanshard's situation was unworkable, and in the wake of the Fort Rupert incident he tendered his resignation in November, only nine months after his arrival.[16]

Blanshard's concerns about 'the impropriety of making appointments among the company's servants' were echoed shortly after his resignation when the Crown named Fort Victoria Chief Factor James Douglas the new governor of the colony. Fifteen independent settlers signed a petition protesting the appointment. 'We and we alone represent the interests of the Island as a free and independent British Colony,' they insisted,

for we constitute the whole body of the independent settlers, all the other inhabitants being in some way or other so connected with and controlled by the Hudson's Bay Company ...

We beg to express in most emphatical and plainest manner our assurance that impartial decisions cannot be expected from a Governor who is not only a member of the Company sharing in its profits, but is also charged as their chief Agent, with the sole representation of their trading interests in this Island and the adjacent coasts.[17]

Because the Hudson's Bay Company was pre-eminently a business enterprise, the independent settlers assumed that its actions would be motivated by self-interest. While this was rational behaviour for private companies and individuals, it was illegitimate for mid-nineteenth-century governments. The role of government in a laissez-faire age was to provide a regulatory framework that would promote individual gain without impinging on the rights of others to do so. Monopolies and governments based on monopoly, like the proprietary government of Vancouver Island, were anathema to this view. According to the petitioners, under Hudson's Bay Company rule the welfare and prosperity of the colony and the petitioners themselves was compromised. There was, they argued, no 'security that the interests of the Hudson's Bay Company shall not be allowed to outweigh and ruin those of the colony in general.'[18] Even those closely associated with the company had doubts about its impartiality. 'We are taught that a man cannot serve two masters,' wrote Chief Factor Peter Skene Ogden, 'but their Honours are of a different opinion – vide Douglas' new appointment not only two but three: C.F. [chief factor] in the Fur Trade, Agent for the Puget Sound Coy. [the HBC's agricultural arm] and Gov. of Vancouver's Island; if there be not a clashing of interests in the management of these different interests – *I wonder.*'[19] But motivated by its own concern for economy, and recognizing that the HBC was the de facto authority on the Island for the majority of its inhabitants, the Colonial Office was unmoved.[20]

The colony's land laws and the appointment of David Cameron as chief justice were the next flashpoints of political discontent on the island.[21] These two problems and the petitions they spawned made explicit the issues at stake in the company's attempt to govern on the basis of its corporate experience as a private monopoly. Those who signed the anti-land laws and the anti-Cameron petitions opposed the company because its policy decisions had the effect of turning its economic monopoly into a political one, and in the process compromised the impartiality of the law.

The 1849 grant was conditional on the company's successfully colonizing the island within five years.[22] Retired company servants were an obvious source of prospective colonists, not only because the company would not have to bear the expense of conveying such settlers to Vancouver Island, but because their familiarity with the native population acted to safeguard the relatively peaceful relations between the two.[23] Free grants of land like those given in the American territories were not used to attract settlers to Vancouver Island. Instead, the company embarked on a plan of systematic colonization guided and shaped by the ideas of Edward Gibbon Wakefield.[24]

Central to Wakefield's theory was the means by which colonial lands were disposed. The anaemic state of many English colonies was, he thought, due to their abundance of land and their small population. These two factors resulted in a shortage of labour, as few colonists would choose to work the lands of others when they could so easily become their own masters. This labour shortage, in turn, would deter investment by moneyed individuals in the colonies, and thus was responsible for the slow development of commerce, as the capital accumulation necessary for the development of economies of scale was impossible. The solution, according to Wakefield, lay in balancing labour and land. By selling land at a 'sufficient price' – that is, at a price low enough to attract prospective colonists, but high enough to prevent all from becoming independent landowners – the preconditions for successful colonization would be met.[25] Moreover, Wakefield's plans for systematic colonization had in them an element of social engineering. If Britain's social hierarchy was replicated in its colonies, social order would be assured. This was done by pricing lands on a sliding scale, each price corresponding to a different 'class' of settler.

The London governors of the Hudson's Bay Company were taken by Wakefield's ideas and recommended them to James Douglas. 'The object of every survey system of colonization,' confided HBC Governor Archibald Barclay to Douglas in 1849, should be not to re-organize Society on a new basis, which is simply absurd, but to transfer to the new country whatever is most valuable and most approved in the institutions of the old, so that Society may, as far as possible, consist of the same Classes, united together by the same ties, and having the same relative duties to perform in one country as in the other.

The Committee [of the HBC] believes that some of the worst evils that afflict the Colonies have arisen from the admission of persons of all descriptions; no regard being had to the character, means or views of the immigrants. They have therefore established such conditions for the disposal of lands, as they trust will have the effect of introducing the just proportion of labour and capital, and also of preventing the ingress of squatters, paupers and land Speculators. The principle of Selection, without the invidiousness of its direct application, is thus indirectly adopted.[26]

Douglas was confident that 'almost every one of the Company's labouring servants would also gladly avail themselves of the opportunity of settling on British Territory, and spending the declining years of life, under the protection of their native Flag,' and because they were 'a hardy tractable, laborious, class of men ... they would certainly form an excellent nucleus for a new settlement.'[27] On Vancouver Island, land was divided into three classes, each reflecting a different social class: town lots (£10), suburban lots (five-acre sections at £15) and country lands (£1 per acre, with a minimum purchase of twenty acres).[28]

Political power was reserved for settlers who could afford to buy twenty acres of country land; for those who aspired to hold office, ownership of a minimum of three hundred acres of country land was necessary. Given that the average wage of HBC labourers was £17 per year while that of officers ranged from £100 for clerks to £350 for chief factors, effective power in the new colony mirrored the division of power in the HBC hierarchy. Thus, the replication of the social and corporate order of the Hudson's Bay Company was one of the animating principles of colonial land policy.

Measured in terms of actual settlement, the company's scheme of systematic colonization was successful, with town and suburban lots and country lands being purchased by the appropriate – in Wakefieldian terms – social classes.[29] If, however, the HBC's efforts at settling the Island are measured in terms of its success as a colonization scheme – that is, its success in attracting immigrants – then the assessment must be less favourable. For despite the Victorian optimism of Barclay and the governors of the Hudson's Bay Company, the population of Vancouver Island grew slowly.[30] Many attributed Vancouver Island's sluggish development to the high price of land, as the 1853 petition from the 'landed proprietors and inhabitants of Vancouver Island' showed.[31] 'The attempt at colonizing Vancouver Island may, so far, be considered a failure,' they wrote. 'One principle cause of which is the high price charged for land, while in Oregon, but a few miles distant ... the United States Government makes liberal gratuitous grants to actual settlers.'[32] Company land laws were squarely to blame for the 'manifest hopelessness of its settlement within any reasonable period,' rather than the colony's 'natural properties.' Vancouver Island's settlers were not the labouring classes of England, whose numbers inspired Wakefield to formulate his scheme of systematic colonization. Rather, as the petitioners pointed out and the company's land records show, those who purchased land in Wakefieldian proportions were already in the colony, brought there by the fur trade or by the company in its capacity as proprietor to work its farms. 'Although there may be now fifty or sixty purchasers of land,' they wrote, 'these persons were, almost without a single exception, previously upon the Island, or in the immediate neighbourhood, and connected strongly with it by their engagements in the service of the Hudson's Bay Company.'[33] To the petitioners, the only solution to the company's mismanagement and the progress of the colony was the intervention of the imperial government.[34]

There was more to the petitioners' concerns than just economic development. On Vancouver Island, Wakefield's plan had the effect of extending the company's rigid occupation-based social hierarchy over the colony, something that the independent settlers thought they had left behind when they emigrated from England. More important, however, land and political authority were linked. By controlling land alienation, the HBC controlled political power. Land law reform went hand in hand with political reform. Not only did the petitioners call for a reduction in the price of land to 'no more than 10 s. per acre' from £1, they also demanded a change in the franchise qualifications. If the petitioners had their way, electors would include 'all persons possessed, for their own use and benefit, of land in the counties worth £10 sterling, or in the towns worth £20 sterling, or occupying houses paying rent to the amount of £10 sterling per annum.' As a logical extension of these demands, the petition also contained a call for an elected Council and Assembly, as well as 'reliable courts of justice.'[35]

Although some company officials dismissed the land petition as the work of 'two or three contemptible propagandists,' the American press did not.[36] The Olympia (Washington) *Columbian* reprinted it along with an editorial in October 1853, and in doing so must have raised the spectre of American annexation in the minds of Douglas and the London governors of the Hudson's Bay Company. 'The language of the petition is very similar to that which our own immortal sires used in their beseeching through vain appeals to the same government,' noted the *Columbian*. 'When Great Britain shall turn her back on her natural-born sons, we will take them to ourselves, foster them as our own and the consequences be upon her head ... American enterprise would thunder a welcome to the STATE OF VANCOUVER.'[37]

David Cameron's appointment as chief justice of the newly created Supreme Court came on the heels of the anti-land laws petition and sparked yet another round of petitioning. Cameron's appointment and the agitation that ensued was just the end of a series of smaller problems that plagued the construction of Vancouver Island's legal system, and that illustrate the difficulties the company encountered when it tried to extend its corporate experience into the civil sphere. The limitations of company authority that were revealed in the course of the construction of the colony's courts did nothing to make the HBC's position as proprietor more palatable to the island's independent settlers. For not only was the company a monopoly – an illegitimate form of association in the mid-nineteenth century – but it also appeared to be inept when it came to administering the law.

Before it was granted proprietorship of Vancouver Island, and through much of the colonial period, the HBC equated the institutions of the law with the regulation of labour. Although there is no evidence that they were appointed, it is significant that the London governors of the company put forward the names of fourteen HBC officers as 'gentlemen ... well-qualified to hold commissions of the Peace under the Act of 1st and 2d Geo. 4th ch 66' for Vancouver Island.[38] Despite his difficulties with the company, and his warning that 'to appoint [representatives of the HBC] magistrates would be to make them judges in their own causes,'[39] Governor Richard Blanshard's first civil appointment went to the HBC surgeon John Sebastian Helmcken. The medical officer was made magistrate for Fort Rupert 'as the miners and laborers there have shown a disposition to riot.'[40] The trend of appointing company officers to judicial positions continued under Governor and Chief Factor James Douglas. In March 1853 he named three company bailiffs – managers of the HBC's farms – justices of the peace.[41] Kenneth McKenzie, the bailiff of Craigflower Farm, and Thomas James Skinner, the bailiff of Constance Cove Farm, were JPs for 'the Peninsula,' while the manager of Colwood Farm, Edward Edwards Langford, was given jurisdiction in Esquimalt. The JP for Metchosin, Thomas Blinkhorn, was not an HBC employee, but did work as a bailiff on a three-hundred-acre farm belonging to Captain James Cooper, formerly of the company's maritime service, then an independent merchant.[42] In September, David Cameron, a manager of the company's collieries at Nanaimo and James Douglas's brother-in-law, was added to the colony's complement of justices of the peace. The JPs held petty sessions on the first Thursday of each month and a general session four times a year.[43] Though there are few records of the proceedings of Vancouver Island's courts before 1858, those that have survived bear testimony to the accuracy of Richard

Blanshard's early impression of the nature of legal activity in the colony.[44] Most of the suits involved disputes between company employees: claims for wages, breach of contract, or desertion. Company servants could also be found on the criminal side of the early court's business, charged with assault or drunkenness.[45]

Though they appeared to be well equipped to handle these cases, it soon became apparent that the justice's courts were neither sufficient nor competent to handle all the legal business of the colony. Although the English laws relating to justices of the peace were received in Vancouver Island in 1849 and were not amended before the appointment of the first JPs, the colony's magistrates appear, from the surviving court records, to have assumed wide-ranging powers inconsistent with their statutory jurisdictions and responsibilities.[46] In June 1853, for instance, Thomas James Skinner was convinced by an 'American adventurer,' Webster, to issue what amounted to an injunction to stop two ships from receiving spars at Sooke.[47] Webster's motive in seeking this injunction was to secure a monopoly on timber exports from Vancouver Island. After ordering the vessels to be released from custody and dissuading both masters of the ships in question from launching proceedings against his justice of the peace, Douglas chastised Skinner for his 'rash and ill-considered' behaviour.[48] His warning seems not to have had any effect, for in September of the same year Skinner awarded damages of $2,213 and costs to the same Webster in a countersuit launched against the Muir family of Sooke.[49] Spurred on by his success, Webster launched yet another case against the Muirs, but left the colony when it became apparent that he would not receive such favourable treatment from the colony's new Supreme Court of Civil Justice.

The establishment of the Supreme Court of Civil Justice of Vancouver's Island with David Cameron as its judge on 2 December 1853 was, as James Douglas wrote, a direct result of 'certain irregularities, in the practice of the Justices Court, arising from the inexperience of the Magistrates ... It was therefore resolved to limit the Jurisdiction of the Justices Court in civil cases, to such simple matters as our Justices are competent to deal with.'[50] The jurisdiction of justices of the peace in civil matters was limited to cases involving sums up to fifty pounds; all other cases fell under the jurisdiction of the superior court. Although the act establishing the Supreme Court was disallowed by the law officers of the Crown in January 1854, it is unclear whether this affected its operation.[51] Certainly the colonists continued to consider David Cameron Vancouver Island's chief justice, though his appointment and the Supreme Court itself were not confirmed until April 1856. Though he had no formal legal training, Cameron drafted the rules and regulations governing the Supreme Court, which gave it jurisdiction in civil matters as well as the power to sit as a court of appeal, bankruptcy, equity, probate, and revision. These were passed by an imperial order in Council in February 1857. Criminal jurisdiction was granted to the Supreme Court in April 1860.[52]

The colonial government established an Inferior Court of Civil Justice, designed to further limit the jurisdiction of the justices' courts in civil matters and in response to the 'comparatively numerous' suits for 'petty debts' in 1857.[53] Essentially, this was a small debts court modelled on the English county courts as established by the 1846 Act for the More Easy Recovery of Small Debts and Demands in England.[54] But in contrast to the situation in England, there was only one Inferior Court of Civil Justice, based in the main population centre of Victoria and presided over by David Cameron. The Minor Offences Act, 1860, and the Vancouver Island Jury Act, 1865, further modified the procedure of the inferior courts in order to accommodate the island's transient and sparse population.[55] The first act gave two justices of the peace the powers of justices sitting as a court of quarter sessions in criminal cases where a material witness was unable to wait until the next sitting of the court of quarter sessions. Furthermore, cases tried under the Minor Offences Act could be heard with a jury of eight rather than twelve men. The Vancouver Island Jury Act amended the manner of taking verdicts in civil cases. Instead of unanimity, judges were authorized to accept verdicts passed by a majority of three-quarters of the jury, provided that the jury in question had been retired for a minimum of three hours. In recommending the bill, Vancouver Island's attorney-general thought that 'in so small a community as that of the Colony where few individuals are absolutely unknown to each other' verdicts were harder to obtain.[56] No doubt he was right: given Vancouver Island's factionalization, reaching any consensus must have been difficult.

By far the most important act dealing with the inferior level of courts on Vancouver Island was the District Court Act, 1866. This act allowed for the creation of several inferior courts of civil justice for the recovery of small debts. Each district court was presided over by one justice of the peace, whose jurisdiction was limited to cases involving sums up to $250.

The evolution of Vancouver Island's courts is suggestive of the limitations of Hudson's Bay Company authority. The inability of the JPs to handle civil cases – something their qualifications as company bailiffs did not prepare them for – led directly to the formation of the Supreme Court of Civil Justice and the Inferior and, later, District Courts. Despite his comments about the incompetency of the bailiff-JPs, old HBC-hand and Governor James Douglas must have held fast to his belief that the authority conferred by the company could still be effective, because he named David Cameron to the superior court. Cameron was just as unqualified for the post as his brother magistrates. According to the independents, not only was he untrained in the law, but his 'improperly close family connexion' with James Douglas and his 'commercial situation as Clerk of the Honble Hudson's Bay Company's coal mines at Nanymo [sic]' also disqualified him for the office of Chief Justice. The Victoria-based *British Colonist* wrote that Cameron, 'instead of being versed in the profound commentaries ... of Blackstone on the Common law, was – so far as can be inferred by his occupation – only versed in the *blackstone* of the Nanaimo mines. Jefferies may have benefitted from the lucubrations of Coke the compeer of Bacon, but our Chief Justice possibly benefitted from the *coke* derived from coal.'[57]

Governor Douglas's appointment of his brother-in-law and a former company employee did little to dispel the fears that Vancouver Island's proprietary government rested on a political as well as an economic monopoly. Unlike the earlier conflict over the colony's land laws, however, Cameron's appointment struck a more direct blow to the idea of the rule of law. Given his past association with the HBC and his familial ties to the governor, each time Cameron took the bench his presence was a symbolic contradiction of the very notion of impartial justice. Moreover, the chief justice's occasional outbursts did not aid his own cause. A Colonial Office memorandum stated that Cameron 'conducted himself on one occasion in Court, shortly after his appointment as J.P., in so disgraceful a manner that the other three magistrates passed a resolution censuring him in the strongest measures ... [H]is conduct was so gross that the whole of those in Court soon actually hissed him.'[58] But Cameron was more than just a symbol. His powers of sanction and reward as chief justice were real, as those who came before him realized. Fines or confinement in irons in the north bastion of the fort made company rule palpable to the colonists in a way qualitatively different from the colony's governorship or its land policy.

It was David Cameron's exercise of his very real judicial powers that precipitated the last flurry of petitioning in the winter of 1853–54. His actions in *R. v. Robert John Staines* (1853) revealed the social as well as the political dimension of the debate over the law and legitimate political authority on Vancouver Island.

'A man full of frills,' Robert John Staines arrived at Fort Victoria on 17 March 1848 to take up his position as HBC chaplain.[59] Six years later to the month, Staines died near Cape Flattery, Washington, when his overloaded ship, the *Duchess of San Lorenzo*, bound for San Francisco, sank. Elected by some of the island's colonists to act as their emissary, Staines was on his way to London, carrying with him two petitions – one addressed to the Duke of Newcastle and the other to the Queen herself – signed by sixty-nine of the 'most dutiful and loyal' inhabitants of Vancouver Island.[60] In these two petitions the colonists

'A Squatocracy of Skin Traders'   45

complained about the island's legal system, and particularly about the chief justice of the Supreme Court of Civil Justice, David Cameron. 'Groaning under the grievances inflicted by the Local Government of this Colony of Vancouver's Island,' the petitioners complained that

there can be no sound basis for happiness amongst a People where the Courts of Justice are not pure, efficient and reliable. We regard this as a fundamental Maxim of Government unshaken and eternal.

It is our most anxious wish to have the laws of our country ably and impartially administered amongst us by men of adequate integrity, ability, learning, and experience, in whom we can repose our entire confidence, and towards whom we can cordially extend our deserved respect.

We therefore most humbly intreat that your majesty would graciously cause a strict inquiry to be immediately instituted into the circumstances of the recent creation of a Court entitled 'The Supreme Court of Civil Justice' for Vancouver's Island ... and the appointment of Mr David Cameron, the Governor's Brother-in-law, as Judge of the same as ... we cannot consider our safety to depend upon our innocence or the rectitude of our cause.[61]

Certainly Staines could relate to the sentiments contained in the petitions. Though he did not sign either document, during his short tenure on Vancouver Island Robert John Staines clashed with its colonial administrators, and had himself been the victim of Cameron's 'notorious and gross partiality, acrimony, malice, and indecorum.'[62] *R. v. Staines* (1853) precipitated both petitions and, despite his death, initiated a protracted discussion of the colony's legal system. Yet despite their lofty rhetoric of justice, the petitions and the documents sent by the island's colonial administration in response had much more humble origins.

On a Saturday morning in the middle of November 1853, George Hawkins, the bailiff of Staines's farm, who had arrived on the *Norman Morison* two years earlier, called on Emanuel Douillet, the managing bailiff of Cloverdale, William Fraser Tolmie's farm.[63] Hawkins told Douillet that he had heard there were pigs on the farm which belonged to him, and which he had come to claim. While Douillet admitted that he had two pigs which did not belong to Cloverdale, he later noted that Hawkins could not pick them out of the herd. Nevertheless, Douillet turned over the two. As he was leaving, Hawkins spotted another familiar pig, and told the bailiff that he would return the following day with a man who knew the animals better and would claim the remainder of his wayward animals. True to his word, Hawkins returned on Sunday at eleven o'clock, armed and accompanied by James McFadden, a labourer and an employee of Staines. The bedridden Douillet was rousted up and told to turn over the animals. He refused, saying that the only two pigs that were not his had already been returned. Hawkins and McFadden accused the bailiff of stealing and left the house without another word. After searching the farm, Hawkins remarked to McFadden that he had discovered three sows that were his. However, the two left without them.

On Monday, Staines, Hawkins, McFadden, James Graham (another labourer) and an unidentified Indian returned to Douillet's, this time armed with a search warrant issued by Thomas James Skinner. With Douillet's neighbours Adolphus Fearon, Baptiste Jollibois, and Jacob Low present, Staines ordered James Graham to read the warrant. The illiterate Graham stumbled, so Staines did the job himself. He then ordered Jacob Low to read the warrant to Douillet in French, but as Douillet later recalled, the warrant said 'nothing about pigs.' The mounted pastor then proceeded to drive all the pigs into the yard, and after picking out five, warned the bailiff not to interfere. He would forgive Douillet once but not twice.

Staines was particular about his pigs. His farm in the vicinity of Mount Tolmie yielded large quantities of wheat and oats, and the pastor himself exhibited a penchant for livestock-breeding. Thus, when he discovered that some of his prized pigs had escaped and, possessed of indiscriminate tastes, had lodged themselves on the farm of an HBC surgeon, Staines felt 'wrathy,' and applied to Skinner for a search warrant.[64] True to his judicial form, Skinner 'issued a simple order, for the removal of certain pigs ... without summoning the party charged with the offense to appear before him, or taking any steps to ascertain the truth.'[65] 'This most arbitrary proceeding excited a general feeling of indignation, and I was not a little vexed,' wrote James Douglas, 'that Mr. Skinner should have so inconsiderately violated in that instance, the forms prescribed by the Law, without any evident necessity, as Douilet [sic], whether guilty or otherwise was entitled to a hearing in his own defence.'[66]

Douillet reported the incident to Governor Douglas, and swore a complaint to David Cameron on 5 December.[67] Cameron then issued a summons for Staines, Hawkins, and Graham to appear in three days to answer charges of 'illegal trespass and forcible taking and carrying away of ... property.' Douillet's three neighbours, Fearon, Jollibois, and Low, as well as Fearon's wife Susan Grant, were examined, and after hearing their depositions and the answers of the defendants, Cameron concluded that there was sufficient evidence to proceed. The three were released, each on his own recognizance of twenty pounds, and the pigs were taken into the custody of the court. On 17 December James McFadden and George Richardson were summoned to answer the same charges, but apparently were released: Richardson because he claimed to be 'a looker on,' and McFadden because he was acting on Staines's instructions.

Because of insufficient evidence, the Crown did not proceed with the case, and the rest of the defendants were released on 5 January. Not satisfied with his exoneration, Staines laid charges against Douillet for theft.[68] Found guilty, the bailiff was fined and imprisoned in the north bastion of Fort Victoria, and the pigs were returned to their proper pastoral surroundings on Mount Tolmie.

'Highly indignant because Mr Cameron received and acted upon the complaint of Douilet [sic],' Staines 'did everything in his power to create an impression that in so doing, Mr Cameron was animated solely by motives of personal hostility.'[69] Ninety of the island's residents signed a petition complaining about Cameron's appointment even before Staines's January hearing. Calling Cameron's appointment 'a measure so obnoxious to the Community at large,' the petitioners outlined their case against the chief justice. The office should be 'reposed only in men of the highest repute for honor, honesty, & impartiality.' David Cameron shared none of these characteristics.

Mr Cameron has barely resided Six months among us, and in that brief space he has not so conducted himself as to have obtained the respect of the Community; he during the short time he has officiated as a Magistrate, has most singularly failed in impressing us with a sense of his integrity and uprightness, he has in the position proved himself most singularly cast and indecorus in his language; he has exhibited the most profound ignorance of the duties attaching to the Commission of the Peace and is tolerably void of the little practical knowledge necessary to conduct the business of a Magisterial Court as have made him a laughing stock; and indirectly brought scorn on the proceedings of the whole Bench of Magistrates.[70]

When the governor turned them away 'with scorn,' the petitioners gathered at the home of James Yates. There they elected a five-man committee consisting of Yates, William Banfield, and James Cooper, all independent merchants, and JPs Edward Langford and Thomas Skinner, and raised four hundred dollars to send Staines to England to present their grievances.

Not to be outdone, those who supported the HBC's proprietorship drafted a petition of their own in response, countering the charges against David Cameron. The chief justice, they argued, was 'a Gentleman of business habits and considerable colonial experience ... the fittest man here of those not already professionally occupied to preside in such a Court.' In contrast, 'but few of the Subscribers to that [anti-Cameron] petition have property at stake in the Island.'

We are further of opinion, that if in this Colony, where there is perfect freedom of action, where life and property are as yet secure, where the market is so extensive and remunerative, and where the produce is so lamentably small, the labouring and industrious classes were to employ their time more in raising wheat and potatoes, constructing houses to live in &c., &c., and suffer themselves less, to be led away into discussions upon abstract political questions; all would gain by the alteration, progress become more decided, and foreigners and visitors, whose good opinion we respect, would say more for our common sense.[71]

After the trial and the imprisonment of Douillet, the two petitions that Staines carried with him to the bottom of the Strait of Juan de Fuca were drafted, bearing further testimony to 'the strong feeling in the public mind against this abortion of a court.'[72]

This obscure trial and the events that led to it reveal much about the nature of litigation and social tensions in the colony. Though the immediate issue at law was narrow in scope — exactly five pigs wide — the case involved people from the very top of the colonial social hierarchy to the very bottom. But Staines's pigs also managed to transcend the merely provincial to reveal both the political and the social dimensions of the debate over law and political authority. Those who petitioned against Cameron saw his connection with the company as a conflict of interest that defeated the notion of the rule of law. 'We cannot,' they wrote, 'consider our safety to depend upon our innocence or the rectitude of our cause.' With Cameron as chief justice, the HBC's political monopoly was strengthened, and it gained a veneer of impartiality through its control of an institution that was traditionally neutral.

But the trial and the petitions that followed also revealed the social polarization that underlay political agitation on the island. Those who opposed the chief justice and company government were late arrivals to the colony and were independent of any HBC affiliation. Like typical mid-nineteenth-century immigrants to British North America, they came to Vancouver Island to improve their economic situation, but found themselves confronted with an obstacle to achieving that end: namely, a colonial government whose economic interests were not favourable to their own, and who, through the law and the courts, could act in its own interests from a position of strength. As chief factor, James Douglas had clashed with Staines over the funding of the company school; he suspected that the pastor was responsible for a series of anonymous letters that appeared in Oregon newspapers criticizing the government of the colony.[73] Staines was among fifteen colonists who signed the 1851 petition protesting Douglas's appointment as governor, and he was suspected of being the organizing force behind the 1853 land petition.[74] Against this backdrop of political agitation, it is not surprising that Douglas gave Douillet a sympathetic hearing and that Staines read this as a confirmation of the partiality of the colony's proprietary government.

Skinner and the other PSAC bailiffs were often at odds with Douglas over the management of the four company farms. As a company agent, Douglas was concerned over the failure of the farms to return a profit, and blamed the failure on the mismanagement and extravagance of the farms' bailiffs.[75] As well, in the June and September before the Staines case, Douglas had been openly critical of Skinner's conduct as a justice of the peace – conduct which, as we have seen, led to the formation of the Supreme Court of Civil Justice. Given this, it is not surprising that Skinner aligned himself with Staines, signing the petitions and sitting with his fellow JP and bailiff Edward Langford and Yates, Cooper, and Banfield on the anti-Cameron committee struck in December 1853.

More interesting are the alliances between those of lower status. Those who supported Douillet were his immediate neighbours, and shared a bond forged during their years as Hudson's Bay Company servants. Douillet and Jollibois had served at Fort Vancouver before being transferred to Victoria, and they, with Adolphus Fearon, had been relatively long-serving company employees.[76] All were French-Canadian. They were bonded together by their shared experience, which included a familiarity with James Douglas who, as chief trader, later chief factor, and still later governor, had also been posted at Vancouver and Victoria. On the other hand, those allied against Douillet had no such long standing HBC connection. All were English immigrants and later arrivals to the colony; Hawkins and Richardson – as well as Skinner – arrived on the *Norman Morison* in 1851 and 1853. Perhaps sensing the disadvantage incurred by the lack of a company connection, they associated themselves with Staines, Skinner, and the anti-company faction as the group that best represented and protected their interests.[77]

These alliances are borne out by an analysis of those who signed the two March 1854 anti-Cameron petitions, as well as a January 1854 pro-Cameron petition (table 1).[78] Those who signed the petitions against David Cameron tended to be literate British servants of the Hudson's Bay Company (many of whom worked on the farms of the Puget's Sound Agricultural Company, an HBC subsidiary) who arrived in the colony after 1849; that is, after the Island ceased to be a fur trade preserve and became a colony. For although the anti-Cameron petitioners were technically company servants, they did not, like those whose association preceded the HBC's proprietorship, consider their interests protected by the company. Unlike the fur-trade-era servants, these later arrivals were brought over specifically as settlers to fulfil the conditions of the company's proprietary agreement.[79] Therefore, they had rather different expectations for their life in the colony. Not only did they expect that the colony would possess the familiar institutions and well-articulated political conventions of British rule, but, as emigrants, they also expected to better their economic posi-

TABLE 1
Anti- and pro-Cameron petitioners, 1854

	Anti-Cameron	Pro-Cameron
N	70	55
Literate	66	26
Illiterate	3	29
British	65	20
French Canadian	0	26
Other	1	8
Unknown nationality	3	1
Arrived pre-1849	1	37
Arrived post-1849	65	15
HBC officer	6	17
HBC servant	49	38
Independent	8	0
Unknown occupation	3	0

tion. With such expectations it is not surprising that they considered the HBC proprietorship the antithesis of proper government and legal administration in a British colony, and aligned themselves against the representatives of the company.

Pro-Cameron petitioners drew their support from the ranks of HBC employees who had arrived during the fur-trade period. The allegiance of company officers is not surprising, but Cameron had support among the HBC's servants as well. Two of these were Emanuel Douillet and Baptiste Jollibois, who were obviously unswayed by their treatment at the hands of company justice, perhaps because their fur trade experience had inured them to the uneven and discretionary nature of paternal rule. Having been with the company when it was solely a commercial concern, the pro-Cameron servants did not have the same expectations as those who arrived later as settlers. For them, little changed with the HBC proprietorship.

The politics of Vancouver's Island just now are disagreeable: but the proceedings of the opposition are so far from formidable, that I really believe had there been a Punch-and-Judy show here to divert the people while the snow was on the ground all this petitioning would never have occurred and the saving in foolscap would have been considerable ...

'A Squatocracy of Skin Traders'   51

The key to the matter is this: two or three contemptible propagandists ... represent the Company as a sort of huge monopoly – a gross fraud – an incubus that broods over the fortunes of the colony, and then we have a parcel of people going about the place roaring British Subject! ... As in the old fable, it doesn't require much penetration to detect the ass beneath this pseudo-British Lion's skin.[80]

From 1849 to 1854 the small European community on the southern tip of Vancouver Island was rocked by rancorous debate over the constitution of legitimate political authority. As the comments above indicate, the colony's independent settlers saw the island's government as a simple extension of the Hudson's Bay Company's economic monopoly, and therefore as antithetical to their rights as British subjects. Law was a focal point of the sort of 'politics' implied in the quotation above. Vancouver Island's land laws had the effect of extending the HBC's corporate hierarchy over island society and of concentrating political power in the hands of those highly placed in the company. Instead of encouraging settlement and economic development, the island's land laws served the 'petty ambitions' of the 'squatocracy of skin traders' who governed the colony.[81]

The construction of the colonial courts provided further evidence of the Hudson's Bay Company's attempts to rule the island using its corporate experience as a private monopoly. Viewing the law as the regulation of labour, James Douglas named the HBC's farm bailiffs justices of the peace and appointed his brother-in-law and the manager of the company's collieries as chief justice. David Cameron's appointment was beyond the pale of acceptable behaviour in the opinion of the island's independent settlers because it contradicted the notion of impartial justice. To the anti-Cameron petitioners, it was 'an abortion' of the rule of law to have someone so closely connected with a business interest dispensing the law.[82]

Although the petitions used the language of rule of law to criticize the authority of Vancouver Island's proprietary government, that language and the notion of impartiality were intimately associated with another equally powerful discourse: that of laissez-faire capitalism. The debate over political authority on Vancouver Island was all about the legitimacy of monopoly as a form of economic, social, and political organization. The very first petition against Douglas's appointment as governor illustrated the interpenetration of these two discourses:

The Hudson's Bay Company being, as it is, a great trading body, must necessarily have interests clashing with those of independent colonists, most matters of a political nature will cause a contest between the Agents of the Company and the colonists. Many matters of a judicial nature also, will undoubtedly arise in which the colonists and the Company (or its servants) will be contending parties, or the upper servants and the lower servants of the Company will be arrayed against each other.

We beg to express in most emphatical and plainest manner our assurance that impartial decisions cannot be expected from a Governor who is not only a member of the Company sharing in its profits, but is also charged as their chief Agent, with the sole representation of their trading interests in this Island and the adjacent coasts.[83]

Self-interested economic behaviour was fine for individuals, and in fact was the basis of the general happiness of a nation in laissez-faire thinking, but it was not consistent with good government. The anti-Douglas petitioners were not convinced that 'a great trading body' could act impartially.

The language of the anti-land laws petition is also suggestive of the close association between law and economy. The petition contended that prospective settlers on Vancouver Island were not rewarded for their individual endeavours because of 'administrative causes' rather than any 'natural' obstacles.[84] The administrative causes referred to were, of course, the HBC's land laws; and they were deemed unnatural because they prevented individuals from reaping the fruits of their own labours. Such criticisms would have been shared by classical liberal economists.

Equally revealing were the petitions generated by the appointment of David Cameron. Both those who supported Cameron and those who opposed him linked his ability to execute his office to his economic associations and his business abilities. In addition to their belief that his close association with James Douglas and the Hudson's Bay Company disqualified him for the chief justiceship, one anti-Cameron petitioner, Bailiff-JP E.E. Langford, also charged that Cameron was a bad businessman, having left a trail of bankrupt enterprises in Scotland and Demerara before he arrived on Vancouver Island.[85] Conversely, but using the same economic standard, Cameron's supporters cited his 'business habits' (probably in his capacity as manager of the company's collieries) and 'considerable colonial experience' as qualifications for the post.

The juxtaposition of these two frames of reference, one provided by the rule of law (impartiality) and the other by laissez-faire, points to the different institutional and ethical basis for political authority in this British North American colony. Unlike their English counterparts of an earlier century or their fellow colonists who had been schooled in the ways of HBC law, Vancouver Island's independent settlers did not ask that their laws and government adhere to a moral standard that bound powerful and powerless together in a unified social whole and ensured some level of distributive justice. Instead they rejected the paternal and discretionary authority that came from a system of mutual obligation, preferring the rule of laws that would allow them to realize their own individual ambitions. Legitimate governments allowed their citizens to pursue their individual wills by providing a formal, rule-bound arena in which competition could occur without unfair advantage or interference. This was the essence of law in a society tied to and shaped by a market economy, and it was given form in the neighbouring colony of British Columbia.

3
Property, Geography, and British Columbia's Courts

The 1858 gold rush diverted the attention of the Colonial Office and the inhabitants of Vancouver Island from their internal political wrangling and towards the banks of the Fraser River on the mainland. On 25 April the *Commodore* deposited the first boatload of fortune-seekers – 400 in all – in Victoria. They were, according to Vancouver Island Governor James Douglas, 'a specimen of the very worst of the population of San Francisco – the very dregs of society.' Nevertheless, he admitted, despite the 'many temptations to excess in the way of drink,' 'quiet and order prevailed.'[1] These 400 were followed in the same year by an additional 25,000, 10,000 of whom arrived in the six weeks between 1 May and 15 June, thereby precipitating the formation of the separate colony of British Columbia on 2 August, with James Douglas doubling as its governor.[2]

Despite the quiet and order on the island, it soon became apparent that British dominion over the mainland was tenuous at best, and perhaps only theoretical. For on New Year's Eve, 1858, just months after British Columbia had become a colony, a man strode into the Fort Yale magistrate's office with nine of his comrades, forced his way into the lock-up, arrested the magistrate and released the prisoners, friends who had been incarcerated for roughing up some 'darkies' in a local saloon.[3] The posse leader was a Californian known as 'Ubiquitous' Ned McGowan, who, along with his friends, wanted to put an end to the pompous blusterings of the local magistrate, 'Captain' Peter Brunton Whannell. Whannell was an Australian; a man, as Ned recalled, 'of fine physique, and had been a Captain in a gold guard in Australia.' 'His good looks was all he had to recommend him, however, for he was an imperious blatherskite and fool. If you addressed him with your hat on, he would threaten to commit you for contempt.'[4] As it turned out, the captain was a simple foot soldier in the infantry who had deserted and run off with another man's wife.[5] He was a dashing cad who loved to exercise his newly minted authority; or, as Ned described it, to 'go charging and slashing about.' It was during one of these fits of judicial energy that the captain decided to clean up neighbouring Hill's Bar by closing down all the saloons and gambling-halls.[6] In doing so, he incurred the wrath of Ned and his colleagues, with the consequences just outlined.

The captain was quick-marched to Hill's Bar, a few miles away, and forced to stand trial before Ned and George Perrier, the colonially appointed magistrate, who must have taken some delight in seeing his rival, with whom he had had a longstanding feud over jurisdiction, in the dock. Whannell was charged with contempt of court, tried, and jailed after getting 'a pretty sharp lecture about his tyrannous and illegal acts.'[7]

Ned McGowan was no ordinary California gold-seeker. He began his public career as a municipal politician in Pennsylvania, then migrated to California in 1849 to participate in the gold rush. Politics attracted him again, and he was soon elected a judge in San Francisco. The position embroiled him directly in the affairs of the Committee of Vigilance, an informal but powerful tribunal of respected men who were the real political brokers in the city and who meted out rough justice to anyone who got in their way.[8] In 1856 McGowan was accused of murdering one of the Vigilantes. But he escaped before he could be lynched, and sparked the longest manhunt in the territory's short history. 'Ubiquitous' was eventually caught, but actually managed to secure a formal trial in 1857. Though he was acquitted, he found California a little too uncomfortable for his tastes and slipped out of Sacramento in July 1858 for the safety of the Fraser River.

Though 'Ned McGowan's War,' as the episode became known, has been described as an *opéra bouffe*, we should not dismiss it too readily, for it can be read as an allegory, revealing the kind of order British Columbians wanted to achieve through the law and the problems that confronted them.[9]

One of the most notable things about 'Ned McGowan's War' was that it was not a war at all: though the colonial government mobilized 25 Royal Engineers and an equal number of Royal Marines for an assault on Hill's Bar and asked the Colonial Office to dispatch an additional 150 members of the Royal Irish Constabulary to British Columbia, they need not have worried.[10] McGowan gave himself up peacefully was tried and discharged with the judge's best wishes. He resurfaced soon afterwards in California with some $47,000 from his share in a Fraser River claim.[11] Moreover, he was not at all 'ubiquitous' in British Columbia. Despite the government's fears, the level of violence in the colony contrasted favourably with that of the gold fields to the south, and was the subject of comment by seasoned miners. 'A Returned Digger' told prospective gold-seekers that 'no body of men upon the whole could conduct themselves more peaceably than do the miners of British Columbia. All disputes are submitted to the Commissioner.'[12] Magistrate Philip Nind agreed, telling Governor Douglas that his six days at Antler Creek hearing mining disputes 'passed off without any disturbance, and though 'all were not satisfied[,] the unsuccessful parties submitted quietly on finding their claims were not supported by law.'[13] Even the Americans were impressed: William Downie, an old forty-niner, was astonished at the calm that prevailed in Antler. 'They told me it [British Columbia] was like California in '49,' he said to Matthew Begbie, the colony's Supreme Court Judge, 'Why, [in California] you would have seen all these fellows roaring drunk, and pistols and bare knives in every hand. I never saw a mining town anything like this.' The 'this' to which Downie referred was, according to Begbie, a collection of 'some hundreds ... all sober and quiet. It was a Sunday afternoon, [and] only a few of the claims were worked that day. It was as quiet as Victoria.'[14]

Observations like those of 'A Returned Digger' and William Downie did not mean that those who came to the colony to seek their fortunes were unconcerned about the issue of order – they were. But the order they wanted to create and preserve was an economic one; one that would favour the security of property and its pursuit. Even amidst the exaggerated fears of violence precipitated by Ned McGowan's War, there were those in the colonial government whose worries over the happenings at Hill's Bar stemmed from concern over the potentially negative effect of such actions on the colony's economic development, rather than over the possibility of bloodshed.

In addition to shedding light on the kind of order British Columbians were concerned with, Ned McGowan's War highlighted one of the difficulties the colonial government faced in making its authority meaningful. Though British Columbia was an independent colony, its seat of goverment was in Victoria, on Vancouver Island. This meant that outbreaks of violence on the mainland could not be contained immediately, but had to await the arrival of the island-based administrators and military. Distance proved to be as formidable an obstacle to the effective and efficient governance of the colony as were the 'clamerous [sic] and politically speaking the most unreasonable People in the world' who lived within its borders and had their own ideas about how they should be ruled.[15]

The problems of creating a favourable economic order and overcoming the colony's great distances were solved through the law. Indeed, the former could not be achieved without accomplishing the latter. Both European British Columbians and those who governed them saw the law as central to economic development. But in the absence of the face-to-face familiarity necessary for a system of paternal control, like that which characterized the fur-trade period, to work, both the colonial government and the colonists moved quickly to formalize and define their relationship, which, given the colony's origins, was primarily economic. That relationship was constituted through a discourse of laissez-faire liberalism that ascribed to the state the role of creating the conditions necessary for the pursuit of individual self-interest. The colonial government, through the law and the courts, was to protect the property of British Columbians by providing them with a rule-bound arena in which to pursue their economic self-interest with a minimum of interference and to resolve any disputes that arose as a result of it.

Creating the kind of economic order British Columbians wanted – a laissez-faire liberal one – required a strong and interventionist state. A well-functioning capitalist marketplace relied upon the imposition of a set of standardized and certain rules of exchange over great distances; and this was achieved by creating local judicial offices. Though doing so was by no means an innovation – indeed, it was something that had its origins in pre-capitalist medieval England – the centralized power that local justices represented and upheld facilitated economic development by providing regularized ways of dealing. But as Ned McGowan's War suggested, the colony's geography could pose a significant obstacle to the effective exercise of state power. The extension of law to create a liberal economic order was hence a spatial and social problem. The mainland colony's great distances and the localism it spawned were overcome by investing local courts and resident law officers with wide powers. Thus, as will be discussed, if the demands of a market economy provided the colonial courts with their *raison d'être*, British Columbia's geography went a long way to defining the ambit of their powers.

When James Douglas issued a proclamation in December 1857 declaring the rights of the Crown with respect to the gold found 'within the limits of Fraser's and Thompson's River Districts' some nine months *before* British Columbia came into being, he knowingly overreached his jurisdiction as Governor of Vancouver Island, fearing that the 'country would become the scene of lawless misrule' because of the influx of American miners.[16] This action set the tone for the government's subsequent policy in constructing the colony's courts. Under the guidance of British Columbia's new puisne judge, Matthew Baillie Begbie, the government moved quickly to establish formal legal institutions in the gold colony, hoping to forestall the development of a strong tradition of local government that characterized the California gold fields.

A third-class Cambridge graduate and a Lincoln's Inn-trained barrister, Begbie was recommended for the British Columbia post by Sir Hugh Cairns, his colleague at Lincoln's Inn and England's solicitor-general.[17] A month after his arrival, Begbie issued an order creating the Court of British Columbia; six months later, the court over which he presided was named 'the Supreme Court of Civil Justice of British Columbia' and was given jurisdiction over all civil and criminal cases.[18] Proclamations issued in 1860 and 1865 augmented the powers of the Supreme Court by making provision for the speedy trial of prisoners and giving it jurisdiction in bankruptcy.[19]

Given the Whannell-Perrier fiasco, Begbie also turned his attention to the appointment of the colony's justices of the peace.[20] His remarks on the magistracy reveal his belief that authority sprang from social status. Those suitable for the position possessed the carriage and demeanour associated with the English gentry. 'Great care would require to be exercised in the selection of these gentlemen,' he informed Governor James Douglas. 'Probably men upwards of thirty years old, with such common sense and good temper as possible – and a little capital, and with country tastes, would be preferable. Personal appearance and even manner and voice are of considerable effect – an Indian can distinguish an Englishman by his voice.' Colonial magistrates should also have a legal education, be married, and bring their families with them to their districts. 'I should hope thus,' Begbie concluded, 'to secure to the colony the advantages of both resident English country gentlemen and stipendiary magistrates.'[21] Despite Begbie's desire for educated gentlemen, the colony's justices were, with one exception, untrained in the law.[22] English sentiment remained the overriding prerequisite for the colonial magistracy. Englishmen who lived in California before travelling north to British Columbia were to be avoided. 'There is usually to be remarked among such persons an alteration in voice, in tone and manner,' Begbie noted, as well as 'an accretion of prejudices as to colour and race, which I think render them unfit.'[23]

Despite their lack of legal education, British Columbia's justices were called stipendiary magistrates, a term usually reserved for barristers with at least five years of legal standing, and were paid civil servants.[24] Most were Anglo-Irish rather than English, and had some previous connection with the military.[25] They immigrated to the far reaches of the empire, like so many others from similar backgrounds, to maintain and perhaps increase their social status. Becoming a colonial justice was attractive for just these reasons. When the Langley JP Charles Bedford learned that the office did not confer the status he had hoped for, he resigned. 'At the time I had the honor to receive from you the appointment of Justice of the Peace ... I was under the impression that ... altho'. the salary was extremely low, my position in the colony would be of some standing,' he wrote to Douglas. 'I find that Justice of the Peace in this colony occupies an inferior position ... I therefore beg ... to resign.'[26] Although Bedford did not achieve the social status and political standing he desired, most of British Columbia's other JPs eventually did, sitting in the colony's Legislative Council after its creation in 1864.[27]

In addition to their political involvement, all of the colony's magistrates held a variety of non-judicial posts concurrent with their judicial offices. The concentration of a variety of administrative functions in the hands of British Columbia's legal officers was probably a hallmark of frontier societies. The colonial secretary informed the newly appointed JP Peter O'Reilly that

[i]n the early conditions of the Colony before institutions are formed and Departments are organized, it is incumbent upon every officer of the Government to afford his assistance in every way in which it may be needed; and under such circumstances, Officers are frequently called upon to render Services which in a more advanced state of the Colony it would never fall to them to fulfil.[28]

These services included acting as the district's land recorder, coroner, postmaster, gold commissioner, Indian agent, and revenue officer, as well as its stipendiary magistrate. Justices of the peace also negotiated the public works contracts for many of the colony's roads and bridges. As Richard Hicks recalled, it was not a job for the lazy or the faint of heart. 'I came to Fort Yale when great excitment existed among the Indians, the population amounted to upwards of five thousand and [included] some of the worst California could produce ... I had to perform every office and work – even to grave digger. My hands were full night and day[.] I worked hard.'[29]

In addition to the duties associated with these offices, British Columbia's justices sometimes found themselves saddled with the responsibility for the social welfare of the district. For instance, after the 1868 fire that all but destroyed Barkerville, the magistrate there dispensed what money he could to help those who had lost everything.[30] At Lytton, Henry Maynard Ball dealt with 'a serious and infectious epidemic of "Diphtheria and Diarrhoea" combined' that spread among the Indian population. 'Common humanity, as well as a sense of duty dictated to me to undertake upon myself the responsibility for the expense,' he informed the colonial secretary.[31] Later, he wrote to New Westminster requesting that 'an Indian Half Breed destitute and sick with a white swelling on his knee' be given some money and sent down to the hospital to have his leg amputated.[32] Cases of insanity sometimes confronted the magistrates, who locked up the afflicted parties until they could be sent to the jail at New Westminster.[33] British Columbia's magistrates were, as contemporaries noted, virtually the government of their districts.[34]

The judicial duties of British Columbia's justices of the peace were defined in part by the gold-rush economy. From the colony's beginnings, cases arising from commercial transactions comprised the bulk of the legal business in the colony. At Yale, on his first circuit in 1859, Begbie reported that there were 'heaps of civil causes here, I don't know how many came rushing at me. Summonses have been issued right & left: and I hear that there will be an equal amount of litigation at Lytton.'[35] Even after the initial rush of suits that accompanied the 1858 Fraser rush, Begbie still considered that nisi prius business occupied most of the court's time.[36] 'It has often happened to me on the mainland,' he wrote after the completion of his 1866 summer circuit, 'that while the criminal business was either nothing at all, or at least extremely light, the nisi prius business has extended over several days or even weeks.'[37] Most of these causes were actions to recover debts, usually involving sums 'almost always under £50 and often under £5.'[38]

By 1859 it was clear that the costly and slow proceedings of the Supreme Court in handling these cases deterred suitors from launching actions. Certainly the forty-five people who petitioned James Douglas in August 1859 thought so. Calling themselves 'Sufferers by there being no Courts of Law in the nature of District or County Courts in the colony of British Columbia to which we can apply ... to recover Debts of small Amounts due by Miners and others, as well as between miner and miner,' the petitioners called for the creation of a number of small debts courts with jurisdiction to hear cases involving up to fifty pounds.[39] Pointing to the '[m]any abuses that had grown out of that state of things, together with a general want of confidence, and an almost entire stoppage of credit transactions,' James Douglas issued a proclamation creating small debts courts in December 1859.[40] Presided over by the colony's stipendiary magistrates, these courts were given the jurisdiction requested by the petitioners (fifty pounds) but were not confined to acting in particular districts because, according to Attorney-General George Hunter Cary, of the 'wandering nature' of the population.[41]

As the rush proceeded up the Fraser, culminating in the 1862 discoveries in the Cariboo, commercial credit became even more widely extended. Attracted by the possibility of profiting from the influx of miners into the colony's interior, Victoria and New Westminster merchants scrambled to get their consignments of goods upcountry. This growing web of credit precipitated calls for greater regulation by the courts. 'Merchants should be protected and assisted by the judiciary of the country,' wrote one Cariboo trader in 1865. '[T]here should be no false delicacy manifested by the Judge to protect the trader, without whom the country never would have been prospected ... for the moment merchants are prevented from recovering their just debts they will shut down all alike.'[42] 'Pickaxe' agreed, and observed that the 'good nature' of the district's stipendiary magistrate had inspired some miners to avoid paying their bills and merchants to withdraw credit. As a result of the magistrate's 'imprudent' leniency, he concluded, 'the poor but honest man is likely to die of starvation, when he might otherwise be profitably employing his time prospecting.'[43] These voices and the others that joined them[44] struck a sympathetic chord with British Columbia's Supreme Court judge. 'Authority might usefully be given to one or more county court judges,' Begbie suggested, 'to deal ... with all matters ... touching the granting of injunctions, the appointment of Receivers and the giving leave to appear and defend actions on Bills of Exchange and promissory notes.'[45] When the county courts were established in April 1866 they were modelled on their English counterparts, but had jurisdiction in cases involving sums up to £100 ($500), a significant increase over the old limit of £50 ($250) set by the 1859 proclamation.[46] Notwithstanding the objections of Attorney-General Crease, the new County Courts Ordinance was, if the Yale grand jury's presentment was indicative, 'looked upon as a most desirable improvement.'[47]

While the small debts and county courts dealt with the general need to regulate credit, more specialized institutions emerged to serve the needs of the mining economy. Created in August 1859, gold commissioner's or mining courts were modelled on the New Zealand institution of the same name and heard all mining disputes arising within a given district.[48] The colonial administration moved quickly to establish formal institutions in the gold fields, hoping to profit from the collection of various licensing fees, but also to prevent the development of a strong tradition of local government of the form that in California centred around miners' meetings.[49] These were informal tribunals consisting of elected miners who regulated conduct in the gold districts, meting out punishment according to local sentiment. In British Columbia, miners' meetings were replaced by a single assistant gold Commissioner who rendered decisions summarily and was armed with powers of enforcement equal to those of the Supreme Court. Additional rules and amendments were made in the next five years, and proclamations issued in 1864 and 1865 further extended and consolidated the provisions of the various Gold Fields Acts.[50] The jurisdiction of the mining courts remained the same until 1867, when the Gold Fields Act was again amended, this time eliminating appeals to the Supreme Court based on questions of fact.[51] As well as sitting in judgment over mining disputes, assistant gold commissioners issued mining licences, collected the various licensing fees, monitored the productivity of the diggings and, presided over locally elected mining boards, which drafted bylaws regulating the operation of the local mines. Like the small debts and later the county courts, British Columbia's mining boards and courts were expected to 'foster and encourage mining enterprise in developing our mineral resources.'[52]

The union of Vancouver Island and British Columbia in November 1866 created a controversy over the Supreme Court, which again underscored the importance of commerce in the life of the colonies and the role the law played in fostering it. As with the inferior courts, the colonial merchants exerted pressure on the government to ensure the security of property through reform of the Supreme Court. Because the Act of Union made no mention of the status and jurisdiction of the colonial courts, it was unclear how the legal apparatus of the now united colonies would work. British Columbia's governor, Frederick Seymour, along with Matthew Baillie Begbie and Attorney-General Henry Crease, contended that upon union the Supreme Court of Civil Justice of Vancouver Island ceased to exist, and that the only valid court and chief justice was that of the former mainland colony.[53] 'When the whole executive [of Vancouver Island] is abrogated,' wrote Begbie to the Colonial Office, 'the judiciary must surely expire with it.'[54] While those on the mainland considered the Act of Union less a merging of the colonies and more an 'extension' of British Columbia 'into a new dominion,' those on the Island had different ideas.

There was little love lost between Joseph Needham, Vancouver Island's chief justice, and Matthew Baillie Begbie, particularly in the wake of the Grouse Creek War (see chapter 6), when Needham was called in to arbitrate an appeal of one of Begbie's decisions. Over and above the personal animosity between them, Needham claimed that because the Act of Union did not specifically abolish either of the colonial Supreme Courts, both continued to exist after 1866.[55] Moreover, by virtue of the 1857 imperial order in council establishing the Supreme Court of Vancouver Island, the local colonial legislatures could not frame or alter the rules and regulations governing the court.

While the Colonial Office sided with Needham on his first point, it rejected the second. 'The object of that Act [of Union], as I understand it, was simply to unite the 2 colonies of Vancouver's Island and British Columbia in as general terms as possible, leaving the Colonial Legislature to work out the details of any changes that might be deemed expedient,' the secretary of state for the colonies, Lord Carnarvon informed Seymour. 'The act was not intended to grant titles, jurisdiction, powers & position of the Judges, and it appears to me that it did not touch them. And if this is so, Mr. Needham is still Chief Justice of Vancouver's Island & with all the same powers & authority that he had before the Act passed.'[56]

To clear up the doubts surrounding the jurisdiction of the two courts, the Colonial Office suggested that the local legislature pass an act declaring the legitimacy of the two chief justices in the united colony but giving each precedence in his formerly separate jurisdiction. Upon the death or resignation of Begbie (chief justice of the mainland of British Columbia) or Needham (chief justice of Vancouver Island), the remaining judge would become the chief justice of British Columbia.[57] After much heated discussion, the Colonial Office's suggestions were embodied in the Courts Declaratory Ordinance, passed in May 1868, almost a year and a half after union.[58]

The ordinance did little to alleviate the practical problems of having two Supreme Courts in a colony of fewer than six thousand people.[59] Both the merchants and lawyers of British Columbia complained of difficulty in securing debts, given the lack of concurrent jurisdiction of the two superior courts. When Joseph Nicholson, an agent of some Victoria merchants, attempted to collect money owed to his employers from Charles Wallace, the capias issued on his behalf by the mainland Supreme Court was ignored by its island counterpart. Needham discharged Wallace as a bankrupt, and the money that was paid into court was given not to Nicholson but to Wallace's other creditors.[60]

Nicholson petitioned the government in December 1868, and in response the Legislative Assembly struck a committee to examine the jurisdictional problems raised by the petition. Of central concern to the committee was 'the very great injustice [done] to litigants', particularly given that 'a very large portion of the law suits are connected with the local trade and commerce of the colony.' The only solution, the committee reported, lay in giving the two courts equal jurisdiction. Without reform, suitors would be compelled to launch actions in both the Island and the mainland courts, an enterprise that was costly and time-consuming.[61]

Concerns about the adverse effects of the Courts Declaratory Ordinance on the commercial life of the colony were raised again by merchants and lawyers a year after Nicholson's petition. 'Nearly all the men of business in the Colony'[62] called the governor's attention to 'the want of concurrent jurisdiction in Civil cases.'

[It] is felt to be a great hardship pressing with great weight on a Commercial community whose interests are identical over the whole Colony. It imposes on litigants a double tax, by compelling them to resort to two Courts before they can obtain the fruits of their Judgement and by giving to Debtors every opportunity of defrauding their Creditors by passing from one Jurisdiction into another and so embarrassing the Administration of Justice.[63]

In addition, both the merchants and 'nearly all the lawyers in the colony' complained about the absence of a colonial Court of Appeal, calling the situation 'disastrous and oppressive.'[64] Before the colonial government was able to respond, the jurisdictional problem disappeared with the appointment of Joseph Needham as chief justice of Trinidad.

The Nicholson petition and the debate surrounding the Supreme Courts after union illustrated the connection between legal institutions and economic development, and specifically the need for standardized rules of exchange not only across individual colonies but between them. As Governor Seymour's successor Anthony Musgrave noted in his report to the Colonial Office, the debate over British Columbia's Supreme Courts 'illustrates the practical difficulty which exists in separating the legal business of the Mainland from the commercial requirements of Victoria, which is the Mercantile focus of the whole colony.'[65] A well-functioning marketplace and the economic prosperity that would follow was possible only through the imposition of uniform rules and the security that came from their predictability.

While the demands of laissez-faire capitalism for a standardized and secure rule-bound arena in which individuals could pursue their self-interest shaped and were embedded in British Columbia's courts, those institutions also bore the imprint of the colony's geography. For the courts to fulfil the role that British Columbians wanted them to, however, the colonial state had to be both strong and interventionist. This was not quite the contradiction it seems to be, for as economic historians have pointed out, even at the height of laissez-faire in the mid-nineteenth century the 'free market' was the product of self-conscious construction and regulation on the part of the state rather than a natural phenomenon.[66] Markets did not just happen as a result of human interaction – they had to be created. If a laissez-faire economic order and state intervention were not contradictory, achieving the former through the latter was problematic in British Columbia, where the colony's geography posed a very real obstacle to standardized, effective, and efficient governance. Imposing and creating order was thus a spatial problem, and it was solved, or at least addressed, by creating local courts and resident law officers and investing them with extensive powers. Before discussing the details of that process, however, it will be useful to consider the problem of distance more generally, and how the law is especially useful in overcoming it.

Despite historians' preoccupation with the place of North American geography in shaping a continental consciousness, its effects on the organization of power have been largely overlooked. Canadian historians are not alone in neglecting the influence of distance on power, for, as the sociologist Anthony Giddens noted, 'there is a lack of concepts that would make space, and control of space, integral to social theory.'[67] According to Giddens, the extension and exercise of power is fundamentally a spatial problem. Distance acts as a barrier to the exercise of power in two ways: first, it is a physical obstacle to surveillance and enforcement. While states may possess absolute dominion over their subjects, if they lack the ability to monitor their subjects' behaviour or punish those who violate their rules, then their power is meaningless. Second, distance encourages localism – the proliferation of parochial meanings and customs –

that prevents the development of a set of common experiences and ultimately hinders the social integration necessary for the creation of a powerful and effective state.

The key to the liberal state's exercise of power lies in its ability to 'stretch' experience over time and space; that is, to break down local practices and replace them with a set of common ones defined and mediated by the state.[68] Without sufficient 'stretching' of common experience over time and space and the social integration that comes with it, governance is difficult because the groundwork necessary for consensus is lacking. By developing a commonality of experience, the state ensures itself a degree of certainty in the behaviour of its citizens. As well, by providing the institutions and the rules through which that experience is constituted and mediated, the state ensures for itself the opportunity for surveillance and control.

One of the ways the liberal state creates a commonality and hence exercises power, I suggest, is through the law. Law is a community of shared meaning and experience, which to a certain degree can transcend space and time.[69] It gives meaning to action by assigning it a value (legal or illegal) and defines social relationships by spelling out the obligations that bind people to each other. As well, it provides a language and a set of procedures and institutions that allow people to deal with each other in an intelligible way. Though conflict brings people before the law, when they go to court they participate in a common, formal, state-sanctioned legal process that limits and guides human relationships over great distances. The process that upcountry miners went through in resolving their disputes through the courts would be familiar to the merchant in Victoria, or in San Francisco or London, for that matter. Formal law can also stretch experience over time: when people submitted themselves and their disputes to the courts for adjudication, they connected themselves to a process and a set of rules that was historical. By virtue of the very nature of the legal process, which assessed present behaviour by linking and measuring it against precedent, the law stretched human experience backward. It also projected that experience forward, prescribing the rules of interaction that would bound and guide future relationships. By transcending space and time in this way, the law was central to the governance of modern societies and societies of strangers.

In British Columbia the problems of distance were exaggerated by a rugged geography. As Attorney-General Henry Crease observed of his colony, 'In every direction we are met by the fact that the centres of population in British Columbia are at the circumference.'

Cassiar is full 1000 miles north of Victoria, making a clear 2000 mile journey thither and back, Kootenay is some 600 miles, 400 of it on horseback, from Victoria, making a journey there and back 1200 miles, Cariboo 400 or 500 miles north from Yale, 700 from Victoria ... Off the [Yale Cariboo] Waggon Road the only mode of transit over all other parts of the province is by packhorse and trails. The Judge has to carry with him for himself and his attendant and packer, tents, baggage, food, cooking utensils, and camp equipage of every kind, and blankets; ford rivers, scale mountain-sides, camp and sleep out seven and six weeks at a time, sometimes subject to an Egyptian plague of mosquitoes.

The Supreme Court Judge as a matter of absolute necessity has to carry with him, in addition to the above, all Law Books he will require in every branch – Chancery, Probate, Common Law ... some 500 lbs., with freight at 25 cents per lb.[70]

Despite Crease's complaints about the barriers confronting those charged with the colony's legal administration, the law was still an important vehicle for exercising state power, particularly in the absence of others. In British Columbia a legal infrastructure was in place within months of the colony's formation, well before the construction of anything more than the most rudimentary roads and bridges. The circuits of Matthew Begbie's assize court adumbrated the boundaries of the law's empire on the Pacific coast (both literally and figuratively),[71] connecting the small settlements in its gold fields – the outposts of its realm – to each other and to the colony's administrative centre.

The problem of distance was not overcome through the simple presence of legal institutions and their officers, however. Their presence was necessary, of course, but the real key to understanding how law aided in the governance of the colony lay in the fact that social relations were mediated and, to a certain extent, created through its forms. The law imposed duties and obligations on individuals, thus setting out the boundaries of and a common basis for their interaction. In doing so it made economic activity possible across the colony because it provided secure and predictable ways of dealing, thus giving British Columbia a coherence that came from the creation of a functioning marketplace. Thus, the conditions that made for effective governance – a commonality that stretched over space – also favoured capitalist enterprise. However, the law also provided the colony the coherence that comes from a engaging in particular conventions of dispute resolution. Not only were parties engaged in a shared experience when they went to court, but through the law's rituals some were also linked to a common past. The courts were a touchstone to the familiar, secure, and sometimes glorious traditions of English common law.

Despite their frontier environment, British Columbia's law men strove to maintain a certain degree of orthodoxy in their trial proceedings. Begbie travelled his lengthy circuit with his robes and full-bottomed wig in tow, and his assizes followed a pattern not too different from that of his English counterparts, even if the juxtaposition of old world forms in a new world context was often jarring, as Arthur Bushby discovered. 'I may record these few days as some of the most remarkable in my life,' noted British Columbia's first court registrar of his and Begbie's first assize in March 1859.

Since my arrival in B.C., Begbie had appointed me clerk of the court, assize clerk, registrar, clerk of the arraigns &c. As I had never been in a Ct of justice before the thing seemed strange indeed to me. I had to open the proceedings by reading the proclamation of silence O Yes O Yes O Yes which I did at the top of my lungs. Then I had to read aloud the different commissions – the Queen's to Begbie and of oyer & terminer & gaol delivery &c. – swear the grand jury, petty jury, witnesses &c., read the indictments twice through, ask the prisoner whether he was guilty or not ...

'It was most strange work,' he concluded. '[H]owever, I got through all right & once I heard my voice tell at the other end of the room I bawled away like fun.'[72]

It would be misleading, however, to assume that the law's theatricality and magisterial qualities were transferred intact from old Albion to the new Eldorado. More often than not, British Columbia's law men wore coonskin (if not literally than certainly metaphorically) rather than scarlet and ermine, and heard cases in a variety of venues, ranging from the 'curious brick and frame designs' of Victoria's legislative buildings (dubbed the 'Birdcages') to the back of an accommodating horse.[73] The shifting mining frontier worked against the establishment, at least initially, of the substantial stone court houses that anchored other colonial communities in British America.[74] Most government buildings on the mainland were dark, windowless structures held together by mud and constant repair, 'a style of architecture ... peculiar in its order,' as one Caribooite observed. 'It is neither Doric, Ionic, nor Corinthian, but decidedly Columbian ... The relative properties of capital, column and base never trouble the mind of the builder.'[75] Even in New Westminster, the colonial capital, the Supreme Court sat in 'an austere frame structure measuring 40 ft by 20 ft,' which possessed an 'open floor, rattling windows, and old sooty cotton lining and ceiling, in many places torn to shreds and fluttering in the breeze like a bird of evil omen over the seat of justice.'[76]

The changes wrought by the immediate circumstances in which the law was administered were not limited to those of venue. Despite its integrating effects, British Columbia's governors still found it necessary to modify the substance of the law in response to the geographical realities of life in the colony. They did this by increasing both the intensity and the scope of court powers; that is, by increasing the number of state institutions (increasing the intensity of state power), and by vesting those institutions and their agents with a wide range of powers (increasing the scope of power).[77] In doing so, the colonial administration made it more likely that individuals would fall under government surveillance and power. Moreover, as the intersection between the agents of the state and its citizens increased, social relations came to be mediated through the institutional forms of the state to a greater degree. A commonality of experience developed as a result, and state power became more effective because it was hegemonic.

The colonial government attempted to increase the intensity of its power through the legal system by creating a set of inferior courts anchored by a resident stipendiary magistracy. By placing legal officers in the gold fields and arming them with extensive powers the government hoped to increase the effectiveness of its courts and make the resolution of disputes more efficient. Though an early plan for British Columbia's legal system called for two or more justices of the peace to be assigned to each of the colony's districts to take informations and issue warrants in all criminal cases, to hold bail or commit prisoners to jail to await the next quarter sessions or assizes, or to hear cases involving petty offences and render judgment summarily, this was never done.[78] Instead, the colony's JPs had the 'power to act in all the said Colony, without distinction of districts and divisions.' The government also dispensed with the need for JPs to sit in pairs to decide cases by endowing 'a single Justice ... [with] all such powers and jurisdiction as ... vested in ... any Stipendiary Magistrate for the metropolitan district of London.'[79] The increased power of the magistrates eliminated the need for the colony's justices of the peace to sit together quarterly. A court of quarter sessions did not exist on the mainland. Instead, a single justice decided all but the most serious civil and criminal cases. These were heard at the annual assize by Matthew Baillie Begbie. This widening of power was achieved without a parallel change in the expertise of British Columbia's legal personnel. For although they were called stipendiary magistrates, the colony's justices were untrained in the law, unlike their English counterparts, who were barristers of at least five years' standing.[80]

The most visible example of the trend towards investing more power in the hands of British Columbia's inferior courts, however, was in the legislation governing the small debts and county courts. There were two ways for a creditor to secure his debt.[81] The first was to initiate a suit to recover his property. If the court ruled in his favour, the debtor was required to satisfy the claim by selling his personal property and then, if necessary, his real property. To this end, the court had the power to attach and sell his goods. If he could not comply, he was jailed until he fulfilled his obligation. The second way of obtaining redress was called the 'mesne process.' In it, the creditor simply swore an affidavit attesting to an overdue debt or the fact that the debtor was about to abscond or sell his property and the court (at the discretion of the judge) issued a writ of capias ad respondendum. This was the method chosen by most British Columbians, because it was faster than the more elaborate trial process. The writ empowered the sheriff or bailiff to arrest the debtor and hold him in jail until he satisfied the creditor's claim. In contrast to the situation in the trial process, however, the court had no power to attach the debtor's goods. The creditor could have the debtor's property (through the longer, more expensive trial process) or his body (through the mesne process), but not both.

The Small Debts Act (1859) gave the colony's magistrates the power to issue writs of capias ad respondendum in all cases of debt above twenty pounds when it could be shown that the debtor was about to abscond. Even this was not sufficient for Yale's stipendiary magistrate Andrew Charles Elliott, who informed the colonial secretary in 1860 that

the exigencies of justice are by no means fully complied with by the 'Capias ad respondendum' not issuing for any less sum [i.e. debt] than £20. [T]he greater number of cases in my Court are, and will continue to be, under that amount and in which I have no power to detain debtors when about to leave the Country. I should respectfully suggest that £5 should be the minimum.[82]

Under the imperial statute that regulated the English county courts, this power was severely limited by a series of stringent conditions that had to be fulfilled before such a writ could issue. No such limitations were defined in the British Columbia act, leading Matthew Baillie Begbie to conclude that 'it wo[ul]d really seem impossible to set aside a capias obtained on such an order,' even though, 'circumstances may be such that I myself wo[ul]d not or co[ul]d not have made the order.'[83] Thus, out of a need to facilitate economic transactions in the frequent absence of the colony's senior law officer, the Small Debts Act endowed British Columbia's magistrates with virtually unlimited powers of arrest in suits involving relatively small amounts of money.

In addition to the power to issue writs of capias, an 1865 ordinance gave magistrates powers in bankruptcy and insolvency equivalent to those held by the Supreme Court, and allowed them to grant immediate protection to debtors instead of requiring that they be held in prison until Begbie's circuit came through the district again.[84] But it was the County Courts Ordinance (1866) that put the final touches on the wide powers of the colony's inferior courts. As well as setting a new limit to the jurisdiction of the county courts (one hundred pounds), the act made no provision for appeal, shortened the time for the return of a summons from ten days to three, dispensed with the need for the plaintiff to prove the defendant's intention to abscond, and gave the judge rather than the plaintiff the right to decide whether a case would be heard before a jury. In addition, the act modified the conditions under which a writ of capias was served. Before the enactment of this ordinance, writs had to be presented to the defendant directly by the sheriff or high bailiff of the court. Under the new act, writs of capias could be served by any person designated by the court to do so. Taken together, the provisions of the County Courts Ordinance not only made it easier for suitors to recover debts and sue for damages, but also vested wide-ranging and discretionary legal powers in the hands of a few untrained men, whose 'country tastes' were of questionable use in ensuring the judicious exercise of the law.

The effects of geography were also felt on the criminal side of the law. The Speedy Trials Act (1860) made provision for criminal hearings to be held by the Supreme Court anywhere and at any time in the colony without a commission.[85] In framing the act, Begbie was well aware that its provisions 'entirely contradicted the spirit and practice of the Courts of Justice as administered in England'; nevertheless he claimed that 'the practise of Criminal Trials as followed in England would render convictions [in British Columbia] in almost every case impossible.'

[I]t would be in the upper country simply impossible to secure the attendance of the witnesses or of the prisoner on a serious charge after an interval which would in England be deemed barely sufficient to introduce between the apprehension and trial of an offender. Your Excellency is well aware of the wandering habits of the population ... the absence of all gaols or places of security[, and] the extremely small number of regular constables ... There would be no means of securing the attendance of witnesses after the interval of a month without committing them to close custody; which in the existing state of things is a physical impossibility.

'I do not recollect one case of a white man who has been convicted of any offence,' he concluded, 'unless the trial were had within a month or so from the time of his apprehension.'[86] The Colonial Office did not share Begbie's pragmatism or appreciation of the problems of distance, and disallowed the act.[87]

As the power of the courts was being extended, the power of British Columbia's juries was curtailed and challenged. The Juror's Act, passed in 1860, eliminated the right of plaintiffs and defendants to challenge the selection of jurymen.[88] In English law, the right of challenge was a check on the possibility of corruption or bias, and was unlimited.[89] When similar legislation was put forward in the island colony, the opposition press predicted that trial by jury would become 'a mockery, a delusion, [and] a snare.'[90] In the eyes of British Columbians, the bench further challenged the effectiveness of the jury. Whether he addressed them as 'a pack of Dalles horse thieves,' altered their verdict, or discharged them and decided the case himself, Matthew Baillie Begbie gained a reputation for his repeated attempts to undermine the decision-making power of juries. So infamous was Begbie's treatment of juries that in 1863 the New Westminster-based *British Columbian* reported 'that it is the intention of our prominent citizens to unite in a declaration that they will not sit on a Jury in our Supreme Court while the Bench is occupied by Mr. Begbie.'[91] Though the Supreme Court judge was within the scope of his powers when he challenged jury verdicts, his actions, when combined with the widening of judicial power achieved through colonial laws, must have contributed to a growing sense of the colonial government's power.

The Sheriff's Act was also passed in 1860.[92] It gave the high sheriff the authority vested in stipendiary magistrates, thus combining the powers of enforcement with those of judgment. Though sheriffs in England had once had judicial powers in civil and criminal matters, by the time English law was received in British Columbia a strict distinction had been made between the two functions, and the sheriff was 'disqualified from acting as a justice of the peace.'[93] This consolidation of offices reflected the exigencies of frontier life. Specialization and the division and diffusion of power were sacrificed, and the risks of consolidation taken in the name of efficiency and economy.

After the union of the colonies in 1866, the colonial legislature passed a series of acts that effectively imposed British Columbia's legal apparatus on Vancouver Island. With the exception of its Supreme Court, the island's tribunals were given the same wide-ranging powers as the mainland's courts.

In response to the economic and social exigencies of the Fraser and Cariboo gold rushes, the institutional foundations of law, order, and authority in British Columbia were laid down with great speed. British Columbians took what legal historians have called an 'instrumentalist' view of the law, seeing it as an essential part of the economic infrastructure of a new colony tied to external markets and experiencing rapid growth.[94] Law was considered a tool for economic development. The colonial government shared that view, though it was also motivated to establish law by a desire to prevent the development of local and informal means of dispute resolution and government and to assert its own power. Both capitalism and the needs of the colonial state were thus fulfilled through the law. British Columbia's courts were shaped by and upheld a laissez-faire capitalist economic order, which contributed to the creation of a functional marketplace by establishing predictable and standardized ways of dealing and the control that came with them over a far-flung, culturally diverse, and mobile population.

The geographical realities of the colony also left their imprint on the courts. British Columbia's great distances, rugged terrain, and scattered population were no small barriers to its effective and efficient governance. In an effort to overcome them, the colony's legal architects increased the scope and intensity of the lower courts' powers. The summary proceedings of the gold commissioners' courts were designed to settle disputes within a formal legal setting, but without the lengthy and potentially costly delays associated with jury trials or Supreme Court proceedings. The same rationale underlay the formation of the small debts and county courts. In these, the colony's stipendiary magistrates had powers of arrest (that is, powers to issue writs of capias ad respondendum), which in England were more tightly controlled and placed in the hands of formally educated and seasoned barristers. On the criminal side, the Speedy Trials Act (1860) did away with the need for separate commissions to be issued for each assize, allowing criminal cases to be heard at anytime and in any place in the colony. Less serious offences were also treated with the twin demands of effectiveness and efficiency in mind, for stipendiary magistrates dealt with criminal offences summarily, sitting alone rather than in pairs at quarter sessions of the peace.

The overall effect of the changes made in response to the colony's geographical exigencies was to enhance the security of property and state power, and hence to make the marketplace even more functional. Property and geography were thus dual and reinforcing influences on the construction of British Columbia's courts; and, as we will see, they were visible in the pattern of litigation that emerged from their operation.

4

'A California Phase': Civil Litigation, Economy, and Society in British Columbia

June 10, 1863
Richfield, B.C.

Dear Sabrina,
    This place is on the celebrated Williams Creek & is called the town of Richfield but it is merely a collection of rude cabins. Provisions are high here, pack animals can come no farther than Van Winkle, 14 miles from Here and everything coming from here to there has to be carried on men's backs for which they get 25¢ a pound. I did a little of it but it is very severe labor ... You must pardon me for writing on such a dirty sheet of paper but it cost me a quarter & I was too stingy to throw it away because it got soiled. It will cost me another quarter for an envelope & two dollars to send the letter to New Westminster. You must pay well for everything you get here ... It may seem extravagant to pay $5 a pound for tobacco but I do like to sit & smoke & think of my far away Nina ... So you see it requires a good deal of money to keep a man going here. Gilbert Munro and Aus McIntosh & I came up together & we still live in a brush tent together. Munro was lucky enough to get work the first day he came making shingles & has been at work every day since. Aus has not had work to do. I have been working at whatever I could get to do but have not got steady work ... Wages are ten dollars a day, out of which you must, of course, board yourself. We live on bread, beans & bacon, with an occasional mess of very tough beef (50¢ a pound) and manage to subsist from three to four dollars a day each ...
    This is the dreariest country you ever beheld or imagined ... If you are willing to spend a number of years in this wilderness, to live like a Hottentot & work like a galley-slave you will probably make some money; at all events you'll be sure to lay in a good stock of rheumatism for your old age ...

                                                        Yours forever Robert[1]

At twenty-nine, Robert Harkness, a general merchant, had been married to Sabrina Wood for nearly six years. They had three small children: Effie and Robert, aged five and three, and Catherine, just two weeks old when her father left for St Catharines to join Thomas McMicking's group of 'overlanders' bound for British Columbia.[2] Running his father's general store in Iroquois, Canada West, had not brought him the financial rewards he wanted, and Robert, perhaps attracted by the promise of gold 'as plentiful as hard words in an English workhouse,'[3] joined the Queenston party in April 1862, leaving Sabrina and their three children with his in-laws in Dixon's Corners. While Sabrina tried to keep body and soul together by teaching, Robert, as his letter suggests, faced a different kind of adversity during his four-year stint in British Columbia.[4]

If his experience is typical, life in the new Eldorado was uncertain, dependent on seasonal wage labour in the mines or on work servicing those who toiled in the hopes of striking it rich. These aspects are borne out by the nature of civil litigation in British Columbia. As suggested in the previous chapter, the courts were constructed to meet the needs of a commercial economy, and the pattern of litigation confirms that that was what they did. Suits for debts incurred in setting up and working a claim comprised the bulk of cases in the civil courts. Actions involving land title or family matters, to name two common types of suits in other more settled jurisdictions, were non-existent.

In addition to shedding light on the nature of the colonial economy and the law's role in mediating it, civil litigation suggests much about gold rush society, revealing the kinds of relationships and the sort of community that existed there. The community that formed around the mines consisted of men like Robert Harkness who had come to make their fortunes in British Columbia but who had every intention of reaping the benefits elsewhere. But the rush also brought others in its wake to service its needs: merchants, saloonkeepers, blacksmiths, butchers, boarding-house operators, and the local doctor, lawyer, and barber: people who, when the mines were played out, stayed behind to form the nucleus of a permanent settlement.[5]

Social relations among these people were highly specialized, and constituted largely as a consequence of economic activity. These British Columbians had limited kinds of relationships with each other – relationships based on consumption and exchange, rather than on affection, kinship, religion, or simple proximity, permanence, and familiarity. They were, to use Bruce Mann's terminology, strangers rather than neighbours.[6] There was a 'flatness' and narrowness to gold rush society which, though rooted in newness and the intentions of its inhabitants, were hallmarks of the modern world.[7] Among strangers, formal law was particularly important in constituting social relationships between different groups of people – that is, in setting out the duties and obligations that bounded and shaped relationships – and in mediating them. Informal law existed within British Columbia's mining population and, of course, its aboriginal communities, and could be a very powerful force indeed (chapter 6 explores just how powerful it was in the Cariboo). But gold rush society consisted of more than miners and Indians. There was no single shared system of informal law within the boundaries of the colony that could be used by all its inhabitants; hence the place of formal institutions in dispute resolution.

It is in this social context that we must situate the meaning and significance of litigation. Because the bonds of community were not sufficiently developed in a new society like British Columbia to allow for the informal settlement of disputes, the formal adjudication of the courts was necessary. British Columbians did not consider recourse to the courts as undesirable or as a sign of social breakdown, but as an outgrowth of human nature – the natural outcome of the pursuit of self-interest. Moreover, going to court was consistent with the demands of laissez-faire liberalism for predictable, certain, and rule-bound mechanisms of dispute resolution. Like all discourses, liberalism created a way of seeing and acting in the world; more specifically, it constructed conflict and formal conflict resolution as natural and rational. Going to court was not a sign of social disorganization and breakdown – of the absence of community; rather, it was an expression of a different kind of community, one that was shaped by the capitalist marketplace and its demands for standardized ways of dealing.

Although British Columbia owed its origins to the Fraser River rush, James Douglas's administration was uncomfortable with the prospect of mining's becoming the linchpin of the colonial economy. 'The miner is at best a producer and leaves no traces but those of desolation behind,' he told the Colonial Office, 'but durable prosperity and substantial wealth of States is no doubt derived from the cultivation of the soil. Without the farmers' aid British Columbia must for ever remain a desert.'[8] However, despite his government's best efforts to encourage settlement, first by implementing a Wakefieldian scheme (as on Vancouver Island), and, when that proved unsuccessful, an American-style homestead policy, Douglas discovered that 'the purchase of Country land is considered a most unprofitable method of investing money in this country.' The 'high rate of interest ... derived from investing money in other real estate, or in mining or mercantile enterprise' kept land and the sturdy yeoman farmer from anchoring British Columbia's economy and society.[9] Instead, as the pattern of litigation in the colony's courts reveals, they were replaced with commercial credit, merchants, and various small-scale entrepreneurs.

Though civil matters have always predominated over criminal ones, the kinds of suits that came before British Columbia's courts reflected the colony's emergent commercial economy and the nature of frontier development. The colony's Supreme Court devoted only one-fifth (18.7 per cent) of its time to criminal trials. Most of the remainder of its energies was expended in civil matters, including civil litigation (22.9 per cent), business in chambers (17.7 per cent), probate (7.3 per cent), and bankruptcy (28.9 per cent). The rest of the Supreme Court's time was devoted to 'administrative' functions (4.4 per cent). The single largest portion of the Supreme Court's time was occupied sitting as a court of bankruptcy. These proceedings dealt with the seizure and administration of the bankrupt's property by a court-appointed trustee and the distribution of that property among the bankrupt's creditors. Activities conducted in the judge's chambers consisted largely of hearing motions (for example, applications to change the venue of trials, delay proceedings, or appeal lower court decisions), issuing writs or orders, and assessing costs. As a court of probate, the Supreme Court oversaw the probate of wills and the administration of estates. Naturalizing aliens, settling land title under the Town Lots Leases Act, and settling corporate affairs under the Companies and Winding-Up Acts were the court's administrative duties in the colonial period.

The bulk of litigation, both civil and criminal, occurred in the two lower courts, and it is these that are the focus of this chapter. The small debts or county courts and the mining courts dealt most directly with securing property and with the largest number of people.[10] The majority of the cases were suits for debts, not an unusual state of affairs in a frontier setting. As Douglas McCalla and Graeme Wynn demonstrate, merchants played an important role in the development of the Canadian frontier.[11] By advancing credit, they absorbed much of the risk and the cost of resource extraction and settlement. On the British Columbia mining frontier the same process can be seen at work. Attracted by the possibility of profiting from the influx of miners into the colony's interior, Victoria and New Westminster merchants engaged in a rush of their own as they scrambled to get consignments of goods upcountry. In May 1860 Magistrate E.H. Sanders reported that 'the business at Yale is rapidly assuming a California phase (and a bad one), viz. a pure credit system. Miners and upcountry traders seldom pay for goods as ordered, but require time, in many cases six and eight months.'[12] By August, Sanders noted that the credit system had gained ground: 'even the Chinamen have their pass-books in trading with white merchants whilst amongst themselves credit is almost unlimited.'[13] The colony's law officers expressed concern over this liberal extension of credit, and dismay over the speculative activities of these merchants. 'The real cause of the depressed state of affairs is the partial exhaustion of the Gold Mines [and] the failure of the Miners and others to meet the unlimited and ruinous credit that had been so freely extended to them,' Stipendiary Magistrate William Cox wrote in 1867.[14] From New Westminster, Police Magistrate Chartres Brew confessed, 'I do not know ... a single Merchant who commenced business with Capital.'

[A]ll obtained their Stock in trade on credit – payment within sixty days to be considered Cash – after that 2 per cent a month interest to be charged on the debt. Merchants who were thus set up in business instead of using their returns in clearing off their indebtedness continued paying this ruinous interest which no reasonable profits could support, and applied their receipts in extending their business prospecting – placer diggings – artesian Mining – Bed rock drain – Bed rock flume – Steam Boat and other Companies scarcely one of which has proved hitherto remunerative ... The result of such a system was inevitable, failure must come sooner or later, and it has come upon many: Numbers of the embarrassed Merchants in Victoria must know that their difficulties are to be attributed either directly or indirectly to dabbling in Mining Stock – many of them went largely into it themselves, and others gave extensive credit to men who ruined themselves and those who trusted them, by entering into that uncertain and hazardous speculation.[15]

The business of the colony's courts reflected a preoccupation with the regulation of the economic activity that stemmed from the gold rushes. The Cariboo was the heart of mining activity in the colonial period, and thus generated most of British Columbia's civil litigation. Although Barkerville was the largest settlement, Richfield, to the south on Williams Creek, was the district's administrative centre. Almost half (45.8 per cent) of all county court actions initiated in the colony originated in the Richfield County Court. Of those actions, three-quarters were civil suits, which, if we can generalize from this particular example, indicates the extent of civil litigation in the colony.[16] The number of plaints entered at the county court level peaked in 1863–4 and 1867–9, coinciding with an increase in mining activity and an extension of credit in the wake of the Cariboo (1862) and Kootenay (1865) gold rushes (see figure 1).

In county court proceedings, prospective plaintiffs had to file an affidavit stating the reasons for their claim with the judge or court registrar.[17] Leave to commence a county court action was left entirely to the discretion of those officials. Once the judge granted permission to proceed, the action commenced with the entry of the plaint in the courts record book. A summons to appear, containing the names of the plaintiff and defendant, the nature of the claim, and the date of the hearing, was issued by the court and served, or presented to the defendant.

Service was carried out by the sheriff or, more often in British Columbia, by a constable attached to the district. The summons had to be given to defendants

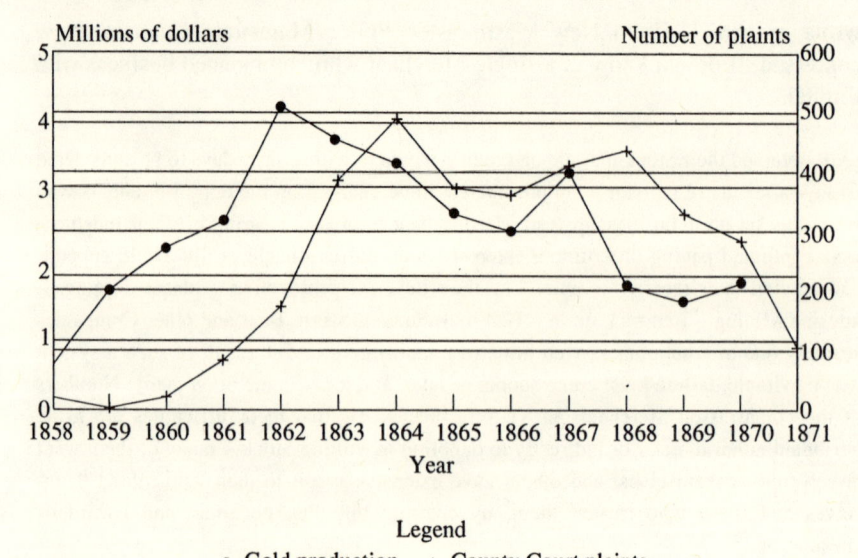

78   Making Law, Order, and Authority in British Columbia

Figure 1
Gold production and civil suits in British Columbia, 1858–71

directly, unless they worked at a mine, in which case it could be left with the person in charge. If the summons could not be served because the plaintiff had misstated the defendant's name, residence, or place of business, or if the defendant had moved, the action ceased. Another action, at additional cost, could be initiated if sufficient information was available.

Once the summons was in the defendants' hands, they had a variety of options. If they admitted their debt as stated in the summons ('confessed the plaintiff's claim') they had to deliver their confession to the court at least five days before the date of the hearing. If they and the plaintiffs came to some agreement as to the amount and method of payment, that agreement had to be registered with the court before the hearing. No appearance in court was then necessary. In either case, the amount admitted and a proportion of the costs had to be paid into the court by the defendant.

Defendants could choose to defend themselves. If they did, they had to inform the court five days before the hearing. In addition, they had to file details of their defence with the registrar, who would deliver them to the plaintiff. Notices of defence could be received by the court only upon payment of court fees for entering and transmitting such information. The defences available

TABLE 2
County Count actions, 1858–71

Action	N	%
n/a	305	8.9
Provisions	1,254	37.0
Mining	33	1.0
Services	94	2.8
Promissory note	789	23.3
Building materials	76	2.2
Room and board	170	5.0
Damages	93	2.7
Freight	37	1.0
Judgement	57	1.7
Labour	363	10.7
Miscellaneous	119	3.5
Total	3,389	100.0

Source: see Note on Sources.

included anything from a complete denial of the claim to proposing a setoff; that is, proposing to pay a lesser sum to the plaintiff. Defendants also pleaded the statute of limitations, coverture, infancy, and bankruptcy as their defences.

Before the hearing, parties to the action could ask the court for leave to examine their opponents or for certain documents to be deposited with the court as evidence. Any time before or during the trial plaintiffs could withdraw their actions and defendants could confess or otherwise settle the action.

With few exceptions (2.7 per cent), the actions brought forward in the colony's small debts and county courts throughout the period were launched to recover debts (table 2). Three-fifths (60.3 per cent) were a direct result of merchants' extending credit for goods sold and delivered (37.0 per cent) or individuals' extending credit in the form of promissory notes (23.3 per cent). While mining activity was dependent on the extension of this kind of credit, the county court records also reveal a second kind of economy in operation in the gold fields. What might be called a 'service sector' grew up around the mines and was responsible for many of the suits launched. Actions for unpaid bills for board, medical attention, legal services, and, occasionally, a haircut or the rental of a billiard table point to the existence of a less transitory community in the Cariboo that was the locus of permanent settlement.

The gold rush not only offered opportunities for men able and willing to swing a pickaxe; it also created possibilities for women, who, finding a market for their domestic skills, commercialized them to their advantage by opening hotels, restaurants, and laundries.[18] In fact, the real fortunes in the Cariboo rush were made in the service sector, particularly in provisioning the mines and miners and in packing goods to the distant gold fields. Thomas Spence made a tidy profit on a consignment of goods purchased in Victoria in June 1863, shipped upcountry, and sold to the miners there. For instance, he sold brandy, which in the colonial capital cost $4 per gallon, to Gold Commissioner Peter O'Reilly for $18 (O'Reilly bought two gallons); pickles that cost $2.50 a dozen were worth an incredible $32.65 in Barkerville; and cheese increased fivefold in value, from 25¢ to $1.25 per pound, on its journey to the upcountry creeks.[19] The cost of food was a constant source of complaint, for prices 'increased as you proceed into the interior and at the Mines, Flour, Sugar, Tea, Coffee [and] Wines are as much as 2 to 5 times the figures for New Westminster.'[20] 'A Returned Digger' warned prospective gold-seekers that 'single meals in restaurants consisting of beans and bacon and a bad cup of coffee cost 2 dollars,'[21] leaving many, like Robert Harkness, to forgo whatever pleasures upcountry restaurants offered and take his meal of 'Cariboo turkey' (bacon) and 'Cariboo strawberries' (beans)[22] 'with the occasional mess of very tough beef (50¢ a pound)' in his tent.[23]

Despite the great potential for profits – some of which was realized, if Thomas Spence's ledger-book is any indication – economic success was still uncertain in the service sector. Richfield's merchants appeared regularly as plaintiffs in the district's county court, suing for overdue accounts.[24] However, some of the same merchants, along with the town's doctor, its lawyers, saloonkeepers, hotelkeepers, and carpenters, also comprised Richfield's 'debtor class' – those who made more than one appearance per year as defendants in debt actions.[25] In the gold fields the margin between solvency and bankruptcy was narrow and, for the individual entrepreneur, constantly shifting.

Uncertainty also characterized the life of the miner. Despite its promise of wealth and independence, gold-mining did not, as 'Sawney,' (the Cariboo's Robbie Burns) wrote, make a man 'free and easy as a Lord.'[26] Many of those who toiled in the Cariboo gold fields did so as wage labourers rather than independent miners. Staking a claim and transforming it into an operating mine required a substantial outlay of capital. Unlike the diggings in Australia, California, or even along the Fraser, most Cariboo gold was not found embedded in the clay, sand, or gravel of the upcountry creeks and thus easily dislodged with water by panning. Instead, the paydirt had to be extracted from great depths, often reached by shafts, and washed with a hand-held rocker or, for larger and more efficient operations, a sluice. Constructing the shafts and sluices was a

TABLE 3
Richfield Mining Court actions, 1864–71

Actions	N	%	Totals
Non-mining			
Judgment	11	1.6	
Wages	165	23.7	
materials	52	7.5	41.7
Money	8	1.2	
Tradesmen's services	14	2.0	
Mining			
Assessment	56	8.1	
Damages	21	3.0	
Disobeying court order	7	1.0	
Drainage	27	3.9	
Interest in a claim	61	8.8	58.3
Partnership	1	0.1	
Obstructing claim	47	6.8	
Right of way	5	0.7	
Trespass	152	21.9	
Water	28	4.0	
Miscellaneous	40	5.8	5.8
Total	695	100.0	100.0

Source: see Note on Sources.

labour-intensive and expensive proposition. As a result, miners often worked for wages or shares in a jointly owned claim.[27]

The pattern of litigation confirms the extent of this wage labour. Suits to recover wages made up just over 10 per cent of the cases in the county court. Though the Mining Court was established to deal with disputes that grew out of mining activity, just over two-fifths of its caseload consisted of disputes not directly a result of mining activity (table 3). Almost one-quarter of the litigation in Richfield's Mining Court arose out of disputes involving wages. Though wages at the mines were reputedly high, ranging from six to ten dollars per day, the cost of living was equally high and the returns uneven.

Though working for wages supposedly eliminated much of the risk associated with gold-mining, Robert Harkness's experience showed that being paid regularly depended on the success of the mine. He arrived on Williams Creek in May 1864 to find 'times very dull, no work going on ... Very many have left & are leaving every day, unable to earn enough to procure grub.'[28] Though his friends had purchased a claim on Lowhee Creek, Robert chose to work for others. 'If their claims turn out well they'll make their piles, if not they'll lose their summer's work,' he told his wife. 'I can't afford to risk losing my summer. I *must* have some money to send home & the only way I can make sure of it is to work for wages.'[29] He did so for the Bed Rock Drain Company, digging a drain to remove some of the water from the richer claims. 'My wages are nominally $9 a day,' he wrote, 'but I have to take my pay in the stock of the company which is at a discount of over 50 per cent so that in reality I am earning but little, though I was fortunate in getting anything at all to do.'[30] A month later, a disconsolate Robert reported that his worst fears had been realized:

I worked for the Bed Rock Drain Co. up to last Saturday, but had to take all my pay in stock, except about 60 dollars. The stock is unsaleable now, money is very scarce, work hard to be got and times dull ... The whole of us are depending on the Montreal claim, if it should turn out a failure we'll all be poor enough again [by] fall ... If it should prove worthless I shall have only to try & procure the means of getting home as fast as possible for I haven't the heart to undertake two or three years prospecting of another claim with but a slim chance of success at the end of it.[31]

In addition to shedding light on the nature of the colonial economy and its precariousness, the pattern of civil litigation reveals how people interacted with each other through the legal system. In essence, it tells us about the social as well as the economic context in which the courts and the law operated. An intractable question regarding litigation is why people chose to go to court at all to settle their disputes. That they did, and in great numbers, is evident from the court record. It is also clear from the petitions and letters sent to the colonial government and the press that British Columbians were interested in their legal institutions – almost exclusively those that dealt with civil rather than criminal issues – as aids to economic development (see chapter 3). But determining why particular individuals decided in specific instances to go to law is more difficult. Several pieces of evidence emerge from an analysis of the court records, which, taken together, construct a context favourable to litigation: first, there was much money to be gained by doing so; second, the cost of going to court was not prohibitive; third, plaintiffs were remarkably successful in winning their suits; fourth, enforcing judgments did not appear to be a problem; fifth, and perhaps most important, the nature of social relations favoured a formal rather than informal means of dispute resolution.

Despite the extension of the county court's jurisdiction from £50 ($250) to £100 ($500) in 1866, over one-third (37.6 per cent) of the cases heard were actions for sums of £10 ($50) or less, and 60.9 per cent were for £20 ($100) or less. Suits launched in the courts of the 'Lower Country' (that is, below Lil-

TABLE 4
Value of County Court actions, 1858–71

Value ($)	Total N = 3,389	Lower Country (%) N = 1,164	Per Country (%) N = 2,225
0	0.3	0.8	0
1–50	37.6	43.5	34.6
51–100	23.3	20.0	24.9
101–200	23.7	21.2	25.0
201–300	10.7	10.8	10.6
301–400	1.8	1.2	2.1
401–500	2.5	2.0	2.8
500+	0.2	0.5	0
Median	$61–70	$41–50	$71–80

Source: see Note on Sources.

looet) exhibited a pattern different from those launched in the 'Upper Country' (table 4). Geography affected the pattern of litigation. With a bit of variation, the farther away one got from the population and administrative centre of New Westminster, the higher the value of the suit. The median value of lower country suits was between $41 and $50, while in the upper country the median value ranged from $71 to $80, some 60 to 75 per cent higher. In New Westminster itself, actions for sums less than $50 constituted almost two-thirds (63.6 per cent) of the business of that court, while suits for $50 to $100, $100 to $150, and $150 to $200 comprised 17.4 per cent, 7.3 per cent and 3.4 per cent of the plaints entered. Conversely, at Richfield, in the upper country, actions for less than $50 made up only 37 per cent of the business of that court. This pattern probably reflects the relative ease with which cases were brought forward in New Westminster, as well as the lower cost of goods there.[32] Because county courts in the interior of the colony served larger geographic areas, individuals who wished to launch actions were often required to travel some distance, thus making suits for debts at the lower end of the scale too costly to pursue. As well, because transporting goods to the gold fields added substantially to their cost, cases launched to recover debts occasioned by the purchase of provisions were necessarily of greater value than similar ones initiated at settlements closer to New Westminster.

Unlike the County Court, the Mining Court's jurisdiction was not limited to suits below a certain sum, even though the same magistrate served as both County Court judge and assistant gold commissioner. Given the higher value of mining property and the higher wages in the gold fields, the average value of Mining Court actions was $523, almost five times that in the County Court. The

TABLE 5
Cost of County Court actions, 1858–71

Costs ($)	Lower country (%) N = 1045	Upper Country (%) N = 1437
0	8.3	0.6
1.01–5.00	53.3	45.6
5.01–10.00	21.6	26.6
10.01–15.00	7.2	16.0
15.01–20.00	3.6	5.9
20+	6.0	5.3
Median Cost ($)	4.50	$5.00

Source: see Note on Sources.

median value of Mining Court cases was two and a half times that for the County Court ($187). Actions for wages in the Mining Court averaged $278 (median $179).

Prospective plaintiffs had much to gain by launching a suit, and they were not deterred by the costs of litigation. Though it was somewhat more expensive to go to law in the upper country, as table 5 indicates, the median costs were not very different.

Without reference to income levels, this discussion of the value and the costs associated with launching a suit lacks meaning. However, because data on standards of living and wages for the colonial period do not exist, I can only venture some informed guesses based on two sources: estimates of wage rates in the Colonial Office's Blue Books of Statistics on British Columbia and contemporary comments of the colony's legal personnel. There was a difference in income between the upper country gold districts and the communities below Lillooet. From the Colonial Office estimates, lower country unskilled labourers averaged between $40 and $50 per month from 1860 and 1870, while skilled tradesmen (carpenters and blacksmiths, for instance) could earn double that or more.[33] At the same time, labourers in the gold fields could earn from $50 to $75 per month, while a miner's income was estimated at $10 per day in 1864, and $6 to $8 per day in 1867–70.[34] Less systematic, though probably no less accurate, were the occasional comments of the colony's law officers, who often complained of the high wages that could be commanded in the gold fields. During his tour of the Fraser at the beginning of the 1858 rush, James Douglas noted that it was 'impossible to get Indian labour at present as they are all busy mining, and make between 2 and 3 dollars a day each man.'[35] Three years later, in 1861, the situation had not improved. '[T]he labourers who can be commanded are very few ... [f]or the large proportion of miners cannot be induced to work a mine for wages at all or otherwise than as owners,' Matthew Baillie Begbie reported. 'The rates of wages, viz. $10 for mining, and $8 for ordinary work, hewing logs &c. indicate the high rate of production in the mines. So do the rates of all the articles beyond the first necessaries. When a man will give $12 for a bottle of American Champagne, his gold must be a burthen to him.'[36]

These figures, rough as they are, put the value of suits launched in the county courts in some perspective. Three-fifths (59.3 per cent) of the suits launched were for sums greater than the highest average monthly income for labourers. Put another way, the median value of a county court suit ($41 to $50 in the lower country and $71 to $80 in the upper country) was equivalent to one month's income for a labourer and about ten day's returns for a miner: a substantial sum. This statistic acquires increased significance given the seasonal nature of mining and the uneven returns experienced even when the mines were in operation. The high and fluctuating cost of provisions, which, according to Magistrate Thomas Elwyn, were 'crippling every man in the mines,' only underscored the fact that much was at stake in the outcome of a county court suit in British Columbia.[37] When the potential gains were so great, it seems unlikely that median court costs of $4.50 to $5 – approximately 10 per cent of a labourer's monthly income, or less than a day's work for a miner – were prohibitive to prospective suitors.

If the amount at stake and the costs associated with litigation were not obstacles to going to court, prospective suitors must have been positively encouraged to do so by the treatment they received before the law. County Court and Mining Court plaintiffs were strikingly successful. Three of every five plaints entered were resolved in their favour. Conversely, defendants were successful less than one in every ten times (7 per cent). Of the County Court decisions resolved in the plaintiff's favour, 34.6 per cent were straight judgments for the plaintiff; 13.6 per cent were confessed (that is, a formal admission of the charge was made by the defendant); and 6 per cent were resolved in the plaintiff's favour because the defendant did not appear to stand trial (table 6). Only 2.6 per cent of the cases resolved in the defendant's favour resulted from a judgment of the court. In fact, defendants won more cases by default (4.5 per cent); that is, when the plaintiff withdrew his suit, failed to appear, or had a non-suit declared. Finally, under the category of 'other' decisions, two figures are especially notable: those for no appearance and no service. In those categories, 4.6 per cent of all cases did not proceed because the plaintiff or both the plaintiff and the defendant did not appear, and 2.3 per cent did not proceed because proper service of the writ of summons was not or could not be executed.

These figures reveal some interesting patterns. First, although judges awarded plaintiffs at least eight times as often as defendants (56.1 per cent ver-

TABLE 6
County Court decisions, 1858–71

General decision	Specific decision	N	%
n/a		126	3.7
For plaintiff	For the plaintiff	1,174	34.6
	Confessed	461	13.6
	Default	202	6.0
	Paid	52	1.5
	Satisfied	14	0.4
For defendant	For the defendant	89	2.6
	Withdrawn	102	3.0
	Non-suit	47	1.5
Other	Settled	206	6.1
	No appearance	155	4.6
	Dismissed	106	3.1
	No service	68	2.0
	Struck out	44	1.3
	Adjourned	36	1.1
	Postponed	33	1.0
	Summons only	22	0.6
	Other	16	0.5
Settled out of court		436	12.9
Total		3,389	100.0

Source: see Note on Sources.

sus 7.1 per cent), defendants chose to settle out of court a little more than once every ten times (12.9 per cent), placing their faith instead on court intervention (87.1 per cent). The court intervened to varying degrees: actions were ended when the defendant confessed the plaintiff's claim (13.6 per cent), paid an agreed-upon amount (1.5 per cent), or otherwise satisfied the claim (0.4 per cent), or after a full trial (38.7 per cent). This willingness on the part of defendants to abide by the forms of legal process is further supported by the figures for actions that were ended by failure to serve the summons (indicating that the debtor absconded; 2.8 per cent), by default (6.8 per cent), or by the non-appearance of the plaintiff and/or the defendant (4.6 per cent). In total, just 14.2 per cent of all actions were decided in one way or another by a failure to appear. British Columbians usually came to court to answer their creditors' claims, indi-

TABLE 7
Richfield Mining Court decisions, 1864–71

Decision		N	%
n/a		15	2.2
For plaintiff	For the plaintiff	285	41.0
	By default	9	1.3
	Confessed	81	11.7
For defendant	For the defendant	63	9.1
	Non-suit	19	2.7
	Withdrawn	16	2.3
Settled out of court		29	4.2
Other	Adjourned	17	2.4
	Dismissed	90	12.9
	No appearance	5	0.7
	Paid	5	0.7
	Postponed	3	0.4
	Satisfied	1	0.1
	Settled	40	5.8
	Other	17	2.4
Total		695	100.0

Source: see Note on Sources.

cating perhaps that the transiency associated with the mining frontier was not as marked as we have thought.

Decisions in the Mining Court mirror those seen for the County Court (table 7). Cases were rarely settled out of court or withdrawn after an action had been initiated. Equally rare were cases where the principals did not appear: default judgments and non-appearances comprised only 2 per cent of all cases, suggesting, as was the case with the county courts, that the miners' proverbial transiency was not as much of a problem as might be expected.

British Columbia's inferior courts showed themselves to be friendly to plaintiffs, rewarding them in almost 60 per cent of the cases launched. The courts' actions would be meaningless, however, if they could not enforce their decisions. Unfortunately, there is little information about the execution of court orders. The colony's sheriff, whose job it was to carry out the decisions of the courts, left behind no surviving records. Given British Columbia's sparse population and the limited numbers of constables, enforcement appears to have been problematic. Despite these concerns, few suitors voiced complaints.[38] Only 1.7 per cent of County Court actions were launched to enforce previous judgments of that court (see table 2). This does not necessarily mean that remaining 98.3 per cent of judgments were enforced successfully. It could mean that plaintiffs recognized the futility of going to court again to get their judgments enforced. However, the comments I have gleaned seem to indicate that the courts could be successful in executing their decisions. On Vancouver Island, David Cameron seized Robert Staines's pigs with the aid of a constable sworn in especially for the occasion. It was an expensive endeavour, costing nearly $140, or about one-third of the chief justice's annual income. When Malvina Jane Toy, a Clinton innkeeper, succeeded in winning her suit against Francis Barnard in 1867, an angry Barnard complained to the attorney-general. The County Court did not grant him sufficient time to comply with its verdict, and seized his property. The sheriff took Barnard's coach and horses and assumed possession of his real estate at Clinton. Had his lawyer not 'paid the money under protest my stage would have been stopped for several days and myself put to great inconvenience.'

Imprisonment was also an option exercised by the court against debtors it considered likely to abscond before a trial, as well as those unable to pay their debts following a judgment against them. Incarceration was no small matter. John and Robert Cranford (whose case I will discuss in chapter 5) were arrested in 1862 for debt and imprisoned for eighty-four and sixty-six days respectively. The 'debtors' prison,' which was part of the New Westminster jail, where the Cranfords were held, was a notorious place. John Robson, the editor of the *British Columbian*, had been an inmate of the jail after the Cranfords' stay. The night he spent there left a deep impression on him, punctuated as it was by 'the shrieks of a dying maniac' and the smells of 'noxious effluvia.'[39] British Columbians were particularly sensitive to the whole issue of imprisonment for debt in late 1862. In the weeks just prior to the Cranfords' trial and Robson's imprisonment, British Columbians had been regaled with stories of the horrors of New Westminster's debtors' prison, which culminated in the death of one of its inmates, James Locke.[40] Such sentiments must have touched British Columbia's colonial administrators, because shortly afterwards the law respecting bankruptcy and insolvency was amended and imprisonment for debt outlawed.[41]

Although the courts had the power to enforce their decisions, their effectiveness still relied on the willingness of both parties, especially the defendants, to abide by judicial rules and proceedings. At least part of the reason for this willingness lay in the barriers to mobility in the gold fields. People could not readily escape a court action. The Gold Fields Acts placed restrictions on the length of time a claim could remain unworked before it was considered abandoned and subject to be claimed by other miners. Miners often invested a substantial amount of time and capital in their claim, which they could not easily leave behind. And of course there was always the eternal optimism of the gold fields – the ever-present hope of striking it rich – that could tie a miner to his claim.

So far we have ascertained that British Columbians went to court because they had much to gain by doing so; that it did not cost them much when they did; that plaintiffs were successful in winning their cases; and that there did not seem to be a problem enforcing the court's judgments: all in all, this was a favourable context for litigation. But this does not explain why defendants chose to let the court decide their fate rather than settling their disputes on their own. In fact, it begs the question. Perhaps the most important reason people went to court when they disagreed was because it was a natural thing to do. Among British Columbians, the use of rules and institutions of formal law to settle disputes was a cultural convention, just as song duels were used for settling conflict among the Inuit or ritual warfare among the Barotse.[42] Going to court and letting the court intervene to the extent that it did – settling nine plaints in ten – apparently was not considered unusual or symptomatic of social decay as it was in other societies governed by English common law.[43] In fact, everything we have learned so far about British Columbians' attitudes to and expectations of the law suggests quite the opposite. From the colony's formation, they *wanted* their relationships with the government and with each other to be constituted and regulated by the law; so much so, in fact, that they petitioned for the construction of courts and took an active and ever-watchful interest in the administration of the law. There was no golden age of informality to serve as a reference point for an alternative form of dispute resolution, and so there were no jeremiads about the decline of community sentiment or predictions about the imminent breakdown of society signalled and created by litigation.[44]

Indeed, in liberal discourse, litigation might be viewed as a normal outgrowth of human nature. Liberalism constructed human behaviour as inherently rational and motivated by the pursuit of self-interest. Two things follow from this view: first, because human nature is rational, behaviour is rule-driven; second, conflict not only is inevitable, but is a natural outgrowth of rational behaviour – the pursuit of self-interest. Given these two aspects of liberalism's view of human nature, the solution to the latter is implied by the former: conflicts can be limited by telling people the rules, and disputes can be resolved through the application of them.

The cultural convention of resorting to formal law and going to court to resolve disputes was supported by the colony's social structure. Relationships among British Columbia's non-Native population were specialized, constituted primarily by economic activity rather than the social ties or kin, family, religion or ethnicity. The latter bonds did exist among particular groups – for instance, there were Cornish, Chinese, and Canadian miners in the Cariboo who formed occupationally and culturally based mining associations and no doubt socialized together – but their *raison d'être* in British Columbia was, first and foremost, economic. When people interacted, they did so in specialized contexts for limited and specific purposes. Contacts were brief and largely transacted for purposes related to mining: buying a pair of boots from the general store, entering into a partnership to develop a claim, slapping down a dollar for a drink and a dance with one of Adler and Barry's Hurdy-Gurdy girls. While each of these contacts could easily develop into more encompassing relationships over time, time was one thing that many of these relationships did not have. In a colony devoted to resource extraction, communities appeared, disappeared, and reconstituted themselves with news of false starts and rich finds.[45]

Instead of having a number of kinds of relationships with a limited number of people, British Columbians had limited kinds of relationships with a large number of people.[46] For instance, the person from whom Robert Harkness bought his foolscap and his tobacco was not likely to be a relation, a neighbour, or a fellow parishioner. He or she was probably one of a number of people who provisioned the miners. Thus, though these relationships were real and important, individuals had less invested in them, emotionally and materially, than they would have had if the social bonds of kin, family, and community were present to reinforce the economic ties. Because of this, there was less at stake when a dispute arose between two people. Whereas formal arbitration might jeopardize a relationship that had many layers in addition to the economic one, and hence would not be worth pursuing, social relations in British Columbia were sufficiently specialized that the potential risk was limited. Moreover, because relationships were so narrowly defined, it was difficult for one individual to get the necessary leverage on another to make informal dispute resolution possible. The courts were a common denominator of communication and a necessary instrument of coercion in a place where commonality beyond that created by the work place and work process was a rare thing.

Litigation in nineteenth-century British Columbia was thus largely an expression of a certain kind of community: a community of individuals who were strangers to one another, and who, in the course of pursuing their own self-interest, came up against others doing the same thing. They turned to the law to resolve their conflicts in the absence of the necessary familiarity to deal with them informally, and because they valued the predictable rationality of the formal legal process. In a world shaped by the marketplace and its demands, certainty was the best guarantee of individual self-interest.

'The history of British Columbia is brief. Gold made it and gold unmade it.'[47] That pithy comment from the English traveller W.A. Baillie-Grohmann encapsulated two fundamental realities of colonial life: the dominance of the economy in British Columbia and its precariousness. Both were confirmed and elucidated by the pattern of litigation. Civil rather than criminal matters preoccupied British Columbia's courts, and actions for debt comprised the bulk of civil litigation in its inferior tribunals, as they did in other jurisdictions.[48] However, both the extent and types of debt cases illustrated that commerce, credit, and wage labour were important parts of the frontier economy and that land was not. Cases involving disputed land title or trespass were almost unknown in the County Court; and while they did comprise just over a fifth (22 per cent) of Mining Court actions, mining properties were part of a larger system of commercial and industrial capitalism rather than a settled agrarian economy.

Resource extraction was an uncertain enterprise, and its uncertainty was exceeded only by that which characterized the business of servicing the mines and miners. Though merchants absorbed much of the risk associated with frontier development through their liberal extension of credit, they did not do so for purely altruistic reasons. The storekeeper, like the saloonkeeper and the boarding-house operator, wanted to strike it rich just as much as the miner did. But they often had to go to court to do so. When they appeared as plaintiffs, however, they were often successful, winning three out of every five cases, while defendants won less than one every ten times. For British Columbia's miners, the plaint was often as effective as the pickaxe in securing their fortunes. Plaintiffs in the colony's Mining Court also fared well, winning at least more than half their cases.

While success might have made British Columbians litigious, it does not fully or adequately explain why they resorted to the courts to resolve their disputes. To understand that, we must take note of two things: first, how British Columbians saw the world and acted in it; second, how this way of seeing was reinforced by the social context in which the law operated. We have already seen how the discourse of laissez-faire liberalism was embedded in the colony's legal institutions. The same discourse also constructed litigation as a desirable method of dispute resolution because the application of a set of formal, standardized laws to economic transactions was the best guarantee of the certainty necessary for a well-functioning marketplace. Within a liberal discourse, going to court in cases of dispute was commonsensical: in short, litigation was a cultural convention of this nineteenth-century gold colony.

That cultural convention was reinforced by the colony's social structure. British Columbia was first and foremost a new society; but it was also culturally diverse (apart from the significant and sizable Native population) and mobile.

These three factors – newness, diversity, and mobility – made it difficult for British Columbians to establish the kind of familiarity necessary for conflicts to be settled informally. British Columbians were strangers to one another, and because they were, the law came to play a central role in mediating social relations and even creating their boundaries.

The heightened importance of the law in nineteenth-century British Columbia, both as a means to secure property and as a sort of social glue, meant that British Columbians took an active interest in its administration. As a result, any maladministration, as we will see, took on added significance.

5

Cranford v. Wright:
Law and Authority in British Columbia

In April 1861 something significant happened in Alexandria, a small settlement in British Columbia's upper country: Stipendiary Magistrate and Assistant Gold Commissioner Philip Henry Nind sat down and wrote a letter to W.A.G. Young, the colony's colonial secretary, declining an appointment as a county court judge. 'I regret that His Excellency has been pleased to nominate me to this post,' he said,

as I am deficient in that special Knowledge requisite to the proper execution of its duties, nor have I any legal works to refer to for instruction and guidance. The population in this district is fond of litigation and many are acquainted with the technicalities of law, and would only be too ready to detect mistakes committed by an inexperienced County Court Judge. I respectfully submit that the appointment be conferred upon someone better qualified by education and experience to undertake its duties.[1]

What lifts this episode from the routine to the remarkable is the fact that Nind, a graduate of Eton and Oxford, felt himself not just 'inexperienced,' but positively 'deficient,' and hence unsuited for the post. Here surely was the sort of 'gentleman ... with country tastes' that Matthew Baillie Begbie thought should anchor the colonial magistracy.[2] Yet Nind did not think his social status would confer the authority necessary for him to do his job effectively.

Nind's letter is interesting because it raises questions about the nature of legal authority in British Columbia and suggests some answers. But before turning to those, it might be useful to discuss briefly what I mean by authority. First and foremost, authority is a type of power, which can itself be defined as the ability to produce intended effects. Authority is distinguished from other kinds of power (such as force and persuasion, for instance) by the means by which it produces those intended effects. Those possessed of authority are able to do things because people obey their commands. Though obedience can be secured by coercion, the obedience that underlies legitimate authority rests on consent. Thus, though authority is a form of power, it also implies a certain social relationship between rulers and ruled. People in authority have a right to command that is recognized by those over whom they rule. Without that recognition and the consent it implies authority is illegitimate; indeed, some would say that it does not exist.[3]

If legitimate authority rests on a recognition of the right to command – on the consent of those governed – on what basis is that recognition and consent given? How do people gauge the legitimacy of authority? As was suggested in chapter 1, fur-trade authority was premised on a particular understanding of society in which mutuality and inequality were the accepted foundations of social order. Labourers accepted their lower status and the arbitrary and sometimes violent rule of HBC officers as long as the latter fulfilled the responsibilities commensurate with their station and power. Philip Nind's letter suggests that while his social status did not confer the authority necessary for him to rule, possession of 'special Knowledge' would. In Nind's opinion, British Columbians measured the authority of the law less by the character of the person who dispensed it and more by his demonstrated knowledge of the 'technicalities of law.' Authority was thus contingent on individual ability and performance. In fact, Nind's comments indicate that the authority of the law could be separated to a certain degree from the individual who administered it: it was the 'special Knowledge' itself, rather than the individual, which possessed authority.

If Nind's letter suggested the broad outlines of two kinds of authority in British Columbia, their details were provided in *Cranford v. Wright* (1862), a prosaic suit for breach of contract and debt that precipitated a storm of controversy over the administration of the law, and in the process revealed more about the right by which the law commanded obedience. The case reveals the standards European British Columbians used to gauge the legitimacy of the law. Those standards, I argue, were derived from liberalism, and they became apparent in the discussion about the case and the conduct of the judge and the principals involved that occurred in the pages of both Vancouver Island's and British Columbia's newspapers. Why was the case so controversial? What were the central issues? *Cranford* was controversial because the presiding judge, Matthew Begbie, appeared to contravene what European British Columbians considered the proper conventions of legal decision-making: he insisted that character assessment play a leading role in decision-making, dismissed important documentary evidence, and was contemptuous of the Cranfords' lawyers' use of legal doctrine – not how they used it, but that they used it at all to make their case. The central issues of debate involved Begbie's interpretation of contract law, his treatment of documentary evidence, and his reaction to the lawyers' use of legal doctrine. In framing their criticisms of the judge, European British Columbians revealed that to them legal authority was rooted in texts and the experts who could interpret them, and that justice or fairness was a matter of the simple application of the rules. Unlike paternal authority, which was based on personal discretion, textual authority and expertise conferred the certainty and predictability that was a precondition of success in the marketplace. Just as laissez-faire liberalism created an institutional structure that both supported and furthered its needs, it constructed an ethical system that did the same thing.

On the basis of a single, albeit high-profile, case, the argument I put forward in this chapter is necessarily speculative – a quality that is only reinforced by the nature of my subject matter, which is the slippery concept of authority. Nevertheless, for all its particularities, I do think *Cranford* is emblematic of many of the tensions in the administration of the law, and of the problems of doing so in a particular social and economic context.

The case of *Cranford v. Wright*, which John Robson, the editor of the *British Columbian*, called 'most lengthy and, to the mercantile community of this and the adjoining Colony, most important trial,' began on Thursday, 4 December 1862, before a densely crowded courtroom, with David Babington Ring and John Foster McCreight representing the plaintiffs John and Robert Cranford Jr, and George Hunter Cary, attorney-general of British Columbia, and H.P. Walker representing the defendant Gustavus Blinn Wright.[4]

This action was a countersuit for $25,000 in damages. Robert Cranford had contracted Wright, a packer, to transport $10,000 worth of goods from Douglas to Lillooet. The original suit, launched by Wright against the Cranfords, was heard in Lillooet before Begbie at nisi prius proceedings in October 1862.[5] Hoping to profit from the demand for provisions in the Cariboo mining district, Robert Cranford had arrived in Victoria in April 1862 with a consignment of goods from San Francisco, which he arranged to be transported from New Westminster to Lillooet by G.B. Wright & Company.[6] In a contract signed on 25 April, Wright agreed to pack the goods for nine cents per pound, payable sixty days after the arrival of the merchandise at Lillooet, and assured his customer that the goods would reach their destination in seven to ten days. Robert Cranford then proceeded to Lillooet where, in anticipation of the arrival of his goods, he contracted another packer to take them to Williams Creek, farther up the Fraser River. Then he waited. And waited. Two weeks later, the second packing company released Cranford from the agreement they had struck, informing him that it could wait no longer. Not until 28 May – thirty-three days after the signing of the contract with Wright – did the first of Cranford's goods arrive at Lillooet. The merchandise continued to trickle in over the summer, a third of it delayed some sixty to seventy-five days and none of it arriving in less than thirty-three days. In all, half could not be forwarded to Williams Creek because it arrived too late in the year or had spoiled; and the portion that did make it to the upper country did not sell at the high prices that Cranford hoped for. During the delay, other enterprising merchants had established themselves in the Williams Creek area, and had glutted the market.

None of this was of concern to Wright, however, who launched a suit against Robert Cranford and his elder brother John in August for non-payment of 'goods sold and delivered.'[7] Claiming a debt of £1,719, Wright convinced the County Court judge at Lillooet, A.C. Elliott, to issue a writ of capias on 8 September for the arrest of both Cranfords.[8] Robert Cranford was arrested at Lillooet on the same day and imprisoned for eighty-four days. His brother John, also a Cariboo merchant, was arrested at Williams Creek three weeks later on 27 September, brought to Lillooet, and imprisoned for sixty-six days.[9] Their case was heard before Matthew Baillie Begbie on 15 and 16 October, and despite their efforts to show that John Cranford was not a partner and therefore not indebted, and that Robert Cranford, by virtue of his contract with Wright which stipulated that payment was not due until sixty days after delivery, was also not indebted, the case proceeded.

When Wright produced the contract of 25 April in the Lillooet courtroom, both Cranfords 'pronounced it altered.' They said 'that the words "*& Brother*" had been interpolated, and that the "&" had been crowded in at the end of the first line, the word "brother" written across the margin opposite the second line, that the "t" had been inserted before "him" to make it read "them" and that the alterations had been made in darker ink.' Even Begbie agreed that the document had been tampered with, noting that 'the dot which had been over the "i" in "him" was still there to show what the word once was.' Nevertheless, the judge 'went on to make apologies for Mr. Wright, saying that it was a private memorandum of Mr. Wright's and that he had a right to do what he liked with it.' Wright, without prompting from the bench or the defence counsel, admitted 'that he had made the alteration of the same day on which it was written.' To this Begbie again interjected that 'it was rather in Wright's favor than against him that he should so boldly show this altered agreement.' 'In this way,' John Robson wrote in the *British Columbian,*

Judge Begbie relieved Wright's Counsel of his duties, and drew a veil over the ugliness of Wright's guilt. In this way Judge Begbie would not see, and did his best to prevent the Jury from seeing, that Wright had virtually committed the CRIME OF FORGERY against J.P. Cranford. How could the memorandum of agreement be a private one with which he had a right to do as he chose, and then bring it forward in a Court to prove an Account!

Despite the sensation caused by this evidence, however, the jury ruled that John Cranford was liable as a partner and that the sixty-day stipulation in the contract signed by Robert Cranford and G.B. Wright had been rescinded. They awarded Wright $9,500, a sum that included court costs of almost $1,000. Robson attributed this decision to Begbie's failure to charge the jury properly. 'If he had done so, fairly, no honest Jury could have decided as they did.' 'In sober truth,' he concluded, 'Judge Begbie ignored a large part of the evidence.'[10]

From their jail cells, the Cranfords were unsuccessful in their attempts to get a new trial, and were released only when they launched the countersuit against Wright, which was heard by Begbie at the December sitting of the Supreme Court. Claiming damages of $25,000, the Cranfords used the same argument they had in the earlier suit. As well as asserting that John Cranford was not a partner and that Wright had breached his contract with Robert Cranford, the counsel for the plaintiffs claimed that Wright had appropriated Cranford's goods, 'having caused the brand and mark of the plaintiff to be obliterated, and his own substituted, at a time, too, when the market was high.'[11] At this point Begbie interrupted the Cranfords' lawyer, McCreight, saying that he 'could not allow imputations of such a nature to be cast upon the defendant, and insisted that they were disgraceful and must recoil upon the head of the person advancing them.' McCreight refused to withdraw his remarks, and Begbie requested that David Babington Ring, the plaintiffs' other lawyer, take over. Ring refused, and the judge subsided until the contract between Robert Cranford and Wright as well as invoices between the two were produced as evidence. Though the contract was admitted, the invoices, addressed to 'R. Cranford, Jr.,' which were brought forward to show that the contract had been altered to read 'R. Cranford & Brother,' were not. Begbie's refusal to admit the invoices 'produced a hot discussion between the judge and plaintiffs' counsel, and a reference by the latter to *Taylor on Evidence*.[12] 'The title of this book,' said the *British Colonist*, 'will never be forgotten by those present at the trial. *Taylor* was invoked nearly every hour of the day.'[13] Relations between the bench and the Cranfords' counsel were not improved on the last day of the trial (17 December), when Robert Cranford attempted to shake Wright's credibility by telling the jury that the affidavit with which Wright obtained the writ of capias in *Wright v. Cranford* was false.[14] Wright swore that the Cranfords owed him £1,719 15s. for 'goods sold and delivered.' This, according to the Cranfords, was not strictly true: the Cranfords, if they owed Wright any money at all, owed it for freight charges. Here

Begbie interjected: 'Oh, Mr. Cranford! I have seen sheaves of affidavits made in this country by persons who never read them. No doubt Mr. Wright did not read that before he swore to it, so that it would be unfair to impute a false oath to him.' Amidst the 'confusion' that followed, proceedings were adjourned, and at Begbie's suggestion all retired to the races.[15] At 6:30 p.m. the court met, counsel presented closing statements, and Begbie charged the jury, telling them first that 'they must consider that the defendants [applicants] (the Cranfords) were strangers, while on the other hand, Mr. Wright was well known to them';[16] and second, that they had three points to decide: whether the contract between the Cranfords and Wright was rescinded, as the defendant claimed, or was still binding; if the contract was not rescinded, what constituted a reasonable time for delivery of the goods to Lillooet; and the value of the goods when they should have arrived and their value when they did arrive, the difference being equivalent to the damages incurred by the Cranfords.[17] Before the jury retired, Ring asked that they be given a 'bill of particulars' outlining the Cranfords' claim to aid them in their decision. To this Begbie reluctantly agreed.

Late the next day, some twenty-six hours after they had been locked up, the jury were recalled, having failed to come to a decision. Begbie refused to accept a majority verdict as he had in an earlier case in the same nisi prius session.[18] Ring asked when the jury had been given the bill of particulars. Begbie was 'considerably disconcerted at this enquiry,' and the court registrar, Greville Matthew, sported 'an unusual flow of blood to his features.'[19] The foreman, 'after considerable shuffling,' told the court that the document in question had not been given to the jury until 'Three o'clock this afternoon!' 'Thus it appeared that a document essential to enable the Jury intelligently to come to a decision had only reached them after they had been locked up for twenty-five hours, and three hours before they had been called before the Court!' Though William Grieve, the foreman, said that considerable progress had been made after they received the bill of particulars, and that a decision could be reached if the jury were allowed to retire again, another juryman disagreed and asked to be discharged. Counsel for the plaintiffs asked Begbie to offer advice or assistance to the jury so 'that justice be not defeated,' but Begbie refused and discharged the jury. Mr. Ring, addressing the registrar, said:

'Mr. Matthew, have you the book in Court which contains the names of the Barristers who practice in this Court?'
Mr. Matthew: 'Yes.'
Mr. Ring: 'Then please *dash your pen across my name.*'

McCreight made a similar request, and 'both gentlemen indignantly withdrew.

Cheers were given and the Court adjourned amidst great confusion and excitement.'[20]

The Cranfords were rearrested and sent to prison, but released when they again made application for another trial – this time in the adjoining colony, on the grounds that their contract had been made in Victoria with a Victoria-based firm. David Cameron never heard the case, however, as it was finally settled out of court in April 1863.[21] Ring and McCreight's dramatic withdrawal created a great sensation in New Westminster, and a 'meeting to mark public disapprobation of the extraordinary course pursued by the Judge throughout the trial' was held immediately.[22] 'Loud applause' greeted the arrival of the two principals in the Columbia Theatre, where both were complimented for the 'firm and manly ability with which ... [they] repelled the insults heaped upon them by the Court during the Cranford suit.' William Grieve, the foreman of the jury, was called upon to address the meeting and 'in a very able and lucid manner went over a large amount of facts and figures bearing upon that extraordinary trial, and showing most conclusively that the Jury had sufficient data before them to entitle the Plaintiffs [applicants] to a verdict.' The meeting soon adjourned, but discussion continued in the pages of both the Island and mainland's newspapers.

What is striking about *Cranford* is the intensity of feeling and the interest that accompanied a case that was, on the surface, a routine suit for debt. If the attention given to the trial by the *British Columbian* is any indication, all of New Westminster's 1,190 inhabitants were riveted by the proceedings.[23] The Cranfords themselves contributed to a good portion of the discussion. 'We desire, through your columns, to present a plain statement of facts for the consideration of the authorities and the people of British Columbia,' they wrote to John Robson, the newspaper's editor.[24] With his help they produced a lengthy three-part series entitled 'A History of the Wrongs of the Cranfords including an Account of the Two Celebrated Suits – Wright vs Cranford and Cranford vs Wright.'[25] The articles related the circumstances leading to the trials themselves and reprinted some of the documents submitted as evidence in the two cases. In addition, the newspaper published nine editorials and four letters to the editor, representing the views of all twelve jurors, in the weeks preceding and following the December trial. Interest was equally keen across the water in Victoria. The *British Colonist* followed the trial closely, reprinting daily testimony and offering editorial comment on the case. The interest generated by *Cranford* stands in marked contrast to the relative lack of discussion given to assize criminal trials, even trials for murder.

Cranford is important because it sheds light on the foundations of authority, revealing the standards British Columbians used to gauge the legitimacy of the law. Those standards, as will be discussed, were derived from laissez-faire liberalism, and were apparent in their assessment of the ends they thought the law should uphold and the means by which it did so. The substantive legal issues *Cranford* raised – points of law involving contract and debt – bore directly on the issue of social obligations and individual responsibility, and thus illuminated the kinds of relations the law upheld and, ultimately, the social basis of its authority. Consistent with the discourse of laissez-faire liberalism, English common law held that obligations between individuals were matters of self-conscious and voluntary contracts. The only obligations that existed between people were those that they agreed to undertake. The law would enforce those, justifying its interference as an extension of individual will, and no others. In addition, common law thinking about debt changed with the increase in commercial activity, again reflecting the impact of capitalist values. In the mid-nineteenth century, imprisonment for debt came to be seen as unjust because it punished people unduly for pursuing their self-interest. Moreover, because it attached even more risk to the already risky marketplace and actually removed some people from it, imprisonment for debt was detrimental to the general welfare because it suppressed economic exchange. The execution of the law in *Cranford* was inconsistent with contemporary thinking on both contract and debt and the social and economic realities of life in British Columbia, and hence was controversial. The furore surrounding the case demonstrated that the law's right to command rested on the extent to which its decisions favoured individualistic capitalist enterprise.

Not only did British Columbians gauge the law's authority in terms of the extent to which it fulfilled capitalist ends, but they also measured the way it achieved those ends: the means by which legal decisions were made. Civil trials placed heavy demands on the decision-making abilities of judge and jury, and this had implications not only for the shape of the trial but also for the authority of the law. The length of the trial, the nature of the testimony and jury deliberation, and the courtroom dynamics between judge and lawyers in *Cranford* demonstrated the inadequacies of character and social status both as a basis of authoritativeness and as a means of reaching decisions in the courtroom. Moreover, the controversy surrounding the case suggested that the foundation of authoritativeness and decision-making was more textual than social: authority was to be found in texts and their interpreters.

In the original suit brought by Gus Wright against the Cranfords and in the subsequent countersuit, the contract between the two disputing parties was the central point at issue. *Cranford* occurred at the height of what the legal historian Patrick Atiyah calls the 'age of freedom of contract.'[26] From 1770 to 1870 the law of obligations, of which contract law is a part, reflected and reinforced the central tenets of laissez-faire. Contract law treated individuals as equal and independent agents whose obligations were limited by and coextensive with the intentional, voluntary, and private arrangements they made with each other. Individuals could be held responsible for meeting only those obligations that they intended to enter into and that were specified in a contract. The role of law in the age of freedom of contract was to enforce these private agreements between individuals. Using the law in this way was not considered paternal intervention by the state, but rather an extension of individual will. The law had almost nothing to say about the content of the contracts; that is, whether they were reasonable or just. Such questions were best left to the judgment of the individuals involved or, at best, lay in the realm of politics. Instead, those who framed and enforced the law operated under the assumption that the greatest happiness and prosperity, as well as the greatest justice, resulted from allowing individuals to 'realize their own wills.'[27]

Matthew Begbie had a different interpretation of the law of contract and the nature of obligation, which got him into trouble during *Cranford*. Although the brothers insisted repeatedly that Robert 'was the only person connected in the business,'[28] Begbie, during the Lillooet trial,

ingeniously helped the plaintiff's [Wright's] case by laying great stress in his charge on the fact that after J.P. Cranford had been employed by R. Cranford, Jr., he had manifested great zeal and energy in conducting the business, and had given the impression ... that he might be a partner. Judge Begbie ruled that J.P. Cranford might, in this way, unconsciously have made himself a co-contractee with R. Cranford, Jr., and so instructed the jury.[29]

According to the *British Columbian*, J.P.'s 'zeal and energy' did not make him liable as a partner, and it was ridiculous to punish him for his industry.

Moreover, according to David Ring, his exertions did not even make him the legal agent of Robert Cranford. In making that argument, Ring drew on agency and contract theory. Most of the law of agency was developed to protect third parties from the actions of principals and their agents, and spelled out the rights and liabilities of principals (to the third parties) that arose out of the actions of those acting as their agents. *Cranford* raised the issue of when and how a person becomes an agent of a principal, and what the agent's responsibilities and liabilities are. It is unclear (indeed, this was the point at issue) whether John Cranford was an agent of his brother Robert. He was not named as such in the contract; in fact, his name did not appear at all in that document, nor did he act in such a way as to imply that he was an agent. Even if he were an agent, however, that would not mean that he was party to the contract (that he could sue and be sued on it). He would be a party to the contract between Robert Cranford and Gus Wright only if the principal was undisclosed; if he purported to be acting on behalf of the principal but was in fact acting on his own behalf; or if he intended and purported to contract for a non-existent principal. According to the Cranfords' lawyers, none of these actions described those of John Cranford.[30]

Begbie's understanding of contract seemed to stem from an older and, by the 1860s, anachronistic understanding of obligation that was rooted in paternalism and a particular understanding of society. For Begbie, obligation was not limited by or derived from a legal instrument such as a written contract. Instead, responsibility was coextensive with the moral obligation incurred by behaviour and social status. It could be, as John Robson noted, assumed 'unconsciously.' J.P. Cranford acted like a zealous merchant and partner and so took on, regardless of his intent, the responsibilities of a businessman. This included paying his bills. Begbie's idea that obligations extended beyond the particular desires and intents of the people involved was rooted in a particular understanding of how society was ordered. In that view, the bonds of obligation were horizontal and vertical and extended between and among all individuals regardless of their power and status. The interdependence among the various parts meant that individual actions had consequences for all, and that for the well-being of the social whole, the power and actions of some had to be curtailed. The role of the law was to protect and reinforce this mutuality and, in doing so, to promote the general welfare. In this way, the rule of law and the notion of how society was constructed fit together to uphold a system of paternal authority.

In the age of freedom of contract and laissez-faire, the implicit mutuality that characterized social relations in the previous century was gone. Individuals existed or could exist outside of society, and society was the result of a social contract between autonomous individuals.[31] In the absence of an organic understanding of society, obligation existed only between equal, independent, and freely contracting people. Individual action had consequences only for those directly involved. Because of this, individual responsibility was limited, and the role of the law was correspondingly circumscribed to encompass only the enforcement of specific obligations. The rule of law was the perfect complement to the market economy and favoured individual initiative. It promised to guarantee a level of predictability and standardization in behaviour, and in so doing limited the uncertainty and risk inherent in economic pursuits. By making the options open to individuals clear, the law provided a level playing-field for each to pursue his economic ambitions with the greatest chance of success.

If the general welfare was tied to the faithful performance of economic transactions, it was also guaranteed by liberal laws pertaining to imprisonment for debt. Part of the controversy surrounding *Cranford* was derived from and reflected a larger nineteenth-century debate surrounding debt and the proper legal response to it. The ethical system constructed by capitalism changed attitudes towards indebtedness.[32] As it became more common, indebtedness shed some of its association with moral failure – among the commercial classes, at least – and was viewed instead as a consequence of respectable economic activity.[33] In this context, imprisoning debtors was immoral because it did not serve the security of property or promote continued capitalist enterprise. British Columbia's volatile economy only accentuated these sentiments, and in the wake of *Cranford* John Robson published two editorials on the subject. As honest businessmen engaged in opening up and developing the colony through the extension of credit, the Cranfords, like other merchants, could not be blamed for an occasional 'misfortune.' By imprisoning a debtor the colonial government deprived him of his freedom to engage in the pursuit of economic gain and hence did great injury to the public welfare. Such sentiments were commonly voiced in many parts of North America, which, like British Columbia, were equally concerned with economic growth. For instance, the American lawyer Daniel Webster felt that changes in the law of debtor and creditor were necessary to 'liberate "human capital" for reentry into the economy.'[34] The legal historian James Willard Hurst agreed. The abolition of imprisonment for debt in the nineteenth century was, he felt, motivated by a desire to 'afford the debtor a breathing spell in which he might regather his strength,' and 'to preserve the general course of his dealings.'[35] Laws that deterred economic activity did not serve justice.

Cranford's more general characteristics as a civil trial, its courtroom dynamics and the public reaction to them, are also suggestive of the economic standards British Columbians used to measure the administration of the law and its authority. Though trials in British Columbia often occurred in unorthodox settings (chapter 3), their actual conduct would be familiar to those who lived in more settled societies governed by English common law. The testimony in a single case could often occupy an entire day, during which large amounts of information were produced and difficult questions of law and fact were raised. The intervention of experts who could guide the decision-making process by ordering the evidence produced and by offering rules and precedents became necessary to meet the demand for predictability and efficiency in the legal process.

The reasons for the lengthy civil trials lay in the number of witnesses brought forward, the nature of their testimony, and the protracted deliberations of the jury. Unlike criminal trials, civil litigation did not proceed 'at a cracking pace.'[36] In *Cranford*, the point at issue was frequently lost sight of in the mass of evidence produced over the nine days of testimony. During that time at least twenty-four witnesses took the stand and produced evidence, on which, even after twenty-six hours of deliberation, the jury was unable to reach a verdict.

Though the existing court record is too incomplete to allow more than an impressionistic view of the pace of civil trials, the outlines it does reveal suggest that *Cranford* was not unusual. The testimony in *Linaker v. Ballou*, heard at the same assizes as the *Cranford* case, occupied a whole day, and the jury required twenty-two hours to reach a verdict.[37] Cases heard in the upper country mining districts were no less complex. For instance, in *H.M. Curry v. Forest Rose Company*, heard at the Richfield assizes in 1865, at least eight witnesses gave testimony and were thoroughly cross-examined before the jury retired to deliberate.[38] Though they were locked up overnight, they failed to come to a verdict and were discharged. It was not uncommon for civil cases tried at the Supreme Court to feature four to eight witnesses who testified over one or two days, and for civil trial juries to take more than an hour to deliberate.

Mining cases, whether they were heard before an assistant gold commissioner or before Matthew Begbie on appeal, could be even lengthier, despite the fact that neither usually involved juries. This was due in part to the greater number of witnesses and the complexity of their testimony, which usually revolved around survey lines and the staking of the claim's boundaries. Assistant Gold Commissioner William Cox listened to eight witnesses over three full days of testimony in an 1865 mining case before rendering his 'summary' decision.[39] In 1867 no fewer than fifteen witnesses paraded before Henry Maynard Ball in a mining case that lasted two days.[40] Mining cases that were appealed to the Supreme Court featured fewer witnesses, but were equally protracted. In these the lawyers took centre stage, arguing points of fact and law to Matthew Begbie. *Borealis v. Watson* (1865) occupied a full day of the assize court's proceedings, but featured only three witnesses.[41] In *Aurora v. Davis* (1866), twelve witnesses gave testimony over a twelve-hour day; the court finally adjourned at 10 p.m.[42]

If the numbers of witnesses at civil trials made for lengthy proceedings, the quality of their testimony also contributed to their slow pace. The *Cranford* witnesses took the stand to establish the nature of the contract between the Cranfords and Gus Wright, as well as to answer more general questions about the business of shipping goods to the Upper Country; the condition of the trails and the possibilities of delay; and the likelihood of spoilage. In general, the civil cases heard at the assizes were characterized by a more detailed and complex (and, more than occasionally, stultifyingly dull) recapitulation of the circumstances and events surrounding the legal question at issue. This was particularly true of the mining cases that came to the assize on appeal: the testimony in these was filled with the riveting details of ditch widths and flume obstructions. One reason for the quality of testimony and evidence in nisi prius cases was the result of the intrusion of lawyers into the court room. In *Cranford*, both the appellants and the respondent were represented by teams of lawyers who made full use of their opportunities to cross-examine witnesses.

The main reason for the length of these proceedings was the nature of the points at issue in civil trials generally. Not only were there likely to be more and better witnesses to a civil dispute than a criminal act, but the range of behaviour and the obligations imposed by civil law made the trials more complex. Rather than assessing guilt or innocence, the *Cranford* jury had to make decisions on a variety of issues: first, whether a valid contract existed between the Cranfords and Wright; second, if a contract did exist, what constituted a reasonable time for the Cranfords' goods to be delivered; and third, what damages, if any, should be awarded. These were difficult questions for twelve laymen to decide. The detail produced over the nine days made Begbie's summation more than a mere preliminary to jury deliberation. Despite his summary, the twelve still needed some of the documentation produced as evidence to help them. Even then a verdict was not forthcoming after some twenty-six hours of deliberation.[43]

It is difficult to say much about what went on during deliberation, but occasionally one gets glimpses of the process that indicate that it could be both lengthy and heated. In 1861, for instance, Begbie wrote to James Douglas to tell him that 'a jury room is much required' in New Westminster. '[It] should be an empty room except [for] benches and one desk. A jury locked up for three hours would utterly destroy any furniture.'[44] Though the *Cranford* jurors left the New Westminster court house intact, the dissension in their jury room spilled out into the press. Some of the jurors wrote letters to the editor of the *British Columbian* accusing their peers of misconduct.[45]

These scraps of evidence revealed more than the tension and acrimony that could be part of decision-making, for they also shed light on the sorts of issues jurors grappled with in coming to a decision. Though Begbie considered character important in *Cranford* and instructed the jury to consider the fact that, while they knew Gus Wright, the Cranfords were 'strangers to the Colony,' the jurors spent most of their time wrestling with more factual and technical issues. The chief points at issue were the contract between Cranford and Wright and the assessment of damages. Was the contract valid, or had it been rescinded by the actions of either party? What damages should be awarded?[46] To decide, the jurors needed proper instruction from the judge. 'As jurors we are appointed by our country, we are sworn to give a true verdict according to the evidence, as we shall answer to God, not the Judge,' wrote 'One of the Jurors' to the *British Columbian*.

The duties of Juries, as I understand them, are very different and distinct from the duties of a Judge. The Judge is undoubtedly the first officer of the Court, and among his other duties I suppose he must see that order and decorum are preserved, that witnesses are not brow-beaten by Counsel, while Lawyers have every opportunity afforded them of extracting the truth; he also takes notes of the evidence, and after the opposing Counsel are through, I suppose his duty is to take the evidence, of which he has copious notes, and comment on it for the benefit of the Jury ... Now Mr. Editor, in this celebrated case of Cranford against Wright we were occupied nine days listening to evidence, when the Judge very coolly told us he was not going to read the voluminous notes he had; and he was as good as his word.[47]

When Begbie denied them both proper instruction and documentation, they considered it an injustice, as did the Cranfords' lawyers, who pleaded with the judge to give the jurors guidance 'so that justice be not defeated.' The *Cranford* jurors were jealous of their role in the legal process, and wanted to perform it well. They could be effective only if they were instructed properly, 'One of the Jurors' noted, and supplied with the necessary documentary evidence. 'Now Sir,' he concluded, 'it seems to me a complete mockery of men to keep them eleven days listening to evidence, Judge and Counsel, then lock them up without giving them the article they most need to enable them to solve what difficulties might arise.'[48]

To the *Cranford* jurors a just verdict was one that was informed by a close reading of the evidence. In this case 'reading' should be taken quite literally, for they assigned great importance to written evidence in truth-finding. The jurors demanded that the 'bill of particulars' be made available to them during their deliberations, and they criticized Begbie for directing their attention to Gus Wright's character in his summation and charge rather than reading from the 'voluminous' notes he had taken during the trial. In addition, both they and the British Columbia press took exception to the judge's refusal to admit invoices addressed to 'Robert Cranford' as evidence that the original contract had been altered to read 'R. Cranford and Brother,' and they positively bridled at this cavalier dismissal of the inconsistencies between Wright's affidavit and his oral testimony: 'I have seen sheaves of affidavits made in this country by persons who never read them,' Begbie claimed.' No doubt Mr. Wright did not read that before he swore to it, so that *it would be unfair to impute a false oath to him.*'[49]

To the Supreme Court judge, however, Wright's oral testimony and his standing in the New Westminster community carried more weight in ascertaining the truth than any documentary evidence that could be marshalled against him. From Begbie's comment, it appeared that Wright was accountable only for what he *said* in court. The fact that the judge considered oral evidence more important than written evidence was not unusual for a judge trained in the English common law tradition. The central premise of the adversary system was the notion that trials and truth-finding consisted of the 'sharp clash of proofs' given orally in 'a highly structured forensic setting.'[50] Judge and jurors were to be afforded the opportunity of hearing accused persons speak for themselves and seeing their reactions to the evidence. What was unusual and anachronistic, however, was Begbie's reaction to how that oral evidence came to be presented in court. Though he laid great emphasis on oral testimony, some kinds were more credible than others. As was the case in criminal trials, decision-makers seemed to want to see and hear the accused respond to the claims made against him or her without the benefit of prior preparation. An 'artless' response was crucial because the true character of the accused would be revealed.[51] Because an assessment of character was the key to understanding behaviour, it was also the key to reconstructing the truth in the courtroom.

The artless response and the larger notion of trial and truth-finding eroded with the arrival of lawyers in the courtroom. Though this was something that had long since happened in England, Begbie tried to postpone it in British Columbia.[52] The judge exhibited great antipathy towards lawyers (despite the fact that he was one of them), and admitted them to plead with great reluctance. With the absence of lawyers at the colony's formation, Begbie became accustomed to conducting cases on his own, taking responsibility for representing the interests of both parties. As he told James Douglas, it was not an easy job. 'The labor and responsibility is in all cases thrown upon the Judge or the Registrar to see that the plaintiff takes out the proper writ or commencement of proceedings that is correct in point of form.'

The Judge is then called by the defendant to point out the most efficacious mode of defence; and then he has to sit in Judgment upon the case so brought forward, embarrassed perhaps by the insertion of unnecessary matter or the omission of details with a mind preoccupied & feelings probably engaged on one side or the other (at all events the suitors think so). I hope that I am not given to despondence: but I should in such a position despair of giving satisfaction to the suitors.[53]

Ring's penchant for citing legal texts and dwelling on what Begbie perceived to be irrelevant technicalities was particularly annoying to the judge. When Ring attempted to convince Begbie to admit invoices made out to Robert Cranford as evidence, he cited *Taylor* and contended that 'the maxim, "qui facit per alium facit per se" governs here.'[54] To the amusement of the public, the judge sarcastically replied, 'Translate that into Chinook, Mr. Ring.'[55] On another occasion, when he tired of the arguments put forth by Ring and McCreight relating to the affidavit on which the writ of capias had been issued, he 'became petulant and sarcastic, asking them "if every i was dotted and all the t's crossed." '[56] Only once did Ring manage to silence the judge. At the end of the case, when Begbie attempted to force a non-suit, Ring said,

This is a most extraordinary power attempted by your lordship. The practice is well understood. The most elementary legal textbook – 'Smith's Actions at Law' – lays down the principle against such an assumption, followed with 'Chitty's Archbold,' another elementary work, [which] ... contains cases deciding the point for a century back.

'Upon this,' noted the *British Colonist*, 'the Judge, who seemed surprised, withdrew from his position.'[57]

With the interpolation of lawyers into the legal process, trials became occasions for the making of a case by advocates rather than the stating of a case by the parties. This bothered Begbie greatly, perhaps because it accorded more power to the lawyers and less to him. In addition, references to documentary evidence, precedents, and texts served, in Begbie's view, to obscure rather than illuminate the central issue in trials – the character of the accused – and ultimately to defeat the ends of justice.[58] The jurors, the Cranfords' lawyers, and the British Columbia press rejected the idea that character was a reliable or encompassing indicator of behaviour and that ascertaining character was central to truth-finding. For them, discovering the truth may have involved evaluating the character of the accused, but it also included a more self-conscious and scientific assessment of a set of facts culled and assigned a value by the rules of evidence that governed the legal process.

The tension between these two notions of trial in *Cranford* and the different forms of evidence that underlay them can be read as a metaphor for a larger tension between two kinds of authority: one derived from social status, as represented by Begbie, and the other from written rules and texts and the experts who could interpret and apply them, as represented by the lawyers. The former, which might be called traditional or paternal authority because it relied on an assessment of character, was fundamentally unsuited to the social and economic context in which trials occurred. For character assessment to work as a method of truth-finding and for social status to be an effective source of authority, there has to be a certain amount of common knowledge and experience among the jurors in the former case, and among British Columbians (and here I am speaking of white British Columbians) in the latter. There has to be, in short, a shared sensibility about what constitutes 'good' and 'bad' character and status. It is unclear, given the colony's age and diverse and mobile population, that this shared sensibility existed. In fact, as we have seen in chapter 4, British Columbians relied heavily on the formal institutional mechanisms of adjudication to resolve their disputes rather than settling them extralegally; therefore it appears that it did not. In the absence of unwritten 'rules' that shaped the way people saw the world, British Columbians turned to written ones. Written rules and, more generally, texts were an important reference-point in a young colony where a commonality of experience was as yet insufficiently developed.

Because it was a characteristic they shared with the rest of the common law world, the primacy colonial British Columbians accorded to textual authority and expertise must be placed within the larger context of the relationship between writing and power. Students of the past have long recognized the connections between the development of writing and the concentration of power in the hands of an élite, and have argued that the evolution of the law is a case in point.[59] Written law derived its power largely from its form: the law's mere 'writtenness' distanced it from the biases associated with the people dispensing it, and thus reinforced its power by objectifying it.[60] Obedience was given not to a person but to a seemingly neutral and universal set of laws that were above the petty ambitions and prejudices of those who administered it. Moreover, the law's written form meant that it could be disseminated widely: writing allowed for the extension of the boundaries of regulation and thus for an expansion of the law's empire. In an important way, then, written law underpinned state formation by transcending the limits of personal authority. Written law was also more reliable than the remembered customary rules of conduct articulated by local authorities: its mere tangibility meant that it could be referred to and deployed with certainty because its meaning was seemingly stable and unchanging, embedded in text rather than on the uncertain and shifting grounds of personal whim. Indeed, though written law created certainty, it also came to symbolize it. In fact, it is this collapsing of the real and the symbolic, of the signifier and the signified, that gives written law much of its power.[61]

The certainty afforded by written law and written authority had an added appeal for British Columbians because of the particular economic milieu in which they lived. The ethical system constructed by capitalism assigned great value to the standardization afforded by textuality and to the predictability, certainty, and efficiency that sprang from it. It is probably not coincidental that the some of the most effective arguments for the codification of the law came in the nineteenth century. Codification was the apex and epitome of the certainty and rationality that written law offered, and it is not insignificant that the most extreme pressures for it accompanied the rise of industrial capitalism and its demands for standard ways of dealing.[62]

While it is important to take note of the form of authority, we must not overlook the kinds of texts that were considered authoritative, for I think there is great significance to be drawn from the fact that authority was not only textual but rooted in textbooks. One of the notable aspects of the *Cranford* case was their lawyers' frequent reference to legal treatises: to *Taylor on Evidence*, *Smith's Actions at Law*, and *Chitty's Archbold*. In fact, John Foster McCreight, one of the targets of Begbie's insults, was noted for his knowledge and his routine citing of textbook authorities in making a case for his clients.[63] McCreight was so wedded to textbooks that dispensing the law was merely a matter of applying their principles – something that made him, as he put it, 'only a machine to carry out the law.'[64] McCreight's metaphor is telling. Far from being undesirable, a machine-like legal administration would have characterized a laissez-faire utopia: a machine that imposed order was far preferable to a person because technology was considered more neutral and more efficient and hence did not pose as great a danger to individual freedom.[65]

Reference to legal treatises was and is a common feature of American jurisprudence, but not of cases heard on the other side of the Atlantic.[66] Indeed, this is one of the main features that distinguishes English from American law. British judges were historically more likely to cite Glanvill (d. 1190), Bracton (d. 1268), Littleton (d. 1481), Coke (d. 1634), Hale (d. 1676), and Blackstone (d. 1780), the authors who comprise the surprisingly small English common law canon. In fact, a textbook literature like that used by McCreight and Ring in *Cranford* only came to be circulated among the legal profession beginning in the late eighteenth and early nineteenth centuries, and even then did not attain the status accorded them on the other side of the Atlantic. According to J.H. Baker, they were viewed as ancillary aids and guides to common and statute law rather than law itself.[67]

Treatises and textbooks like *Taylor*, with which British Columbians became tiresomely familiar during *Cranford*, appealed to lawyers because they were the only systematic and reflective treatments of law available. They set out the relevant cases and derived what amounted to first principles from them, and they discussed the more general problems of interpretation and application.[68] In that sense they were more useful and easier to use than the multiple volumes of law reports, which were considered by judges to be superior to treatises, and taken together represented the English common law.[69]

Because the treatises Ring and McCreight used were essentially systematic digests of the common law on particular subjects (evidence, crime, confessions, torts, and so on) they were useful in a colonial context, where frontier conditions – especially the combination of long circuits on horseback and the absence of well-stocked libraries – made reference to the shorter and more manageable works a practicality. Frontier pragmatism led to a shift in principle, however, for despite Begbie's reluctance to recognize their authority (even though he had written a treatise on the law of partnership), the interpretations in these texts came to have the status accorded to law.[70] They also came to be a recognized part of legal education and legal argument. Though Begbie may not have appreciated the rhetorical skills of the lawyers who appeared before him, many British Columbians did. Both the Cranfords' lawyers were treated like heroes and lauded for their legal reasoning; although they may not have understood the law's intricacies, British Columbians appreciated a 'perspicuous and able argument.'[71] Quite apart from their content, merely referring to textual authorities lent a significant amount of rhetorical power to legal utterances. A well-turned argument had a recognizable form, even if its content remained mysterious to most of the gallery of onlookers.[72]

The reliance on written law marked a move away from, or at least a modification of, the hierarchy of laws that characterized the common law tradition.[73] Written law became paramount in the latter half of the nineteenth century; and in British Columbia, at least, it was written law that was systematized and digested.[74]

Cranford pitted legal liability against social responsibility; specific, documented action against a general long-term assessment of 'character'; written against oral evidence; lawyers against judges; and, above all, textual against paternal authority. The case revealed that the ethical basis on which British Columbians measured the legitimacy of the law's authority was one constructed by laissez-faire liberalism and reinforced by the economic and social realities of life in a new colony of fortune-seekers. The authority of the law rested on an assessment of its efficacy in achieving certain ends consistent with individualistic capitalist enterprise. Moreover, British Columbians insisted that those ends be realized in a particular way: disputes arising from the pursuit of economic gain were best resolved not by a seemingly arbitrary assessment of the character of the principals, but by a systematic and careful reading of the evidence and the application of the appropriate rules. Thus, the authority of the law also rested on the means by which disputes were settled; means that were consistent with the demands of laissez-faire for rationality, predictability, and certainty in the marketplace.

However, the legal order represented by this kind of authority was not unitary or consistent. In making explicit the tensions that ran through *Cranford*, there is a danger of distortion; for, despite the dualistic manner in which I have presented them, none of these aspects was exclusive of the other. Indeed, Matthew Begbie embodied many of these seemingly contradictory characteristics: his penchant for paternal rule was visible in *Cranford*, but he was also trained as a chancery lawyer and was the author of a treatise on the law of partnership –

both characteristics that would, one might think, make him sympathetic to the rule of 'black letter,' textbook law.[75] Though the tensions that ran through the case were in part emblematic of the transition from what Weber called 'traditional' to 'legal' authority, that transition was not absolute; for, as we will see, these tensions continued to characterize the liberal 'black letter' system of law that found its fullest expression in the mid- to late-nineteenth century.

6

The Meaning of Law and the Limits of Authority on Grouse Creek

In the middle of October 1866, just as the mining season was coming to a close, a small item – a few lines, really – appeared in the *Cariboo Sentinel* informing its readers of a rumour that William George Cox, the district's assistant gold commissioner, was to be relieved of his duties.[1] The notice seemed innocuous enough, and in an edition that contained a blow-by-blow account of the London prizefight between Mace and Goss and news of the arrest of James Barry for the murder of the miner Charles Morgan Blessing, chances were that it would be missed entirely by all but the most discerning or bored readers. In any case, it was not the sort of piece designed to elicit comment. Or was it?

Just weeks later a petition, several pages in length because of the 490 signatures appended, was making its way to New Westminster and Governor Frederick Seymour's desk.

We the undersigned inhabitants of Cariboo having observed with regret a paragraph in the "Cariboo Sentinel" to the effect that W.G. Cox, Esq., the resident Gold Commissioner for this district would probably be removed to some other locality, beg respectfully to request that your Honor will fully consider the matter before making any such change ... from the very long acquaintance we have had with Mr. Cox, and the intimate Knowledge he has acquired of mining in Cariboo, we consider him much better qualified for the office than any other gentleman in this Colony.

Mr. Cox's conduct since he has resided here has been such as to inspire the public with the utmost confidence in his integrity and fitness for the position he now holds, while his judicial decisions have had the effect of materially checking litigation, and under the circumstances we consider that no benefit could accrue from the removal of a man of his experience, but on the contrary that the result might possibly prove injurious to the interests of the residents of this district and the Colony in general.[2]

Moved by neither the petitioners' sentiments nor their numbers, Seymour posted the magistrate to the Columbia district, where he remained for a year before returning to Victoria to sit on the Legislative Council.[3]

Cox was a favourite of the miners, if not of his wife Sophie Elizabeth Webb, who had herself petitioned Seymour for assistance in getting the cad she had married to support her. Nor was the governor particularly enamoured of him. Seymour told the secretary of state for the colonies that 'the manners which have made him popular with miners and Indians are not quite those which I should wish the American population ... to think characteristic of an English public officer,' and complained that 'Mr. Cox wishes to be entirely uncontrolled. He will avoid co-operating with another officer if he can, or attending to instructions which are not commands from the Governor.'[4]

Whatever shortcomings the magistrate may have had, for the people who signed the petition Cox's authority as an officer of the law stemmed from his 'intimate Knowledge,' something which, as we will see, was distinct from the 'special Knowledge' *Cranford* revealed as central to legal authority. Indeed, the two could be at odds, perhaps irreconcilably.

The existence of these divergent views challenges the consensual picture I have painted of British Columbians' desire for a system of uniform and predictable laws in the name of a laissez-faire order. More important, it raises the possibility that the making of law, order, and authority in the colony was problematic. Indeed, I will argue that the extension of the kind of law and authority British Columbians wanted created a certain amount of disorder. In British Columbia, law and order were notions that were negotiated and contested, sometimes with force and intimidation. The extension of law and the imposition of a capitalist order occasioned some conflict, but that conflict was not rooted in the social disorganization of the frontier and the individualistic values it supposedly inculcated. In British Columbia, at least, some conflict sprang from the very developments that historians contend contributed to its absence: the rapid extension of state organization and control over the frontier. The Grouse Creek War (1867) and the two court cases that preceded it show that the imposition of standard, predictable, and efficient ways of dealing by the colonial courts left little room for local parochialism in legal administration, and that it was a deafness to local voices that created problems. The conflict surrounding the Grouse Creek War was not an expression of Turnerian individualism, nor was it random. It was a manifestation of collective sentiment, its target was specific and rooted in different constructions of the law: one local and customary, as exemplified by the Cariboo miners, and the other colonial and formal, represented by Matthew Begbie. As will become apparent, the existence of multiple meanings of law placed limits on its authority.

The three cases that lay at the centre of the controversy over the colony's judicial administration were all disputes over the ownership of mining claims.[5] Each is rather unremarkable on its facts, which were limited to the recording and rerecording of claims and the placement of stakes.[6] Once the cases were appealed to the Supreme Court, however, the issues of fact in these cases became secondary to Begbie's actions. The judge's behaviour in the three cases and the public reaction to it neatly illustrate the problems associated with administering the law in British Columbia, and adumbrate the limits of formal, institutional, and standardized dispute settlement.

The first of these cases, launched in 1865, pitted the Borealis Company against the Watson Company. After the assistant gold commissioner's decision awarding the disputed claim to the Watson Company was sustained by Begbie, the Borealis Company took the case to the Chancery Court. There, sitting as Chancery Court judge, Begbie reversed his earlier decision, and awarded the disputed ground to the Borealis Company. By all accounts the mining community of the Cariboo was incredulous, and the colony's three main opposition newspapers wasted no time in adding their voices to the growing cries of indignation over Begbie's rulings. Most distressing to British Columbians was the use of the Chancery Court as a court of appeal, a process that was not only expensive and protracted but was also capricious, because decisions appeared to be unfettered by any reference to statute law. 'The late decision in the Borealis & Watson case strikes me as being the most flagrant and arbitrary stretches of power that has ever been committed by an individual occupying the position of Judge,' wrote 'Miner' in 1866:

[W]e have mining laws containing explicit provisions as to the manner in which claims should be taken up and held, but at the same time that any parties having money enough to stand the costs of a Chancery suit may omit to comply with these provisions and set the law at defiance; it tends to create a feeling of insecurity as the value of every title, no man is secure if he strikes a good claim, as after strictly complying with the law which he supposed to be protection and spending his last dollar in prospecting, he may find when he thinks he has reached the long hoped for goal of his ambition, that some more favoured individual had intended in taking up the same ground long previously, but had neglected ... staking it off or recording it, a grave error certainly, but one which can be expiated by filing a bill in Equity, making a score or two of affidavits, and paying his own costs in a Chancery suit, and this is what is called 'Equity.'[7]

Less measured was the commentary of the *British Colonist*, which contended that the 'endless round of litigation' in British Columbia's mining districts was 'ruining claimholders, shutting up the country's wealth and causing disasters in communities hundreds of miles away from the scene of the dispute.' 'The risks of mining are a mere bagatelle,' the newspaper concluded. 'It is the risks of Begbie's Chancery Court that terrify the miner.'[8]

Public indignation over Begbie's actions in *Borealis* scarcely subsided when his handling of another mining dispute drew the attention and the wrath of British Columbians. After issuing an injunction ordering the Davis Company to cease work on disputed ground, Begbie discovered that the Supreme Court seals necessary to validate the injunction were unavailable; they had been detained, with the rest of his luggage, on a wagon that had broken down en route to Bridge Creek. Undeterred, the judge sent a messenger to Richfield with the injunction and orders for William Cox, the stipendiary magistrate and assistant gold commissioner to attach seals to the injunction in his capacity as deputy registrar of the Supreme Court. Cox, whose decision Begbie had overturned in issuing the injunction, declined to act as ordered, claiming that he held no commission as deputy registrar and that in any case he found the whole business disagreeable and contrary to his conscience.[9] Although delayed by Cox's 'decisive stand,' as the newspapers labelled it, *Aurora v. Davis* came to trial before Begbie and a special jury on 18 June.[10] After deliberating until midnight, the jury awarded half the ground to each side, because 'the Aurora and Davis Companies have expended both time and money on said ground in dispute.'[11] According to the *Sentinel*, the jury's decision met with the general approval of the entire mining community. 'There is probably no instance on record where trial by jury has been so fully appreciated ... We are convinced that there is not a single miner on the creek that would not gladly submit his grievances to the decision of seven disinterested fellow citizens, and thus avoid the expensive and vexatious proceedings in Chancery.'[12]

Despite the satisfaction with the jury's verdict evinced by the *Sentinel*, Begbie insisted that a decision by his court 'would not end the litigation, and the expense of actions in one or two other branches of this Court would be heavy on both parties.' Instead of accepting the jury's verdict, the judge suggested 'that the whole matter be referred to me, not in my capacity as Judge, but as an arbitrator and friend, and that whatever decision I may arrive at will be final and absolute.'[13] The two sides agreed, and the following day, 19 June, Begbie rendered his decision to an 'anxious' courtroom. Perhaps hoping to forestall any criticism, the judge made it a point to downplay the irregularity of his actions and to praise the jury as an institution. 'I have always had every reason to be satisfied with the findings of juries during the whole period of my own official experience in this colony,' Begbie remarked; but if 'a jury finds a verdict contrary to the evidence, resulting from ignorance, fear, or any other cause it is [the judge's] privilege to set aside their verdict.' Observing that 'when men go to jump ground they do not see their enemies' stakes,' Begbie ruled against the Davis Company and awarded all of the disputed ground to the appellant.[14]

Reaction was immediate. Five or six hundred miners and residents of Cariboo gathered in front of the Richfield Court house on a rainy Saturday night six days after Begbie's decision to discuss the administration of the colony's mining laws.[15] Amid a great many speeches lasting well into the night, the participants passed three resolutions:

RESOLVED, 'That in the opinion of this meeting the administration of the Mining Laws by Mr. Justice Begbie in the Supreme Court is partial, dictatorial, and arbitrary, in setting aside the verdict of juries, and calculated to create a feeling of distrust in those who have to seek redress through a Court of Justice.'

RESOLVED, 'That the meeting pledges itself to support the Government in carrying out the Laws in their integrity, and beg for an impartial administration of justice. To this end we desire the establishment of a Court of Appeal, or the immediate removal of Judge Begbie, whose acts in setting aside the Law has destroyed confidence and is driving labor, capital and enterprise out of the Colony.'

RESOLVED, 'That a Committee of two persons be appointed to wait upon His Excellency the Administrator of the Government [Arthur Birch] with the foregoing resolutions, and earnestly impress upon him the immediate necessity of carrying out the wishes of the people.

With three cheers for 'Judge' Cox, the *British Colonist*, the *Cariboo Sentinel*, and the Queen (in that order), and three groans for Judge Begbie, the meeting adjourned.[16]

As a result of the mounting public pressure for reform, the colonial government amended the Gold Fields Act in April 1867, limiting appeals from the Mining Court to questions of law.[17] For all intents and purposes, this amendment made the decision of the assistant gold commissioner final, which worried the colonial government greatly. 'This change was made against the general feeling of the Legislative Council, at the insistence of the Members nominated for the Mining Districts and especially the urgent representation of the Mining Board of Cariboo,' Attorney-General Crease wrote. However, 'experience shews the power of appeal to be a safety valve for the preservation of the peace in the Mining Districts of the Colony.'[18] These were prophetic words. But for the next two months, at least, all was quiet in Cariboo.

Borealis v. Watson and *Aurora v. Davis* set the stage for the final and, according to one magistrate, most 'humiliating' part of this mining trilogy: the Grouse Creek War.[19] Having found Chancery and arbitration wanting and his government colleagues sensitive to public pressure, in 1867 Matthew Baillie Begbie found only one option remaining: to adhere to the newly amended Gold Fields Act and refuse to hear appeals from the Mining Courts. This course was not successful in restoring British Columbians' faith in the administration of the law.

In late April 1864, the Grouse Creek Bedrock Flume Company, a Victoria-based joint stock company, applied to Peter O'Reilly, Richfield's assistant gold commissioner, for the rights to a certain portion of land on Grouse Creek. O'Reilly granted the Company title for ten years, provided that it fulfilled the usual conditions of occupation, licensing, and recording of the claim as outlined in the Gold Fields Act. During 1864 and 1865 the 'Flumites,' as they came to be known, developed their claim, investing $20,000 to $30,000; but in late 1866 the company ran out of money, and the claim was left unoccupied from September to November. During this time the Canadian Company, a local association of free miners, entered the Flume Company's claim and finding it apparently abandoned, applied for rights to it. Warner Spalding, who had replaced Peter O'Reilly as interim assistant gold commissioner, duly recorded the ground in the Canadian Company's name. At the beginning of the next mining season, in March, the Flumites renegotiated their lease to the Grouse Creek claim with the Crown, managing to extricate themselves from all previous conditions regulating their occupation of the ground. Inexplicably, Warner Spalding, who had just six months earlier granted the same piece of land to the Canadian Company, presided over this renegotiation on behalf of the Crown. It was only a matter of weeks before the two companies clashed, and the dispute was taken to the district's Mining Court, to be heard by Spalding.[20] There Spalding ruled in favour of the plaintiffs and ordered the Canadians off the disputed ground.[21] The Canadians gave notice of appeal, but obeyed the commissioner's order.

Though the Canadians left quietly, they were back on Grouse Creek in a month. At the end of May, Anthony Melloday and three other Canadian Company members commenced work on the Grouse Creek Flume Company's claim. This time, however, the Flumites took their complaint to Magistrate's Court, laying criminal charges of trespass against the Canadians. The foreman, Melloday, received the heaviest sentence: one month's imprisonment. The others were sentenced to terms of one or two weeks.[22] Noting that the earlier injunction served on the Canadian Company by Spalding had been 'given to their foreman ... in an oral and extrajudicial manner, and not in the form of an order of Court,' the *Cariboo Sentinel* contended that the Canadians had been operating under a 'misconception' and that the punishment meted out was 'rather severe.'[23]

At the beginning of July Begbie informed the two companies that, in keeping with the newly amended Gold Fields Act, he would not hear the appeal. Though he underscored his opposition to the new act, the judge told the appellants that he was not willing 'to drive a coach-and-four through this clause, [just] because I conjecture that it may prove mischievous or work hardship.'[24] Undeterred, the Canadians regrouped and, now thirty or forty strong, returned to Grouse Creek. Three constables and one surveyor were dispatched to eject the Canadians, but were prevented from doing so when the company's men 'surrounded [them] ... without showing any hostile disposition, or making any threats of violence, but simply claiming that as they all acted as one man, if any one was liable to arrest they all were.'[25] The constables left.

Local sentiment seemed to be very much on the side of the Canadians, particularly in the light of Begbie's refusal to hear the company's appeal of Spalding's decision awarding the claim to the Flume Company – an ironic situation, given that it was local sentiment, and notably the pressure of the Canadian Company's principals, John MacLaren and Cornelius Booth, that had led to the 1867 amendment in the first place. Writing on behalf of the members of the Canadian Company, Booth insisted they were not 'acting in opposition to the law of the land.' Since they could not appeal, they were more than willing to force a new case.

Since the Supreme Court sat, they have made the most strenuous efforts to bring their case into court, not with a view of setting aside, but carrying out the decision of Commissioner Spalding. Their case would not be heard at any time, and any action they have taken since is simply with the object of coming into court in such a manner, that the rights they contend for may be contested on the real merits of the case, supported by evidence, which is, I opine, the spirit of British law.[26]

He said the same thing to a public meeting of five hundred people gathered to hear 'a full and truthful statement of the grievances and position of the Canadian Company.' The crowd passed a resolution recording their sympathy with the Canadians and their commitment to aid the company 'by all lawful means to obtain their rights.'[27]

The goodwill manifested toward the Canadians made itself apparent the next day, when the district's magistrate proceeded to Grouse Creek, backed this time by twenty-five or thirty of 'the most prominent businessmen, and respectable citizens of this town' who answered court summonses to act as special constables. Once there, the 'posse comitatus' exchanged 'the most friendly greetings' with the Canadians and the nearly four hundred eager onlookers who had 'splashed through mud and mire, knee-deep, in haste to reach the rendezvous.' All settled in for a long and probably anti-climactic afternoon of negotiation. In the end, with no hope of settlement, the magistrate read a writ of injunction to the Canadian Company and asked it to leave the claim. '[A] unanimous NO was returned, whereupon Mr. Ball, along with his constables, left Williams Creek, and the crowd dispersed.'[28] The magistrate immediately telegraphed the governor, requesting that a detachment of marines be sent to assist him.[29] The Royal Navy refused to intervene, and Seymour, grumbling at the 'very considerable inconvenience,' proceeded to Cariboo.[30]

It was this stalemate that greeted the governor when he arrived in Richfield a few weeks later, on 7 August. Seymour, along with the rest of the colony, had been treated to a series of alarmist reports of 'mob law' on Williams Creek from the *British Colonist* and the *British Columbian*, and no doubt expected the worst. 'In our most important gold field the arm of justice hangs powerlessly by her side, while a company of men, under the most hollow and hypocritical professions of a desire to respect the law are wantonly and openly trampling it underfoot,' insisted the *Columbian*: 'It is simply a question of British Law vs. Lynch Law ... [with reference to Governor Seymour's visit] To go to the scene of strife unarmed with a force to *compel* submission will simply to be to toy with outlawry while the coveted treasure is being grabbed up.'[31] Calling for the imposition of 'martial law,' the *Colonist* noted that 'by offering armed resistance to the mandate of a court' the Canadians were 'criminals' who 'went into court determined to obey the law if it was *with* them; [and] to break it if it was *against* them.'[32] The *Cariboo Sentinel* took issue with its competitors' treatment of the Grouse Creek 'War.' 'Victorians,' the *Sentinel* speculated, 'no doubt wrought up to the highest pitch of excitement by the graphic descriptions of the warlike attitude of the Canadians, would be surprised if they were here. Canadians and Flumites may be seen daily in the streets of Barkerville, habited in the usual miners' garb, saluting each other without the slightest appearance of hostility.'[33] The *Sentinel*'s attempts to emphasize the peacefulness of the Cariboo were not aided by the events that followed, however.

A few days after Governor Seymour's arrival, the Canadian Company strode into Richfield, not, noted one anonymous writer 'in obedience to any order or summons,' but at the suggestion of their leader, Cornelius Booth. Though Booth, the 'Talleyrand of the band,' assured his compatriots they would not be arrested, seven of their number were. Conveyed immediately to the courthouse, the seven received three-month sentences for resisting arrest (stemming from Magistrate Ball's earlier attempt to eject the Canadians from Grouse Creek); with the exception of one man, all refused to go to jail. Instead, they 'warned the constables not to touch any of them, and abused and blackguarded the Commissioner on the Bench!'[34] The seven told the court 'that if they had treated the Commissioner to more champagne &c. they would have won their case.'[35] Ball left the courtroom, and the governor requested a parley with Booth. After extracting a promise from Seymour to commute the sentences to forty-eight hours' imprisonment, Booth *'persuaded* his comrades to walk towards the gaol, promising them that they would not be confined three days!'[36] This concession to the form of law was continued when the redoubtable Canadians arrived at the Richfield jail. There, wrote 'Crimea,' 'they would not allow the doors of the jail to be locked upon them and had free access to all the Court house grounds during the term of their imprisonment. By all accounts, their experience of prison life must have been very agreeable, for their sympathisers supplied them bountifully with grog; what with games and songs, interspersed occasionally with a derisive hoot at the officials, they were the jolliest convicts ever seen.'[37]

When Seymour left Richfield he left behind conflicting impressions of his accomplishment. The Canadian Company believed they had secured a promise for a new trial, while the *Colonist* and the *Columbian* were convinced that Seymour had merely offered the services of Joseph Trutch, the colonial surveyor, as arbitrator. Added to this confusion was yet another round of vitriolic newspaper reports from Victoria condemning the governor's actions. Claiming that the actions of the Canadian 'mob' were legitimated by the governor's negotiations, the *Colonist* predicted an end to the 'security of life and property in the country.'[38] The Canadians rejected arbitration, insisting that they would 'accept nothing less than the law allows them': a new trial.[39] Less lofty were Cornelius Booth's sentiments about Trutch's arbitration.

It appears to me passing strange that a case which has already, through the blundering of incompetent, or possibly interested officials, assumed an unpleasant and dangerous magnitude, should be proposed to be submitted to the decision of an individual in whom the Canadian Co. and the miners of Cariboo in general have no more confidence as to his ability to understand and administer British Law or British Justice than they would have in the ability of a dancing dervish to understand and expound the ten commandments.[40]

Seymour then appointed Joseph Needham, Vancouver Island's Supreme Court Judge, as arbitrator. Needham arrived in Richfield in mid-September, prepared to try the Grouse Creek case (as well as other mining appeals) de novo.[41] Noting that every court had the power to suspend its rules if 'any technicality arises that might tend to defeat the ends of justice,' the judge began hearing evidence in the *Canadian Company v. the Grouse Creek Flume Company* on 17 September. After two weeks of testimony, Needham awarded the disputed ground to the Flumites. 'I cannot be blind to the fact that much public excitement has existed with regard to this case,' he told the court.

But I do hope and believe that all will acquiesce in the decision of this court; I can only say that it has been arrived at after anxious consideration, and a simple desire to administer justice according to the law. I hope, and firmly believe, that armed alone with the authority of the law, a child may execute this judgment, and that no one will here be found whose wish is not to uphold and obey the judicial tribunals of this country tribunals which have always been regarded by Englishmen as the fountain of justice, and the bulwark of freedom.[42]

With this plea for peace Needham ended one of the most protracted disputes in the colony's short history, one that was noted for the bitterness engendered as much between island and mainland as between the rival mining factions. It also ended Begbie's stormy tenure as judge of the Mining Appeal Court. After 1867 the 'tyrant Judge' heard few mining cases, perhaps because his judicial capriciousness deterred prospective suitors from initiating cases.[43]

British Columbia's historians have paid little attention to the three cases presented here, categorizing them as causes célèbres when they take note of them at all, and rooting the conflict in the clash of Matthew Begbie's imperious nature and the untutored opinions of miners.[44] Though the Grouse Creek War and the events preceding it were in no way typical of the colonial legal experience, their significance lies beyond what they reveal about individual personalities. *Borealis*, *Aurora*, and *Grouse Creek* were emblematic of the difficulties, to quote Joseph Needham, 'of administering justice according to the law.' The chief justice's distinction is an important one, for it implies that justice and law were different things. If they were, what accounted for the gulf between them? Why was it difficult to reconcile notions of fairness (justice) with a set of concrete rules, procedures, and institutions (law) which, by and large, had been created in response to the miners' demands and welcomed by them? The answer lies in understanding how the miners and Caribooites understood their world. The Grouse Creek War lets us recover the sensibility that conditioned the way Caribooites saw the law and its administration and assessed justice. The law was not simply a set of hard-and-fast rules and ways of dealing but part of a way of apprehending reality that was socially constructed, rooted in a particular cultural and geographic milieu.

The rhetoric surrounding *Borealis*, *Aurora*, and *Grouse Creek* reveals the discursive elements of that sensibility. While the language of laissez-faire and English common law were shared by disputing parties and thus provided the grounds for discussion and a meeting of the minds, a third element shaped the way Caribooites understood the law: common sense. Not only did the law have to promote economic exchange and development within the framework provided by English common law and institutions, it had to do so in a commonsensical manner. Despite its implied universality, common sense was imbricated in local social relations and a particular locale. Common sense incorporated the discourses of economics and the law, but transformed them in the crucible of local experience into a dialect: a distinctive variation of a common language which had the potential for unity as well as for misunderstanding and division. It was this that made 'administering justice according to the law' difficult.

Despite their differences, Flumites and Canadians used the same language of property and liberty to frame criticisms and justify their actions. The New Westminster *Columbian* and the Victoria *Colonist* contrasted 'British Law' with the Canadians' 'Mob rule,' and predicted an end to 'that security of life and property in the country which has ever been our proud boast. Capital, finding its tenure insecure, will fly to countries where people are made to respect the laws, and where possession of property rests upon a more stable and secure foundation.'[45]

At the same time the Canadian Company, that 'mob' of 'footpads' and 'filibusters,' used the same language and law of property to predict the same ends if its demands were not met. 'There are three things the most despotic governments claim,' Cornelius Booth told a crowd of five hundred gathered at Fulton's saloon,

namely the right to take property, liberty and life. The first of these have already been taken from the Canadian Co., and there is but one step to the last. I repeat that these men do not wish to be looked upon as outlaws; they consider they have been unjustly shut out from having a hearing; and would be perfectly satisfied in obtaining one, even if a decision was given against them.[46]

The crowd agreed, as they had done in the wake of *Borealis v. Watson* and *Aurora v. Davis*, when they informed the colonial government that its laws and Begbie's administration of them were driving 'labor, capital and enterprise out of the Colony.'[47]

Just as they used the same language and agreed that the law served to promote economic development and secure property, British Columbians on both sides of the Grouse Creek War recognized the same process of dispute resolution. The ends sought by those who opposed the government's administration were always to be achieved within the existing structures of formal dispute settlement provided by English common law. In *Borealis v. Watson*, Caribooites criticized the use of the Court of Chancery to resolve mining appeals because its ponderous proceedings were singularly unsuited to mining activity. But what did the miners propose as a solution? The establishment of a Court of Appeal.

Similarly, in *Aurora v. Davis*, arbitration was rejected in favour of trial by jury. And in the Grouse Creek War, the Canadian Company did not ask for public sanction of extralegal action (in fact, it did not consider that it was acting in an illegal manner), but for *'nothing less than the law allows us'*: a full hearing of its case.[48] Indeed, both Cornelius Booth and John MacLaren visited Begbie in early July 1867 to ask for his intervention – surely an indication they had not lost faith in the existing legal options.[49] Even after seven company members were arrested in August, the Canadians still demanded that the 'tyrant judge' or his island counterpart replace Joseph Trutch as arbitrator.[50] It is clear that those who took issue with British Columbia's legal administration did not reject the very structures of dispute resolution; rather, they looked to the official framework of British institutions for relief.

When the Canadians and Flumites framed their demands in the language of the law, they were not just legitimating their actions. By invoking the law, both parties were attempting to deploy the considerable semiotic power of 'British Justice' to their advantage.[51] The law stood for reason and reasonableness against arbitrariness and tyranny; and in cloaking their demands in the language of the law, those on both sides of the Grouse Creek dispute were saying that they were possessed of the same qualities and that their actions were connected to a long and glorious tradition that had existed since 'time out of mind.'[52] Moreover, it is not insignificant that in criticizing Begbie's conduct in adjudicating these mining disputes, the colony's newspapers called his court a Star Chamber, compared him with with James II and Judge Jeffreys, both infamous for their despotism and arbitrary rule, and, as a counterpoint, quoted Baron Garrow, a noted English defence counsel and a man associated with the elaboration of prisoners' rights, on the proper behaviour of English judges.[53] These historical comparisons were rhetorical devices designed to place Begbie within a particular frame of reference and thus help readers to assess his actions and to determine their own. If Matthew Begbie was like James II and Judge Jeffreys, then the proper response would be to resist and overthrow his rule just as the English had resisted and overthrown Stuart tyranny. The particular language and imagery employed to describe the administration of the law in British Columbia was not neutral and did not simply convey meaning. Rather, it created meaning by shaping the way people saw the world and acted in it.

If British Columbians agreed about the ends of the law and the broad institutional framework in which they were to be achieved, they took issue with the means and manner in which those ends were realized. Justice was all about *how* mutually agreed-upon results were reached. As *Cranford* suggested, British Columbians considered that a technical and scientific body of rules applied evenly and predictably ensured justice. 'Special Knowledge,' to return to Philip

Nind's term, was a valued commodity in the colony's gold fields as well. Reflecting on *Borealis* and *Aurora*, the *Colonist* located the cause of the trouble in Begbie's lack of legal experience. 'Unlike Judge Needham,' the newspaper reported, Begbie 'had no legal experience to recommend him, and it is by no means a matter of surprise that his decisions instead of partaking of that judicial clearness and point which are the universal characteristics of the decisions of English judges, should be generally rambling, disconnected and irrelevant.'[54] Both the *Sentinel* and the Canadians dismissed the colonial surveyor as a suitable adjudicator for the same reasons and called for the intervention of the Supreme Court: 'He lacks the legal acumen which is necessary to unravel those knotted points of law that are inseparably involved in the settlement of the dispute in question.'[55]

The legal acumen and skill that Caribooites wanted was at odds with their demands that the law also be self-evident, and with the kind of authority sketched out in *Cranford*. Miners wanted 'simple, practical regulations,' not 'a network of complex laws, which will not only crack their brains, but those of the regiment of lawyers they will need to unravel the tangled skein.'[56] Indeed, James Burdick considered that the need for lawyers was an evil the government should correct. 'When our laws are such that it takes the highest talent in the colony to interpret them, it is certainly time they should be altered,' he told a meeting of miners gathered to protest the administration of justice. '[T]he more simplified our laws are and the easier they are to understand the better they will be for governing us.'[57] His sentiments were echoed and elaborated on by 'A Miner' from Cameronton, who argued that '[w]here lawyers are there is always too much of that tedious circumlocution and formalism which clogs the wheels of practical business.'[58]

In the wake of *Borealis* and *Aurora*, Caribooites argued that common sense was the chief hallmark of just laws and just administration. The *Cariboo Sentinel* published a telling editorial that emphasized this point by contrasting the conduct of Peter O'Reilly (the previous magistrate) conduct with that of his predecessors and his successor, William Cox. Until O'Reilly's arrival, the mining court 'was virtually, if not nominally, a Court of Conscience.'

Then the mining laws consisted of only a few proclamations issued from time to time by the Governor, and the Commissioner supplemented these with his own judgment. Since then extensive mining laws have been passed and partially consolidated. It was not until the administration of Mr. O'Reilly that this Court, by his false pretensions to legal ability, declared itself to be a Court of Equity or Law, or both combined ... The policy of Mr. Cox, on the other hand, was quite different: he made no pretensions to legal ability, yet his policy was at once most agreeable to the miners; he converted this

Court back once again almost wholly into a Court of Conscience, and presided in it with no little success.

In the absence of explicit rules governing conduct in the colony's gold fields, able magistrates exercised their own judgment in settling disputes. Even after the appropriate legislation came into effect, the *Sentinel* argued that a magistrate's conscience rather than a mechanical and, in Peter O'Reilly's case, 'pretentious' application of the law should guide his actions. This was what made William Cox, O'Reilly's successor, popular and effective. Cox's success, the *Sentinel* concluded, was due to the fact he was guided by 'common sense rather than a smattering of law.'[59]

The newspaper's placing of common sense and conscience on the one hand and law and equity on the other is confusing, and significant. 'Courts of conscience' and 'equity' were other names given to chancery courts, so it is unclear why the newspaper would oppose equity and conscience. Moreover, though *Borealis* revealed the miners' distaste for courts of chancery, the *Sentinel* editorial argued for a return to the days when conscience, which was the same as chancery, guided legal proceedings.

The seemingly contradictory character of this editorial was not due to a lack of legal understanding on the part of the author, but to a different understanding of law. To recover it, we need to first sort out the details of the chancery courts' evolution.[60] The Court of Chancery grew out of the Chancery, the department of state whose responsibility it was to keep the great seal: the symbol of the sovereign's authority used to authenticate documents, including common law writs. It was this latter duty that connected the Chancery and the chancellor to the administration of justice. In hearing petitions for writs, the chancellor made his decision by applying the 'standards of what seem[ed] naturally just or right, as contrasted with the application ... of a rule of law, which might not provide for such circumstances or provide for what seems unreasonable.'[61] Decisions in chancery were thus guided by the chancellor's 'conscience,' and the justice they represented became known as 'equity.' By the early nineteenth century, however, the principles of equity became a body of settled law rather than the more personal and subjective assessment of fairness.[62] Ironically, then, though equitable jurisdiction evolved as a corrective to the inflexibility of the law, the Court of Chancery acquired a reputation as a morass of legal complexity and delay into which unwitting suitors could fall and never gain a settlement.[63]

When Caribooites equated Peter O'Reilly's tenure as magistrate and assistant gold commissioner with a 'Court of Equity or Law' and contrasted it unfavourably with Cox's 'common sense,' they revealed that they considered the two kinds of knowledge to be antithetical. The complexities of equity and law were far from the self-evident truths common sense implied; in fact, they were 'pretensions' that caused unnecessary delays and thwarted justice. Cox's common sense cut through all this. He circumvented legal technicalities by letting 'conscience' be his guide. To Caribooites, Cox's 'court of conscience' was the surest route to justice. But courts of conscience were merely another name for courts of equity or chancery. Why was Cox's 'conscience' – his ability to apply 'standards of what seems naturally just or right' – superior to Begbie's? Why, in short, was the magistrate's common sense superior to the Supreme Court judge's?

Caribooites recognized the magistrate's decisions and actions as commonsensical because he was part of their community. 'Common sense' implies a commonality of experience that cuts across political, social, and economic divisions – indeed, this is part of its strength. The concept is a historical one, but it is also a geographical one. Concepts of common sense are tied to particular times and locales; they are, as the anthropologist Clifford Geertz contends, part of 'local knowledge.'[64] Common sense was bounded by place and rooted in specific constellations of social relations that included local government officials. Because the colony's magistrates were part of the communities they administered, they quickly became enmeshed in the politics of familiarity, a situation that both aided and limited their ability to execute the law. As noted, William Cox's knowledge of miners and mining won him the admiration and support of 490 of his neighbours, who petitioned against his removal. 'From the very long acquaintance we have had with Mr. Cox, and the intimate knowledge he has acquired of mining in Cariboo, we consider him much better qualified for the office than any other gentleman in this Colony,' they wrote. 'Mr. Cox's conduct ... has been such as to inspire the public with the utmost confidence in his integrity, ... while his judicial decisions have had the effect of checking litigation.'[65] These judicial decisions were often unconventional: one time the magistrate settled a Mining Court claim by making the disputing parties race from the steps of the Richfield Courthouse to the disputed ground – winner take all. On another occasion Cox swore in Chinese witnesses by decapitating a chicken instead of administering the usual tidier and less spectacular oath, and when he was at Rock Creek he assisted the miners in actually 'drumming out' an Englishman who had been stealing from their sluice-boxes.[66] Actions like these made him, as James Douglas put it, '[p]eculiarly well adapted for frontier service, where tact and a resolute will are indispensible qualities in managing the rough characters met with there.'[67]

Cox's 'intimate Knowledge' was 'special,' but not in the same way as that revealed in *Cranford*, for it consisted of a proper understanding of community morals and a willingness to let local sensibilities guide his application of the law. Those sensibilities were powerful. In the Grouse Creek War, community sentiment about what was right and wrong made it impossible to keep the Canadian Company under lock and key. Henry Maynard Ball, whose misfortune it was to preside over the Grouse Creek dispute, failed because 'he had but little experience in the mining districts.'[68] Familiarity was also behind the ineffectiveness of enforcement. For the most part, policing was done by special constables, sworn in from the local population as the need arose. In Grouse Creek the special constables, who as men of capital and business presumably stood to lose from the unrest, were of no use in ejecting their neighbours; nor could the district's jailer incarcerate the Canadians. 'The public feeling was rather in favour of the Canadians,' complained Frederick Seymour. 'At all events no one would come forward to assist the Government in an emergency.'[69]

Despite the constraints of familiarity on the execution of the law, Caribooites would have it no other way. Because outsiders did not have the same depth of knowledge of the community they governed and were not known by its members, their interventions were considered nonsensical, even when undertaken by a figure as magisterial as a Supreme Court judge. In this context, juries became an important bridge between law as a set of overarching rules and a set of socially constructed norms. '[T]his community,' reported the Richfield Grand Jury, 'owing to its isolated position, the peculiarity of its interests, and especially its national origin, has a decided preference for local trial by jury, and is extremely jealous of all verdicts by its peers.'[70] The *Cariboo Sentinel* was even more direct, asserting that 'a man is wrong when almost every person in the community thinks and says he is wrong.'[71] When Begbie overturned the jury verdict in *Aurora v. Davis*, he not only breached what Caribooites perceived to be established practice, he also burned the only bridge between his notion of law and that of the community in which the dispute occurred. The judge's cavalier treatment of the jury in this and other cases led many Caribooites to conclude that Begbie did not consider them qualified to pass judgment on their peers and that their notions of law and justice were illegitimate and somehow wanting.

When one brave (or foolish) supporter of Begbie suggested that the judge's critics were 'men who neither by education or association are competent to judge of the fitness of things in connection with the Law,' Caribooites answered in no uncertain terms.[72] 'Miner' argued that his criticisms of Begbie's administration were in keeping with the virtuous spirit of 'the revolution of 1688 which secured to our forefathers the liberty of which as Englishmen we boast,' while 'Caustic' noted that a 'strict vigilance on the public' was necessary to avoid 'the subversion of ... justice,' and the editor of the *Cariboo Sentinel* reminded both Begbie and his supporters not to be too quick in dismissing the miners' sentiments. 'The ragged garments worn in Cariboo are quite a different emblem from those of Newgate [prison],' he observed, making the point that despite their rough and untutored appearance, this was a population well qualified by education and experience to pass judgment on the law.[73]

Caribooites also considered the Grouse Creek Flume Company an outsider. Not only were the Flumites based in Victoria and headed by one of that city's most important merchants, they also represented 'big capital' in a region where small, independent entrepreneurs had been the norm.[74] The Canadians styled themselves a 'company,' but their Victoria opponents were the real thing. The Grouse Creek Flume Company was a joint stock venture, capitalized to $50,000. The Flumites were harbingers of a different kind of resource entrepreneur in British Columbia. By the late 1860s most of the easily accessible surface gold in the Cariboo was gone. Continued success on the upper country creeks depended on a hydraulic process, which required a substantial capital investment. Such an investment was beyond the means of most individual miners. Part of the support for the Canadians and the wrath directed at Begbie must have stemmed from an antipathy towards the large corporate enterprise that would eventually dominate resource exploitation and push out the smaller upper country operations.

The sensibility that shaped the way Caribooites perceived and measured the colony's legal administration constructed the law as a local variation of two common discourses. Like other British Columbians, they used the rhetoric of laissez-faire and British justice to frame their criticisms of colonial law and to buttress their demands that it be predictably and efficiently administered in the interests of economic development. However, they incorporated all of this in a shorthand term that simultaneously reduced these criticisms and demands to a single phrase – common sense – and introduced a new and important element. The law had to be administered 'commonsensically.' By labelling their demands 'common sense,' Caribooites demonstrated how firmly laissez-faire ideas and British forms of law had entrenched themselves in the sensibility that conditioned the way they saw the world. The strength and influence of common sense lies in its taken-for-granted nature.[75] Calling something 'common sense' meant that Caribooites did not have to question it: it was a universal truth that needed no explanation. At the same time, however, common sense was rooted in their experiences with a particular kind of law. To an important degree, how Caribooites saw the law, measured its legitimacy, and framed their criticisms was conditioned by their localized experiences with it and with the people charged with its administration. Common sense was not common at all, but 'a distinctive way of imagining the real' that was consistent with their demands that law be predictable, but only within a specific locale that framed a particular set of social relations.[76] Despite the fact they shared a common language of economics and law, then, Caribooites spoke and thought about the law in a different dialect, one constructed by their particular experiences with it and fostered by their geographic isolation. And it was because of this that administering justice according to the law was difficult.

The conflict surrounding the colony's legal administration that culminated in the Grouse Creek War demonstrated the limitations of the law's authority. Despite what *Cranford* revealed, the law was not simply a set of rules and procedures that could be applied mechanically to achieve certain ends, but a social construct that could not easily be detached from the local relations it mediated and was a part of. Law was pre-eminently a social activity that could not be deaf to local voices.[77] Certainly William Cox's experience confirmed this, as did that of John Boles Gaggin, another gold fields magistrate and a contemporary of Cox's. At the end of June 1862 one hundred miners returning from the Cariboo boarded the steamer *Henrietta* in Douglas for the trip to New Westminster. They refused to pay for their passage, claiming that their misadventures in the upper country gold fields had left them 'starving and broken' as well as broke. Despite the obvious illegality of the miners' actions, the Douglas magistrate John Boles Gaggin advised the master of the *Henrietta* to 'take the men on, and on arrival at New Westminster, apply to the proper authorities for redress.'[78] The colonial government chastised the magistrate for his 'want of nerve and judgment' in allowing 'the occurrence of so lawless a proceeding.'[79] 'It appears,' noted Colonial Secretary W.A.G. Young, 'that you consider yourself vested with discretionary power to temporize with your duties, and that you are unaware that, while rigidly dispensing the laws for the protection of life and property, a Magistrate may act with perfect temper and discretion.'[80]

While the 'rigid dispensing' of law was what the government expected of its law officers, the magistrates' success in doing otherwise showed that despite the miners' prior demands for the rule of a predictable, efficient and universally applied set of laws, the social context in which those laws were executed was still very important in resolving conflict and in shaping attitudes towards the law. Their very authority depended on it.

It was a failure to appreciate the power of local voices and community sentiment that got Matthew Begbie in trouble on the upcountry creeks. When he tried to follow the letter of the law in *Borealis* (when he based his decision in the unintelligible rules of equity rather than on statute law), in *Aurora* (when he overturned a jury verdict), and in *Grouse Creek* (when he refused to hear an appeal), he was severely criticized and his authority challenged. In each case he disregarded community sentiment, believing that his own authority or that of the black letter of the law would prevail. The conflict that was precipitated by his actions attests to the dangers of decontextualizing the law, of detaching it from the social context that gave it meaning and effect.

Begbie's failure to recognize that the law was socially constructed was not entirely due to any shortcomings he may have had as an individual, however, nor were his difficulties peculiar to the nineteenth century. The events on Grouse Creek illustrate two related and general problems in using the law as a means of ordering social relations. The first is the problem that comes from simply formalizing relationships in law. British Columbians, and in particular those engaged in mining, were anxious to formalize their relations with the colonial government and with each other, and greeted the construction of the courts with a good deal of approval and enthusiasm. By embedding their relationships in law they hoped to guard against arbitrary government and to secure a degree of certainty in their dealings, especially their economic dealings, with each other. The extension and elaboration of law was thus synonymous with the enlargement of freedom. However, by formalizing relationships in this way, some of their flexibility was sacrificed. 'Legalizing' relationships meant that they had to conform to the law, even when ignoring the rules or 'winking' at them, as in the fur-trade period, would make things more comfortable and less contentious. As the events on Grouse Creek showed, the expansion of formal rights could be accompanied by the contraction of informal freedoms. With the construction of courts and the passage of the Gold Fields Acts, it was no longer possible to adjudicate mining disputes as William Cox did – by running a footrace or decapitating a chicken – because it was no longer *legal*.[81]

The second problem actually consists of two related problems, both of which have to do with conceiving of the law as a set of rules, and of social order as flowing from their recognition and enforcement. Order, according to this formulation, is achieved by informing people of the rules that should guide their conduct and applying those rules and the sanctions they impose in cases of dispute. Though this black letter or positivist interpretation of the law is a common one, it relies on an unspoken and usually unchallenged assumption: that of the universality of human behaviour. The whole idea that a society can be governed by a set of laws of general applicability is workable only if we accept the fact that all people are more or less the same – that they are rational – and that their similarity overrides the infinite differences that spring from historical contingencies. In other words, it assumes that individuals can exist outside of society and that these 'pre-social individuals' are essentially similar.[82] As the controversy surrounding Begbie's disposal of the three mining cases illustrates, such assumptions are, if not unwarranted, then certainly suspect.

In addition, there is the associated problem of accommodating universal rules to particular circumstances. Because it is impossible to draft laws for every aspect of human interaction, administering the law involves using generally applicable rules to regulate specific behaviour. This is a difficult task in itself because of the inevitable disputes about which law to apply and which interpretation of it is closer to the intent of the framers. The administration of the law is further complicated by the need to strike a balance between two notions of equity: one that sees it as resting on uniformity – on receiving equal treatment before the law and achieving similar results in similar cases – and another that roots it in a recognition of and a sensitivity to differences.

These general problems were magnified in British Columbia because of the social and cultural context in which the law operated. As was discussed in chapter 4, the economic, demographic, and geographic realities of the colony led British Columbians to rely heavily on the courts to settle their disputes. The law and its formal institutional processes of conflict resolution were an integral part of social relations. Going to court had implications beyond the usually narrow legal point at issue. Law was deeply implicated in the way British Columbians constituted themselves as a society, and because of this they took an active interest in its administration. Given how much was at stake and the heightened awareness of things legal, any controversy in the administration of the law threatened to dissolve one of the important bonds that tied the colony together.

While the social context in which the law was dispensed magnified its significance and heightened the difficulties of administering it, the broader cultural context provided by laissez-faire also created problems. The prevailing sensibility of the age reinforced the notion that human action was rational and reducible to rules and made standardization and equal treatment before the law rather than a sensitivity to local sentiment the ideal and the engine of administration. Not only were informal solutions to problems like the one Ned McGowan attempted greeted with alarm and suppressed, but even the less imaginative variations on the execution of formal law tried by William Cox and John Gaggin were also censured because they undermined the idea that equity was best achieved by equal treatment before the law. Recognizing and accommodating local parochialisms in executing the law not only encouraged the kind of potentially disorderly localism that was responsible for the violence of California's gold fields, but ran counter to the thrust of much of its legislation. Localism was anathema to commercial capitalist enterprise, and much of the colony's legislation was aimed at dissolving it by constructing a set of rules and institutions that would be administered colony-wide to create an arena for maximal economic exchange.[83] By imposing a standard system of regulation over the colony, the government and most British Columbians (for they were in favour of it as well) completely overlooked the fact that a sensitivity to local sensibilities was essential for the peaceful and satisfactory resolution of disputes. Without it, conflict was almost inevitable. The administration of law that British Columbians wanted was thus deeply implicated in both the control of conflict and its creation and perpetuation because of the elevation of the notion of equity as standardization.

7

Bute Inlet Stories: Crime, Law, and Colonial Identity

'Things are not as they were,' observed the *British Columbian* in the fall of 1864. 'A few years, or, indeed, a few months, ago, who would have dreamed of the murder of a few whites by the Indians calling forth such a demonstration in the vindication of the law as this Colony as recently witnessed?'

One of Her Majesty's gunboats might possibly have been despatched somewhere, and we might have heard of a naval demonstration against an Indian village without the slightest reference to its inhabitants being concerned in the murder, with a flourish of trumpets over old and superannuated Indians and squaws, with a large percentage of papooses, who were killed or wounded in the grand and successful operation! How all of this has changed now. Not only were the most thorough measures taken for the apprehension of the murderers, but the most careful discrimination between the guilty and the innocent [were] observed ... We look therefore, upon this as a redeeming feature of the Bute massacre that it has afforded the Government an excellent opportunity of most forcibly illustrating to the Indian tribes the great superiority of British Law.[1]

Written after the capture of the Chilcotin Indians thought to be responsible for killing eighteen European workmen in the vicinity of Bute Inlet, this self-congratulatory response and the connections it made between law and progress lie at the heart of this chapter. Having seen how liberal discourse structured British Columbians' expectations of law and authority and how the making of a liberal order in the colony was uneven and contested, I turn now to a consideration of how a liberal notion of law – the idea of equality and equal treatment before the law – was central to European British Columbians. The 'superiority of British Law' referred to by the *British Columbian* was, I will argue, both an emblem and a measure of the superiority of those who promulgated, enforced, and were bound by it. In short, law was central to the identity of British Columbians.

That identity and the process of its formation are explored through a close examination of what became known as the 'Bute Inlet Massacre.' Like all stories, the ones that were told about Bute Inlet were cultural artifacts that embodied the central suppositions underlying the teller's and the audience's understanding of the world in which they lived and ultimately who they considered themselves to be. For in discussing what happened at Bute Inlet, why it happened, and what they should do about it, European British Columbians revealed as much about who they thought they were as they did of the event and its perpetrators. There was, as sociologist Robert Miles put it, 'a dialectic between Self and Other in which the attributed characteristics of Other refract contrasting characteristics of Self, and vice versa.'[2] It is towards an understanding of the dynamics of that dialectic between Self and Other – the process of identity formation, of being and becoming – as well as an explication of those attributed characteristics that this chapter is directed.

My subject, then, is the subjectivity of a number of Europeans who lived in British Columbia in the mid-nineteenth century as revealed through the accounts of a mass killing. Crime and crime stories, it is argued, can be especially revealing of the subjectivity of the law-abiding population. Lincoln Faller considers criminals a 'social resource' from which a community takes and sustains its identity, while Martin Wiener argues that because crime was 'the central metaphor of disorder' in the nineteenth century, responses to it not only tell us about identity but also adumbrate the larger contours of social order.[3]

The content and constitution of 'Otherness' or 'alterity,' as Peter Mason calls it, is a topic that has been addressed in the Canadian context to a certain extent, though not necessarily by those names and not always with links, either explicit or implicit, to a larger theoretical literature, whose foundation was laid in large part by Edward Said in *Orientalism*.[4] While this work has described the content of the images and beliefs about the Other and in some cases offered explanations for changes over time, it has, curiously, been less effective in tracing and understanding the continuities in the discourse of Otherness. Part of what follows, then, is an attempt to identify those continuities in the stories that were told about Bute Inlet and to suggest how the historical context in which they were articulated – including but not limited to the impact of liberal discourse – gave them a certain meaning. In other words, I want to suggest why images that had in some cases persisted for centuries might have had a certain resonance in a particular time and place. As well, I am interested the way identity structured action. In pursuing that line of inquiry, I found I also had something to say about the 'Self/Other duality' that has shaped so much of our understanding of identity and its formation both past and present. Like so many dichotomies that have withered under the post-modernist gaze, this one proved to be no exception. The distinctions that European British Columbians drew between Self and Other proved to be less clear-cut than they would have liked; not only did Bute Inlet show that it was more appropriate to speak of the colonial Self as being constituted through and against a variety of Others, it also revealed that this Self was not singular or unitary, but potentially fragmented. Rather than referring to Self and Other, then, we might think of the relationship as being between Selves and Others. Moreover, these different identities, these different Selves, could also be contradictory, existing in a tension that reflected a similar and fundamental one in the rule of law between justice based on a recognition of differences and justice based on an acknowledgment of similarities.

But these are esoteric matters. To reach that high ground and to appreciate the view from the top, we need to start our journey at the beginning of the road from Bute Inlet.

'That respectable old fool Waddington.'[5]

John A. Macdonald's description of Alfred Penderell Waddington could easily have served as an epitaph for him and perhaps many other British Columbians, for he represented both the circumstances and the spirit of many of the European immigrants to the gold colony. Of his respectability there was little doubt: Waddington was born in 1801, the sixth son of an English merchant and banking family. After being educated at the Ecole Spéciale du Commerce in Paris and the University of Göttingen, he embarked on a series of business ventures, none of which was especially successful. With nothing to keep him in either England or Europe, his spirit of enterprise (and a little bit of money from his favourite brother Frederick) led him to California in 1850. San Francisco's gold rush economy proved so buoyant that even the previously luckless Waddington failed to sink, and indeed the wholesale grocery firm in which he was a partner prospered. When news of the Fraser River discoveries broke in 1858, Waddington joined the rush northward to open a branch of his business in Victoria, arriving as 'one of the oldest as well as the best educated' of the fortune-seekers.[6]

Like some other English emigrants, Waddington found being back in British territory to his liking, and he became an active participant in the political and economic life of Vancouver Island and British Columbia.[7] Though he was elected to the island's House of Assembly in 1860, he resigned a year later to begin the project that earned him the second part of Macdonald's label – 'old fool' – and led him to Bute Inlet.

Just as 'Fraser River fever' threatened to turn into 'Fraser River humbug,' British Columbia's fortunes, not to mention those of merchants like Alfred Waddington, were given another, more sustained boost with the discovery of gold in the Cariboo.[8] Unlike the lower country diggings, however, those in the Cariboo were more difficult to get to, and involved a lengthy and arduous journey.[9] In the absence of proper wagon roads, prospective miners had to make their way north from New Westminster along old fur-trade brigade trails. Lying in bed one day, incapacitated by gout, Waddington's mind turned, as it often seemed to, to contemplating his own fortunes.[10] He sent out for a map of the colony and a ruler and, using both, became convinced that it would be quicker and easier to reach the Cariboo via an overland route from one of the inlets along British Columbia's coast: specifically, Bute Inlet.[11] Prospective miners would travel by canoe or steamer 200 miles north from Victoria (their initial port of arrival) along the east coast of Vancouver Island to the head of Bute Inlet. From there, the gold fields lay a mere 160 miles inland,[12] instead of the more than 300 rugged miles from New Westminster.[13]

Anxious to realize his idea and the fortune that would accrue to the person who could secure a government charter to build a road from Bute Inlet, Waddington lobbied the colonial government, made plans to establish the Bute Inlet Wagon Road Company, and began to garner public support. If the newspaper reports are to be believed, Victorians proved no less susceptible to 'Bute Inlet fever' than they were to Fraser River malady.[14] Without doing anything except the most cursory survey, Waddington, armed with a map that was little more than 'a waggish distortion of rivers and mountains,' claimed that his Bute Inlet route was quite literally the road to prosperity, and estimated that it would bring £100,000 of foreign capital into the colony.[15] His enthusiasm won him a charter in 1862 and the confidence and hard currency of investors who had probably seen a speculation or two in the gold rush town.[16]

Construction began almost immediately, and by the end of 1862 almost thirty-three miles of the Bute Inlet road had been completed, a rate of progress that fuelled Waddington's enthusiasm and that of his investors and worried the residents of New Westminster, who stood to lose if Waddington's folly (as they saw it) proved successful. Like the gold rushes themselves, however, the overblown optimism surrounding the Bute Inlet road soon gave way to a harsher reality. Eighteen-sixty-three saw Waddington's road crew repairing flood damage to sections they had completed the previous year and encountering the formidable Homathko canyon, whose terrain proved less amenable to 'improvement.'[17] Waddington's problems were compounded by the government's decision to begin construction on two other roads to Cariboo, one from the head of Harrison Lake and the other from Yale, both of which looked as if they would be completed before his. Though his investors were dismayed and sold their shares to him at a loss, Waddington was undeterred, and sold his Victoria property to finance the next year's construction.[18]

If the newspaper reports and government investigations into the events at Bute Inlet are to be believed, money was an ongoing concern of Waddington and his Wagon Road Company. He attempted to limit his expenditures by hiring Chilcotin labourers to pack supplies and equipment to the construction site and by paying them in trade goods rather than cash.[19] This practice proved to be a point of contention with the Chilcotin, who wanted wages and felt that the road party should have provided them with a certain amount of provisions.[20] Though they continued to work for Waddington's party, their disaffection with their treatment probably contributed to a larger and growing sense of uncertainty concerning their relationship with the European population. Until the arrival of Waddington's party at Bute Inlet, the Chilcotin had had little contact with the white population.[21] Within a short time, however, a number of changes manifested themselves, which taken together, may have been enough to transform their disaffection into direct and violent action: not only did the arrival of the whites at Bute Inlet in 1862 coincide with a smallpox epidemic that decimated much of the coastal native population, but the construction of a road through the heart of their territory threatened to bring further encroachment.[22] Moreover, the retirement of James Douglas as the colony's governor in 1864 signalled the possibility of a further disturbing change: no longer could natives count on the old fur trader's paternalism to protect them.[23]

If any of this uncertainty and latent animosity existed, it was not apparent to the twelve men who, in the spring of 1864, laboured at the main road camp forty miles from the head of Bute Inlet, or to the five members of the advance party who were busy two miles farther on.[24] Indeed, so comfortable and secure were the road-makers in their relationship with the Chilcotin that 'among 17 men there was but one gun.'[25] Nothing transpired on the evening of 29 April to make Waddington's men think differently; so confident and so tired were they that '[e]ven the precaution ordinarily in the bush of having one to keep watch was dispensed with.'[26]

At daybreak eighteen Chilcotin descended on the main camp, shooting at the sleeping men through their tents. As the tent poles collapsed, those whom the bullets missed were trapped and killed soon afterwards. A similar scene was being played out at the advance camp. Of the seventeen road men, three managed to escape, and, though wounded, managed to make their way to the head of the inlet and then to Victoria to break the news of the 'Bute Inlet massacre.'[27]

As news of the killings greeted the readers of the *British Colonist* and the *Daily Chronicle* on 11 and 12 May, another party of Waddington's men, led by Alexander Macdonald, was making its way to Bute Inlet from the interior to work on the road from the opposite direction. Their progress was slow, and loaded down as they were with some twenty-eight horses carrying full packs, they proved an easy target for the Chilcotin. Were it not for a well-timed warning from the native wife of one of the party, it is likely that all of Macdonald's men would have been killed. As it was, three of the eight died, along with William Manning, the only settler in the district.[28]

Though public reaction to the deaths of eighteen whites was swift and sure, concrete action was a little less so. The colony's distances and geography had already kept news of the killings from reaching Victoria and New Westminster, and they further hampered the government's response. Not only was there the problem of organizing and launching a campaign to the far reaches of the colony, the costs associated with doing so threatened to bankrupt the colonial coffers.[29] Though Governor Frederick Seymour accompanied Magistrate Chartres Brew and twenty-eight special constables to Bute Inlet in mid-May to investigate the scene of the initial killings, it was not until the end of June that the 'Bute Inlet Expedition,' as it became known, was fully underway. Two parties, one starting from New Westminster and under Brew, and the other starting in the Cariboo and under the command of William George Cox, made their way to the Homathko in pursuit of the massacre's perpetrators.[30] The difficult and dangerous task of capturing the Chilcotin was made even more problematic because of the absence of anything but the vaguest descriptions of the killers.[31]

As it happened, the Chilcotin solved this problem for the expedition: eight surrendered themselves to Cox's party on 15 August. Klatsassin, said to be their leader, Telloot, Chee-loot, Tapitt, Pierre, Chessus, Chedekki, and Tnanaki were taken to Quesnelmouth, where they were tried at the September assizes. Five of them were hanged.[32] 'Justice,' Frederick Seymour reported, had been done 'legally as well as faithfully.'[33]

In discussing the Bute Inlet killings, the perpetrators, and their own response, European British Columbians erected a series of dichotomies between reason and passion, civilization and savagery, and culture and nature, all of which served to construct the Indian 'criminals' – and Indians in general – as 'Others' against whom they articulated their own identity. The first newspaper report of the 'massacre' published by the *Colonist* illustrates the cant of criminality.

The intelligence received yesterday morning ... of the massacre by Indians of fourteen men, who were working on the Bute Inlet route, is the most startling thing of the kind that has yet taken place in either colony. There is something almost fiendish in the manner in which this treacherous massacre was perpetrated. Sixteen able-bodied Indians, who had been accustomed to pack for the workmen, accompanied by a number of youths, steal upon ... the sleeping white men, and with gun, and knife, and axe, fire and cut and hack at their surprised and helpless victims. Three of the men escaped with their lives, though not entirely unscathed, two having been severely wounded. The other portion of the wagon-road party, four in number, were making preparations to commence the day's work when they were ruthlessly shot down and savagely mutilated. The cause of this Indian outbreak was, so far as at present can be ascertained, entirely one of plunder. The men who have returned say that the Indians have been treated in the kindest manner, and that there was not the slightest indication of ill-feeling amongst them prior to the murdersome attack ...

No time should ... be lost in endeavouring to bring the guilty parties to justice ... It is evident that an example – a terrible example – must be set to our Indian tribes. That they are sometimes forced into shedding the blood of the white men through the white man's own injustices, we do not deny; but there is also the more deplorable fact staring us in the face, that covetousness or fancied slights are quite sufficient to impel the natives to deeds of murder. Fear is the only power that can keep such savages in entire subjection. Let them feel, as they will if our government acts with vigor, that every uncalled-for attack upon the white man will be punished promptly and severely, and we shall hear of but few Indian assassinations. Let justice follow inevitably the footsteps of Indian crime – justice uninfluenced on the one hand by a morbid sentimentality, and on the other by a reckless and brutal indifference to savage life, and we shall not likely have again to recount so heartrending a story ...[34]

Little is notable about this newspaper report apart from the colourful prose. That is just the point: stories cannot be considered 'apart from' their prose. The language used was not just a matter of style. It was rhetorical in the broadest sense – it was meant to persuade – and like all discourses this one was also constitutive of Other and, I will argue, of Self.

The Chilcotin were 'treacherous,' 'ruthless' and 'murdersome' 'assassins,' 'impelled' (like animals) to 'fiendish' acts by 'covetousness' and 'fancied slights.' They were never 'men.' In fact, the article does not even refer to them as the 'Chilcotin;' just as 'savages' or 'Indians.' The slippage between these terms is important because it implies that one might generalize from the particular; from specific individuals who had allegedly committed particular acts to all members of a perceived racial group that encompassed not just the Chilcotin nation but all Native peoples. Their lack of humanity, their otherness, stands in contrast to the way their alleged victims were described. The men killed were 'men' and 'victims' who had treated the Indians with 'kindness.' They were also 'white' 'workmen' and at the time they met their ends they were 'helpless' – everything their killers were not. Though the author recognized that whites may have perpetrated injustices on the Indian population that resulted in bloodshed, the Indians' behaviour was somehow a 'more deplorable *fact*.'[35]

By using this kind of language and melodramatic construction the writer asks us to see all Indians – not just those who allegedly killed the Bute Inlet men – as savage animals, in contrast to the rational and civilized white population, and to act against them accordingly.[36] At the core of Indian criminality was a lack of restraint: that the Chilcotin and indeed all natives were slaves to their passions is evident and elaborated on in subsequent commentary on the crime itself and the motives behind it.

Descriptions of the massacre emphasized the extreme violence of the attack, underscoring the perpetrators' irrationality and savagery. Attracting particular comment was the mutilation of workers' bodies. When Brew's party arrived at the end of May to make their preliminary investigation, Victoria's *Daily Chronicle* reported that they found evidence of an 'indiscriminate attack,' and observed that '[t]he wretches, not content with depriving the poor fellows of life, hacked and mutilated the bodies in the most shocking manner ... the heads of some had been hacked off – others ripped open, and the fiends, in more than one instance, had quartered the bodies of their victims.'[37] Similarly, the *British Columbian* alleged that the foreman, Brewster, had been 'horribly mutilated ... [his] left breast having been cut open and his heart torn out, and according to the statement of the friendly natives, barbarously eaten by the savage murderers'[38] in what Reverend Robert Christopher Lundin Brown described as an 'infernal repast.'[39]

If the massacre itself was savage and senseless, so too was the destruction of property that accompanied it. Stories of the Indians' wasteful destruction of property seemed as reprehensible and incomprehensible to European sensibilities as the killings themselves.[40] According to the *British Columbian*, '[t]he savages had wantonly destroyed everything they could not carry off, even to the few books in the possession of the unfortunate party ... [T]he ground was completely strewn with tea, coffee, apples, sugar and other stores, recklessly scattered about and trampled underfoot.'[41] The same sense of puzzled disgust underlay Seymour's description of the death of William Manning. The Indians had not been satisfied with killing the settler and 'plundering' his stores, but had 'burnt buildings, hay stacks, all that could be destroyed, and even went to the trouble of breaking up the ploughs and agricultural implements.'[42] To reinforce the descriptions of this wilful wastefulness, the Bute Inlet stories often contrasted the Indians' actions with the more rational, calculating work ethic of the men who were killed. For instance, Waddington's road party and Macdonald's packers were 'brutally butchered' while they were 'sleeping the sleep of hard-working men,'[43] and William Manning's death was particularly unjust and undeserved because he, unlike the native inhabitants of the area, had 'improved' the land he occupied.[44]

If European British Columbians emphasized the Indians' lack of restraint, their otherness and particularly their lack of reason was further accentuated in explanations of the massacre. In attributing motives to the Indians, European British Columbians identified three aspects of the native character that contributed to their criminality, all of which were consistent with the view of Indians as slaves to their emotions, 'impelled,' to use the *Colonist*'s word, by their passions: the massacres were motivated by the Indians' fickle and treacherous nature, their superstition, and their covetousness. With a few exceptions, most of the accounts of the massacre emphasized that the Chilcotin had not been abused and, indeed, that they had been well treated – 'rewarded liberally'[45] – and had received 'presents of tobacco and other articles, besides food.'[46] Moreover, according to the survivors and Waddington himself, there had been nothing in the Indians' behaviour towards the work party to lead them to suspect that relations had soured, much less that they had deteriorated to the point of violent conflict. In fact, as Seymour informed the Colonial Office, relations had been so good that Waddington's men had 'with each returning spring, [become] more and more confident of a friendly welcome.'[47] It was this background of apparent good relations that made the killings all the more treacherous and disconcerting to European sensibilities. White British Columbians had to be ever-vigilant, for as Frederick Whymper warned, '[t]hough civilization may have varnished his [the Indian's] exterior, beneath the crust the savage nature lurks, ever ready to break forth, like those volcanic mountains whose pure snow only hides the molten lava within.'[48]

As further evidence of the Indians' inconstant and changeable nature, Lundin Brown wove the conduct of native women into his Bute Inlet story, playing on the stereotype of female fickleness and using the rhetorical and conceptual distinction between princess and squaw which, from Daniel Francis's description, was a variation of the madonna–whore dichotomy.[49] He introduced his readers to 'Klymtedza,' the wife of one of the white packers in Macdonald's party, who out of loyalty and thankfulness to her husband for delivering her from the hardships of native life, and despite considerable danger to herself, warned the packtrain of the imminent attack – much as the legendary Pocahontas did for Captain John Smith in the Virginia colony generations earlier.[50] Though she escaped, Brown speculated that Klymtedza, in true tragic tradition, killed herself out of grief.[51] Not all women, and certainly not all native women, were so honourable. In contrast to Klymtedza's decision to stand by her man, Brown points to 'Nancy,' William Manning's native partner, whose anglicized name was emblematic of the degradation thought to befall many Indians after prolonged contact.[52] Complicit in orchestrating the attack on Manning's farm and his murder, Nancy is presented as the quintessential designing woman: not satisfied with or grateful for the generous treatment she received from Manning, and recognizing that her immediate interests were best served by allying with Klatsassin's party, she betrayed her husband.[53]

If their fickleness pointed to a lack of reason, European British Columbians argued that the Indians' superstitious nature reinforced it and made relations even more difficult. Actions on the part of whites that were considered innocent at best or thoughtless at worst, but certainly not malicious, were, in the eyes of the superstitious Indian, transformed into 'fancied slights' that precipitated a response out of proportion to the offence. In formulating his explanation for the attack on Waddington's men, Lundin Brown recalled an incident in the fall of 1863 involving the theft of some flour from the supply store at the head of Bute Inlet. The Chilcotin were suspected, and when they refused to admit to the theft, the white in charge of the stores took down their names and threatened them with sickness. His action had the intended effect of alarming the Indians, but rather than make them compliant, it precipitated the killings; for, as Brown argued, Indians were superstitious creatures, given to believing in the maleficent powers of what they did not understand. 'They have ... a very special horror of having their names written down,' he asserted. 'They look upon paper as a very awful thing.'

Writing is, they imagine, a dread mystery. By it the mighty whites seem to carry on intercourse with unseen powers. When they're writing, there's no telling what they're doing. They may be bidding a pestilence come over the land, or ordering the rain to stay in the west, or giving directions for the salmon to remain in the ocean. Especially is the Indian appalled when he sees his own *name* put on paper. To him the name is not distinct from the person who owns it. If his name is written down, he is written down. If his name is passed over to the demons which people his hierarchy, he is sure to be bewitched and given as a prey into the teeth of his invisible foes. So when those Chilcoaten [sic] saw their names taken down and heard themselves threatened with disease, they were only too ready to believe it.[54]

And, as Lundin Brown concluded, to kill.

'Covetousness' and 'cupidity' also identified as part of Indian criminality. The impoverished Chilcotin, it was argued, were attracted to the goods carried by the road party and were unable to resist the temptation to possess them. Though Magistrate Chartres Brew observed that 'there was in camp a store of all the things most coveted by Indians: clothes, powder, balls, sugar, flour, [and] meat,'[55] Frederick Seymour thought 'the property of small value.' The 'rough clothes and poor provisions' should have 'offered but a small temptation to the commission of so terrible an outrage.'[56] And they would have if the Indians had been calculating or possessed of reason. That they were attracted to the road party's poor supplies and provisions merely underscored the irrationality of the Indians, as did the reckless way the Indians treated their 'plunder,' strewing the goods that had so tempted them over a wide area or destroying them outright.

Many of the elements in what might be called the discourse of savagery that ran through the accounts of Bute Inlet had an ancient genealogy. The sheer animality of those deemed savage – a term that encompassed the Chilcotins' alleged inconstancy, covetousness, cupidity, profligacy, and passion – was a characteristic that had been used to distinguish the barbarian from the civilized since the time of the Greeks. Christianity designated those traits as sins, and they continued to define savagery and provide a rationale for colonialism long before the Europeans ever realized their imperial aspirations on the Pacific northwest coast.

Particularly notable were the repeated references to the Chilcotins' alleged cannibalism and Lundin Brown's observation of their reaction to the written word. Cannibalism (or, as it was known until the fifteenth century, anthropophagy) was and is an especially resonant and enduring characteristic of savagery, one that has been used since at least the fifth century BC to distinguish 'us' from 'them.'[57] Long before the Chilcotin came to be placed beyond the pale of civilization because of their alleged cannibalism they were preceded by the Scots and Picts, the Jews, the Irish, much of the population of Africa and the Indian subcontinent, as the indigenous peoples of Central and South America, all of whom were apparently 'man-eaters.'[58]

The power of the label 'cannibal' to consign entire populations to a kind of moral exile and thus to serve as a rationale for self-proclaimed civilized communities to suspend their own morality in dealing with those deemed beyond the pale lay in a complex constellation of beliefs, some Christian and others not. As Anthony Pagden notes, cannibalism involved killing another human being, and so for Christians violated the sixth commandment. More than that, cannibalism denied victims their right to be buried in a place of their choosing. This is significant because for Christians the day of judgment involves the resurrection of the body, and burial and its attendant rituals are of crucial importance. Beyond these Christian dicta against cannibalism, however, other and perhaps more basic beliefs contributed to the revulsion elicited by cannibalism.[59] Humans were not to eat other humans, nor any creatures their own kind, for legitimate sustenance came only from those creatures who occupied the lower orders. Thus, Pagden argues, '[c]annibalism demonstrated that they [Indians] could not distinguish between the rigid and self-defining categories into which the natural world was divided.'[60]

Like cannibalism, the fear and fascination which writing was said to hold for Indians had a long history. Though it is now the stuff of grade-B westerns, the

Indians' reaction to and capacity to understand the written word was a recapitulation of the centuries-old Greek definition of barbarism, which at its core was grounded in language.[61] Barbarians originally were those who did not speak Greek. Over time, however, different levels of savagery were distinguished by different modes of communication, and transcription, or the 'writtenness' of language, became the central feature of civility and civilization. A written language allowed the society that possessed it to reach beyond its grasp, and to attain a certain level of intellectual and moral sophistication that came from the exchange of ideas made possible by and through the written word. Thus the absence of a written language, and a dread fear of it, was an indictment of Chilcotin culture both present and future.

Though ancient, the historical context in which the discourse of savagery was articulated gave it a particular and added resonance. The ideology of liberalism, ascendant in the nineteenth century, provided new standards by which to measure the Chilcotins' alleged savagery; standards that, though new, worked to reinforce the old images and beliefs that were embedded in the savage discourse that ran through the stories about Bute Inlet. The killers' actions affronted liberal sensibilities because they were antithetical to rational human nature, namely, the pursuit of individual self-interest. This pursuit rested on an ability to look ahead and to calculate the course of action that would bring the greatest rewards. Because this often involved a denial of immediate pleasures and short-term gains, restraint was also a key characteristic of rationality. The Chilcotins' actions on Bute Inlet – not just the act of killing but the manner in which the killings were carried out – was evidence of their irrationality and only confirmed their otherness.

The Chilcotins even looked different: their physical otherness was emblematic of the moral distance that separated savagery from civilization. 'A set of men and women more squalid and repulsive I have rarely beheld,' said Lundin Brown of the Chilcotin. 'Dark faces, big mouths, black eyes, narrow foreheads, long tangled hair black as night; their thin and sinewy frames with little on them save dirt and a piece of blanket or a deerskin.'[62] Frederick Whymper, an artist who had left the road party before the killings, described the Bute Inlet natives as 'creature[s], half child-half animal' – a combination of innocence and danger – who had been degraded by their contact with European civilization, presumably because they lacked the self-discipline to resist its temptations.[63]

The Natives' physical appearance was something that Europeans had commented upon since the first contact, and had served to distinguish them as Other. By the nineteenth century, at least, the connection between the physical otherness of cultural groups and the hierarchy of development and civility it suggested were buttressed by the emergence of anthropology and Darwinian ideas regarding the origin of the species. Both gave scientific credence to existing beliefs about the 'great chain of being,' transforming a social and religious concept into a scientific one and thus providing another rationale for colonialism.

At the same time, anthropological language and concepts, what Martin Wiener calls the 'ethnological imagination,' were being deployed by Victorian social critics to understand and colonize the 'dark continents' nearer to home: the slums and particularly the criminal rookeries of London.[64] Despite the racial differences, much of the language and many of the concepts of otherness used by European British Columbians to describe and understand the Chilcotin killers were identical to those used by English social critics of the Victorian period.[65] The 'intertextuality' of colonial and imperial discourses of crime suggests that an overarching language of otherness existed and could at least to some degree transcend the differences imposed by race and class and, more generally, by the different social contexts in which they operated. Placed side by side, descriptions of English criminals differed little from British Columbian descriptions of Natives. Mayhew's 'nomadic street people' bore a striking similarity to Lundin Brown's and Whymper's Chilcotin. 'There is,' Mayhew said of the street people, 'a greater development of the animal than of the intellectual or moral nature of man ... they are more or less distinguished for their high cheek bones and protruding jaws ... for their lax ideas of property – for their general improvidence – their repugnance to continuous labour – their disregard of female honour – their love of cruelty – their pugnacity – and their utter want of religion.'[66]

Though English reformers like Mayhew could use the word 'tribal' to describe London's criminal class, European British Columbians had the real thing: a group that appeared indolent, dissipated, and prone to drunkenness or other kinds of excess; a group that was shackled by custom and that perpetuated cruelties in its name; and, perhaps most significantly, a group that was distinguished by separate language, rituals, and physiognomy. In British Columbia the criminal classes were quite literally 'savages': signifier and signified were collapsed – criminological imagination met ethnographic reality, and the intersection of the two discourses on Bute Inlet heightened and reinforced the sense of Indians as Other.

Finally, and perhaps more tangibly, the Bute Inlet Massacre occurred at a time when racial attitudes, both in the colony and the empire generally, were hardening. As Robin Fisher argues, the 1858 Fraser River gold rush marked the beginnings of a shift in attitude on the part of Europeans towards the Native population of the colony. No longer dependent on the cooperation of Native peoples as the fur traders had been, miners and settlers like the unfortunate William Manning came to view them as obstacles to their own economic gain, which was part of the 'progress of the colony.'[67] Given this conflation, the Bute Inlet Massacre took on a larger allegorical significance. The eighteen labourers who lost their lives at the hands of the Chilcotin were building a road through a 'trackless' wilderness: and not just any road, but one to the gold fields – literally, a road to prosperity – to be travelled by men possessed of the same vigorous spirit of enterprise that animated its promoter and developer, Alfred Waddington. In a sense, the Bute Inlet road stood for the European penetration of North America, and the massacre of the roadmen for the violent clash of civilization and savagery, reason and passion, progress and backwardness, and culture and nature.[68]

As well, there were probably few in this British colony who could fail to draw parallels, justified or not, between the massacre at Bute Inlet and the Indian Mutiny just seven years before, an event that precipitated a hardening of attitudes towards indigenous peoples throughout the empire and influenced colonial policy for at least a decade afterwards.[69] In both cases a small group of English men and women found themselves in an alien land surrounded and outnumbered by an equally alien and potentially hostile population who did not, curiously enough, seem interested in availing themselves of the opportunity for moral uplift.

In the wake of Bute Inlet, European British Columbians constructed the Chilcotin as an Other against whom they defined themselves. With that otherness established, the European population gained at least one point of triangulation by which to locate themselves in a new world context. However, the polestar that guided them was not as fixed as they would have liked, and their identity was not as certain as it seemed. In emphasizing the Indians' otherness they became self-conscious and reflective about their own behaviour, and discovered, to their dismay, that despite their best efforts to distance themselves from the Indians the gulf between them was not as wide as they wished. Not only was the man in the animal visible, but, even more disturbing, the animal in man was also ever-present, always threatening to obliterate the distinction between them. For all their adamant assertions and tightly drawn distinctions between reason and passion and savagery and civilization, one of the most palpable sentiments evoked by the Bute Inlet stories was uncertainty. For historians this uncertainty raises questions about the utility of the Self/Other duality in understanding identity and how it is formed, as well as how action was structured as a result.

Though the Bute Inlet stories laid great emphasis on the swift, sudden, and unexpected nature of the attack, contrasting the Indians' passionate nature against the more methodical, calculating, and reasonable response of the white expedition that pursued them, there was a sense in at least some of the accounts that the Chilcotin had carefully planned the massacre; and thus that they were not creatures 'impelled' into action, but a people possessed of a level of calculation and rationality. In his initial investigation of the killings, Chartres Brew learned from other natives that 'the murderers had been concocting their villainous scheme for some time, 'and had waited over a week for the arrival of Mr. Waddington, hoping by his death to break up the road undertaking. This, from what could be gathered from the Coast Indians, seems to have been their main object, rather than plunder.'[70] Victoria's *Daily Chronicle* muddied the distinction between reason and passion in the same way when it described the attack as 'indiscriminate'[71] and insisted that 'plunder was no doubt the main object they [the Chilcotin] had in view,' but then noted that 'the plan of slaughter ... seems to have been formed with military precision, each Indian selecting his man.'[72]

The larger dichotomy that animated the Bute Inlet stories – that of savagery versus civilization – was also not as fixed and rigid as European British Columbians would have liked, for they recognized that the man in the animal – the potential for civility – was never completely lost, and the line between the civilized and the savage was not absolute. On meeting Klatsassin, the Chilcotin chief said to be the instigator of the killings, Lundin Brown pointedly observed that his 'face, narrow at the forehead, wide at the centre; and high cheek bones indicated the characteristics of the North American savage.'[73] Nevertheless, despite the chief's savagery, the missionary could not help but comment on 'his strong frame, piercing dark *blue* eyes, aquiline nose; and very powerful underjaw, [which] proclaimed the man of intelligence.'[74] 'One could hardly look at Klatsassan,' Lundin Brown concluded, 'without feeling that there was about the man something awful, and something winning – in fact, something *great*.'[75]

If the man in the animal was never completely absent, neither could the animal in the man be completely domesticated – a disconcerting and disturbing prospect for European British Columbians. In discussing Bute Inlet, some European British Columbians used the occasion to reflect upon their treatment of Indians more generally, and to engage in a degree of social and self-criticism. Though most of the speakers at the emergency meeting called in Victoria at the end of May roundly condemned the 'devils in red skins' for their actions, C.B. Young offered a more balanced and more disquieting analysis of the massacre. Though Young 'approved of punishment, severe punishment, being dealt to the Indian,' he reminded his compatriots that 'justice should be even-handed. 'Their potato patches had been appropriated by white men and fenced in. Was that justice? – Compensation had been promised to the Cowichan Indians. Had they ever received anything? – At Nanaimo an Indian reserve was made; [but] a cricket ground was wanted [and] it was formed of the reservation. Was that justice?'[76] The answer, clearly, had to be in the negative, and because of this some measure of doubt was cast on white British Columbians' self-proclaimed civility.

If the Self/Other duality fails to capture the ambiguity of colonial identity in British Columbia – the lack of distance and distinctiveness between Self and Other – it also fails to explain the response to the Bute Inlet killings. Having constructed the Chilcotin as savages and their actions as senseless, European British Columbians should have been justified and comfortable in embarking on a policy of destruction: savagery had to be met with savagery.[77] As the *Colonist* put it, there was no place for 'maudlin sentimentality' in dealing with the Chilcotin. When the fate of Waddington's road party became known, demands for immediate action were not long in coming. The *British Columbian* called for the citizens of the island and mainland colonies to unite 'in dealing out speedy justice, at whatever cost, to these sixteen devils done up in red skins,'[78] while the *Weekly British Colonist* expressed its 'hope that the ridiculous farce of bringing them down to New Westminster and trying them by jury will not be attempted in case of their apprehension. A summary examination, and a hempen noose for each from the nearest tree, in the presence of all the tribe, would have a hundredfold more effect on all the Indians of all the coast that the solemn and (to them) unintelligible mummery of a trial by jury.'[79]

News of the attack on Macdonald's packtrain reached Victoria a week or so later and led the *Colonist* to harden its already rigid position: There are hundreds of bold hardy spirits who would at once volunteer to march against the savage murderers,' it reported. 'Let them not stay their hands till every member of the rascally murderous tribe is suspended to the trees of their own forests – a salutary warning to the whole coast for years to come.'[80]

And yet there were doubts about whether this was the proper and civilized course of action. Sentiments like these greatly worried the colonial government and some European British Columbians who managed to avoid getting caught up in the swirl of emotion that seized the island and mainland capitals in the wake of the killings. 'We are too apt,' the *British Columbian* argued, 'in the first flush of excited indignation, to cry out for the utter and indiscriminate extermination of the savages, dealing out to them Lynch Law instead of British justice ... [W]e hope to see the same impartial justice brought into requisition in dealing with the aborigines that we would desire to have meted out to ourselves.'[81] They feared the outbreak of an all-out war between themselves and the more numerous Indians if such sentiments were acted upon, but they were also disturbed by them at a much deeper level. Calls for the enforcement of the law had been conflated with calls for revenge: 'speedy justice' was transformed, almost without comment, into 'summary vengeance.'

Thus it seemed that the uncertainty that surrounded their sense of identity also characterized European British Columbians' reaction. In deciding on the proper course of action, European British Columbians were once again influenced by a sense of themselves articulated through the construction of an Other: but not the same Other. It was the American rather than the Indian who served as the foil against which they structured their identity and their actions.

The experience of Americans, particularly those who lived in the west, stood as a cautionary tale for British Columbians. In the absence of the familiar old world distinctions provided by family, class, ethnicity, religion, and occupation there was little, it seemed, to anchor social identity on the frontier. Mindful of this, European British Columbians were fearful that the alien environment in which they found themselves would transform them into the savages whom they loathed and from whom they drew their identity.[82] They needed to look no further than the United States for an example of the dangers of 'going Native.' California and the 'californization,' to use the contemporary phrase, of the white population implied both an accretion of American prejudices and a razing of all the social distinctions that gave meaning to civility.[83] The restraints imposed by those distinctions held society together, and without them even Englishmen could slip into savagery. Certainly there were many who considered HBC men – even those who occupied positions in the colonial government – degraded by their long contact with the Native peoples of North America.[84] The Anglican Bishop George Hills noted the beginnings of a similar process of degradation at Yale in 1861. Like Indians, the miners there 'had become reckless.' They were away from home-ties and restraints of society, so they gave themselves up to do whatever they were tempted to do; so gambling, drinking [and] sensual pleasures soon wasted their substance away.'[85] Thus, the conduct of European British Columbians towards the colony's native population was a measure of their civility.

Certainly Frederick Seymour was concerned with conduct. In commenting on the Bute Inlet volunteers under William Cox, the majority of whom were Americans, the governor observed that they were 'not much disposed to relish the restraint which I put upon them in carrying out operations against the Indians,' and though they seemed both appreciative and respectful of the British authority he represented – they gave him three hearty cheers upon his arrival in camp – there was a marked difference between their comportment and that of the English volunteers. 'The men raised in the Gold Districts, mostly Americans, passed the greater part of the night in dancing or playing cards to an accompaniment of war whoops and the beating of tin pots,' he reported. On the other hand, 'The New Westminster expedition, almost exclusively English, and comprising many discharged Sappers [Royal Engineers], spent the evening in the usual quiet soldier-like manner. No spiritous liquor was in either camp, yet the amusements were kept up in one long after total silence prevailed in the other.'[86]

Seymour's sentiments regarding the Americans were given popular expression in the colony's mainland newspaper, which, after some thought, argued for a more measured, calculated, and above all discriminating response in keeping not with just white but with British civility. '[T]here are those amongst us who are disposed to ignore altogether the rights of Indians and their claims upon us, who hold the American doctrine of "manifest destiny" in its most fatal form,' observed the more reflective *British Columbian.*' [U]nder the shadow of this unchristian doctrine, the cry for "extermination" is raised at every pretext. Very different, however, are the views and sentiments held ... by the British Government.'[87]

Meting out justice according to the law was what separated British Columbians from Americans, and a failure to do so would surely mark the beginnings of 'californization,' and a descent into savagery. The rule of law stood as a bulwark of individual freedom, but it was also emblematic of European British Columbians' identity, of their membership in the community of civilized British nations. Adhering to the rule of law meant, as the *British Columbian* indicated, treating everyone who came before the courts similarly. Indeed, as Matthew Begbie recalled, since the colony's creation Indians had been told

> that all men are on a level before the Courts of criminal justice ... That they are amenable to the same Tribunals, for the same offences, triable by the same methods and ceremonies and liable to the same punishments as white men, exactly.
>
> They have been told most emphatically that their own old methods of investigation and punishments and licenced retributions and compensations &c. are annulled; and that we are 'showing them a more excellent way.' They have been told that the same line of conduct is therefore expected of them as from the Whites and they have acquiesced and seen the logic of the proposition.[88]

While adhering to the rule of law may have confirmed their British civility against the savagery of American manifest destiny, doing so required British Columbians to deny the very differences they had so carefully drawn between themselves and the Indian savages. As we have seen, in understanding the killings as a 'massacre' British Columbians constructed the Chilcotin as a savage Other and themselves as civilized. But in order to conform to the standards of *British* civility, an identity formed in opposition to the American Other, British Columbians had to behave as if those differences did not exist.

Colonial identity, it seems, was not unitary but fragmented. Because different Selves were constructed by different Others, the relationship between identity and action was complex, historically contingent, and potentially contradictory. This antinomy was apparent in Frederick Seymour's efforts to organize and instruct the two expeditionary forces sent to pursue the Chilcotin. On the one hand, Seymour had authorized the creation of a military force in recognition of the state of 'war' that gripped the colony; on the other hand, he was well aware of the greater significance of the force's conduct, and he continued to insist that they treat the Indians according to the strict standards of the rule of law.[89] In his initial dispatch to the Colonial Office, the governor made it clear that he and his officers sought 'the capture of the murderers and the *vindication* of the law,'[90] and 'to show what had not previously been seen in this part of the world[:] a Government calm and just under circumstances calculated to create exasperation.'[91] It is clear that Seymour considered the expedition's purpose as both practical and symbolic: to capture the killers in a manner that would establish the merits and superiority of British justice over that of the Americans and the Indians. The manner was to be strictly legal: Seymour insisted that the volunteers under Brew and Cox be 'sworn constables – for we wish to proceed *legally*.'[92]

This concern for comportment placed some curious constraints on the military expedition. For instance, Cox was instructed 'to proceed to the headquarters of Alexis, great chief of the Chilcoaten [sic] tribe, shew his warrant and explain that the Queen's law must have its course,' Seymour reported. 'He will support his application for redress by showing my proclamation offering a reward of £50 for the apprehension of each of the murderers.'[93]

Despite the naïveté or the arrogance of the assumption that the Chilcotin, when confronted with the irrefutable logic and reasonableness of British justice in this way, would simply comply and turn over their brethren, Seymour's plan worked, or appeared to. Eight Chilcotin surrendered to Cox's party in mid-August and, in doing so, vindicated the law. It was an epochal moment: just as 'those who hold with the Yankee doctrine of "indiscriminate extermination" were beginning to triumph over their opponents,' British justice had proved itself.[94] More important, European British Columbians had proved themselves to be possessed of the civility they had claimed. 'Things are not as they were,' observed a self-congratulatory *British Columbian*. 'A few years, or, indeed, a few months, ago, who would have dreamed of the murder of a few whites by the Indians calling forth such a demonstration in the vindication of the law as this Colony as recently witnessed?'

One of Her Majesty's gunboats might possibly have been despatched somewhere, and we might have heard of a naval demonstration against an Indian village without the slightest reference to its inhabitants being concerned in the murder, with a flourish of trumpets over old and superannuated Indians and squaws, with a large percentage of papooses, who were killed or wounded in the grand and successful operation! How all of this has changed now. Not only were the most thorough measures taken for the apprehension of the murderers, but the most careful discrimination between the guilty and the innocent [were] observed ...

'We look therefore, upon this as a redeeming feature of the Bute massacre,' the newspaper concluded, 'that it has afforded the Government an excellent opportunity of most forcibly illustrating to the Indian tribes the great superiority of British Law.'[95] And, I would add, the episode served to validate European British Columbians' own identity.

Or did it? Questions about the circumstances surrounding the surrender of the Chilcotin were raised at the Quesnelmouth assizes. Just when European British Columbians were beginning to reassert their civility and superiority, they discovered that the distinctions they had made were not as certain as they would have liked. Though the Chilcotin five were hanged, the uncertainty surrounding their execution precipitated a degree of self-criticism. The incident, and British Columbians' reaction to it, shows that identity is never decided once and for all; it is never fixed but always in formation. Because actions structure identities, British Columbians were always being and becoming.

The Chilcotin, as it turned out, may have come into Cox's camp under false pretences, believing that they would be granted a meeting with the governor, not that they would be arrested and detained. Certainly their capture came as a surprise to Alexis, chief of the Chilcotin, who told Begbie that 'Mr. Cox must have two tongues.'[96] Trickery on the part of Cox's party tarnished the law's victory and raised questions about the justice of hanging the prisoners.[97] There had been questions about Cox's honour during the course of the expedition, making the possibility of his malfeasance less remote. According to the diary of a volunteer, it appeared 'that Mr. Cox, anxious to secure all the glory of bagging the murderers, sent a messenger to tell them [the Chilcotin] that Mr. Brew's party would kill them all ... whereas *he* only wanted to talk to them and make terms.'[98] So concerned was Matthew Begbie about the possibility of duplicity that he took the unusual step of speaking to Klatsassin privately after the trial and before sentencing. After the interview, Begbie concluded that '[b]oth Mr Cox and Klatsassin leave me under the impression – in fact they expressly state – that the latter was completely in the dark as to the consequences of his entering Mr. Cox's camp.' 'It seems horrible to hang 5 men at once,' the judge concluded, 'especially under the circumstances of the capitulation.' But he resigned himself to necessity, observing that 'the blood of 21 [sic] whites calls for retribution. And these fellows are cruel, murdering pirates – taking life and making slaves in the same spirit in w[hi]ch you or I w[oul]d go out after partridges or rabbit shooting.'[99] The Chilcotins' otherness prevailed; the need for Terror outweighed the need for British Justice.[100]

The morning of October 26th [1864] broke bright and frosty. With that feeling of heartsickness which those who know who have had to approach the King of Terrors, and stand by when, with all its fearful ceremonial, the Law puts forth its hand deliberately and violently to take away life, I rose and hastened to the prison. The Indians were already at their prayers ... I then entered the cell, and asked if they were ready to receive the Holy Communion? They said they were most desirous. In celebrating, I said the principal parts of the service in their language; the rest in English. This, of course, they did not understand; but they knew the general meaning. They were very devout in receiving, and seemed cheered and encouraged by the Sacrament.

After the service the prisoners took breakfast, then the gaoler called them out, one by one, to be pinioned. As they went I shook hands with each one, bidding them farewell. First went young Pierre, who wept a little, thinking, no doubt of his young wife and child at home. Then there was Chessus, now a changed man, his face no longer fiendishly hideous as at first, but softened and beautified by the touch of Faith. The rest followed. Klatsassan was the last to leave. He grasped me warmly by the hand, and thanked me ...

I noticed ... someone offering Klatsassan a drink, and his refusing. I don't think he ... refused the liquor from any notion save a sense of impropriety of the thing, and a heroic kind of feeling, as if he thought it nobler to meet the worst with all his faculties about him, and face death manfully ...

The prisoners were then led on to the scaffold. There was a large crowd of Indians and white men round, but perfect silence and decorum reigned throughout; prayers were said in Chilcoaten; very short, of course; such is not the time or place for more than a brief commendation of the souls about to depart. I remember saying to each one, as in turn they were blindfolded, and the rope adjusted, and they were placed on the drops, '*Jesu Christ nerhunschita sincha coontese*' ('Jesus Christ be with thy spirit'). As I was going to repeat this to Taloot, a voice was heard; it was Tapeet. He first called out to his comrades to 'have courage.' Then he spoke two sentences to the Indians round the scaffold. They were of the Alexandrian tribe, and at feud with the Chilcoatens. Still, in such a moment such feelings must be forgotten. So he addressed himself to them, and said, '*Tell the Chilcoatens to cease anger against the whites.*' He added, 'We are going to see the Great Father.'

One instant more and the signal was given; the drops fell. All was done so quietly and so quickly that it was difficult to realize that the frightful work was over.

The remains were interred with Christian burial, after the Anglican rite, in a wood near Quesnelmouth, not far from the Cariboo road. A wooden cross with a rude inscription was set up to mark the spot where those poor fellows sleep.[101]

While Matthew Begbie may have had doubts about whether the Chilcotin had been treated justly, the Reverend Robert Christopher Lundin Brown, the Anglican priest who ministered to the prisoners in their last days and the author of the quoted above account (written several years later) did not. Though Lundin Brown admitted that the Chilcotin came to a melancholy end, he considered it the only fitting one: justice demanded that such a heinous crime be met with the ultimate sanction of the law. Lundin Brown's eyewitness account of the fate of the Chilcotin five was also fitting in a different sense of the word: it was made to fit the needs and expectations of the teller and the audience. Lundin Brown told a story of sin, repentance, and salvation, setting out a perfect, almost predictable, and self-contained resolution to a tragic series of events that invoked a kind of moral closure on them. Here we have men described as 'cruel, murdering pirates' wholly repentant in the end, accepting of both their fate and of a Christian God, who, through their embrace of him, and him of them, transforms the Chilcotin both physically (in the case of the once 'hideous' Chessus) and spiritually, and lends them comfort and fortitude to face the 'King of Terrors' in a composed manner. 'Composed' is the key here: for not only did Lundin Brown's Chilcotin face death with great calm, but they and their story were actually *composed* – created – to leave no doubt in the minds of those who read the account about the inevitability and justice of the Chilcotins' fate and the justice of those who meted it out.

The artifice evident in Lundin Brown's composition is heightened when we compare it with Begbie's uncertainty and the ambiguous boundaries between Self and Other that we explored earlier, and it demonstrates a final point about identity: any presentation of the Self as unitary is a wilful and rhetorical construction that masks an ongoing process of being and becoming.[102] Colonial identity, as we have seen, was not fixed, but potentially fragmented and constantly shifting in relation to the context in which it was formed and the actions it inspired.

The road from Bute Inlet proved to be an interesting and instructive one; its bloody beginnings were revealing of both the form and the content of beliefs about Native people – and hence the form and the content of the European colonial identity. These beliefs, though ancient, were revived and reinvented by the intellectual, political, and material contingencies of a particular historical moment. Along the way, however, it became clear that the distinctions between Self and Other more blurred than that duality indicates, and that more than one Self was formed against more than one Other. Both the Indian and the American were important in articulating British Columbians identity as civilized and British, an identity that was symbolized and realized by adherence to the rule of law. While this notion was fine in the abstract, it proved problematic in a specific instance. In addition to revealing the complex relationship between Self and Other and the limitations of the conventional characterizations of that relationship, Bute Inlet illustrated a constant tension between two different conceptions of justice in liberal societies: one rooted in a recognition of differences (themselves constructed in part by liberalism) and in acting upon them, and the other premised on overlooking those differences as insignificant and treating everyone similarly in accordance with liberalism's universalist tendencies. Despite the peculiarities of this particular nineteenth-century manifestation, it is a tension yet to be resolved.[103]

CONCLUSION
Law and the Limits of Liberalism

Instead of reiterating my argument and showing how each of the previous chapters contributes to it, I want to draw out what I believe to be its larger significance by exploring the links between law and liberalism and the possibilities for justice revealed by these case studies. Broadly speaking, my subject has been colonial state formation, and my concern has been to show how the discourse of liberalism was central to making law, order, and authority in a particular mid-nineteenth century British North American colony. Liberal discourse structured European British Columbians' expectations of the law and its administration, and was embedded in both institutional form and social practice; that is, in, both the courts and in the way people conceived of their relationships as being managed.

Having made that general and rather sweeping argument, I also point out that constituting a liberal order through the law was an uneven and contested process. From Mount Tolmie, where a pastor's wandering pigs gave us the opportunity to see the terms on which British Columbians contested the paternal rule of the Hudson's Bay Company proprietorship, to the New Westminster courthouse, where the Cranford brothers' argument with Gus Wright over, among other things, a lot of spoiled 'Cariboo turkey' (bacon), revealed the tensions between 'black letter' law with its textually based authority on the one hand and a more discretionary form and the socially based authority derived from it on the other, and finally to Grouse Creek and Bute Inlet, there was nothing automatic or natural about the creation of a liberal legal and social order.

The unevenness of the law's development and its contested nature are of greater interest to me here, for they expose liberalism's limitations in achieving justice – or, perhaps more accurately, the kinds of justice that are possible within a liberal framework. The shortcomings of the rule of law in achieving justice were chiefly created by the existence of two different ideals: one that emerged out of a desire for the rule of a set of standardized and evenly enforced laws and like results in like cases, and another that reflected an equally strong desire for a set of laws that would recognize, honour, and privilege the particularisms – the constellations of social relationships embedded in a particular locale and time – out of which disputes arise. The first ideal of justice was most apparent in *Cranford*, and was hostile to a recognition of the particular and the larger social context in which the dispute occurred. It mattered not, for example, who the disputing parties were, or that Gus Wright was well known in the district while the Cranfords were strangers. Such facts were deemed irrelevant, and their introduction diverting and counterproductive to resolving the case. This was, in short, a notion of law and justice that suppressed the differences that emerged from and were associated with place.

The razing of the differences associated with place – of local law-ways and other kinds of customary behaviour – through the imposition of formal law is something that other commentators have argued is central to liberal state formation and the expansion and consolidation of capitalism.[1] After atomizing us by denying the legitimacy of our customary roles and severing the connections we make through them, the law tells us how to behave by constructing new legal roles for us – roles that come with responsibilities it will enforce – and by prescribing formal channels through which we can reconnect and go on in our relationships.[2] In British Columbia we saw how, in an effort to forestall the establishment of local informal government in the gold fields, the colonial government framed the Gold Fields Act, a statute that created the 'free miner' and deemed that only those so designated (by a state-controlled licensing system) were eligible to mine. Moreover, disputes between free miners were to be settled through the state-constituted gold commissioner's courts rather than the informal and locally constituted miners' meetings, as was customary elsewhere.[3] While the gold commissioner's courts performed many of the same regulatory functions as the miners' meetings did in the gold fields of California, Australia, and New Zealand, they were fundamentally different because the conditions of their operation and dissolution, as well as their authority, were derived from the state rather than the local community they regulated. The same process of atomization, reconstitution, and regulation can be seen in the statutes that governed the recovery of debts and the creation of small debts courts, the other set of laws and institutions that were the focus of British Columbians' concern and criticism.

Thus, colonial administrators used formal law to construct an arena of exchange in which economic actors were free to enter into associations within a framework of known rules imposed and enforced by the state and designed to safeguard their economic liberty by setting out their obligations to each other.

This was the proverbial 'level playing-field,' and it was (and is) considered crucial to capital accumulation because it created a degree of standardization in dealing that minimized risk by maximizing predictability. However, the same standardization and predictability that facilitated the pursuit of individual self-interest was also the key to state formation and state power. Indeed (and somewhat ironically, given that historically the state has been considered the enemy of individual liberty), it is this *conflation* of self-interest with state interest that was the key to modern governance, or 'governmentality.'[4] As a result of this conflation, more and more aspects of social life are voluntarily mediated by and through state institutions, thus providing more and more opportunities for state surveillance and control. Populations are rendered self-regulating and self-policing. The need for overt coercion on the part of the state is eliminated or at least minimized, and its role in social, political, and economic ordering obscured. Such, ironically, is the nature of the freedom created by the marketplace.

This notion of justice as emerging from a 'level playing-field' drew on an understanding of society as pervasive as it was partial; an understanding derived from liberalism. In the liberal view of the world all individuals are similar and their identities inherent, springing from a rational essence rather than contingent on their particular subject position as members of certain social groups or their relationships with other individuals in circumscribed locales. Relationships are understood as equal, fluid, and interchangeable, motivated as they are by self-interest. Liberals assume that relationships exist only as long as it is in the interests of the parties involved that they do so. If and when they fail to meet this demand, they end, and other relationships are entered into. By defining value in terms of economic self-interest, such an understanding of social interaction deems any other kind of attachment to particular places and sets of relationships of secondary importance and, indeed, perhaps irrational in shaping behaviour and hence in resolving conflict.[5] If, as liberals believe, all people are similar and their relationships similarly motivated and constituted irrespective of place, then treating them similarly as the rule of law requires is in fact the only way of treating them justly.

In conceptualizing social interaction as occurring in the blank and identical *spaces* of an abstract playing-field rather than in textured, complex, and unique *places*, such a notion of justice ignores the possibility that individuals, their relationships, their disputes, and their resolutions are actually constituted by particular associations with and within specific locales. This possibility proved to be a reality on Grouse Creek. The Grouse Creek War bore testimony to the power of place and the very real constraints it can impose on exercise of rule of law. In so doing, the Grouse Creek War also illustrated the limits of a liberal notion of justice. Both the meaning and the dimensions of this mining dispute and the proper course to take in resolving it were embedded in locale; and as Matthew Baillie Begbie discovered, solutions that ignored the local context were doomed to fail or at least be met with great resistance.

It is this recognition of differences that lies at heart of the second ideal of justice. When Matthew Begbie attempted to administer the law to its black letter in adjudicating a mining dispute, his decision was criticized for its lack of 'common sense.' But common sense was not common at all: it was rooted in community sensibilities. Right and wrong gained their meaning largely from the local context of disputes. As the *Cariboo Sentinel* put it, 'a man is wrong when almost every person in the community thinks and says he is wrong.'[6] Thus, for all its 'blackness' – its 'writtenness' and 'knowability' – black letter law was more intangible, more alien and at odds with the tacit (but more intelligible and meaningful) common sense that Caribooites saw as the basis of just legal administration.

Many argue that ignoring differences, whatever their source – place, race, class, gender, or sexuality – rather than acknowledging and perhaps embracing them can only perpetuate injustice. This argument for difference is made most forcefully by a number of feminist legal scholars.[7] Largely inspired by the work of the psychologist Carol Gilligan, whose work on the development of moral reasoning exposed the gender-biased nature of psychological theory and argued that boys and girls reason differently about morality, this school of jurisprudence seeks to entrench the 'ethic of care' – the 'different voices' in which women speak – into law.[8] Unlike a liberal jurisprudence, which privileges the autonomous individual – something Robin West considers 'irretrievably masculinist' – law should reflect women's true natures, which, because of women's ability to bear children, centre on 'connectivity' and nurturing. Not only would such a jurisprudence liberate women, West argues, it would also liberate men, for connectivity and nurturing are qualities that benefit everyone.[9]

However, recognizing differences can be part of producing and reproducing relations of dominance.[10] Despite the lessons of *Grouse Creek* and the powerful jurisprudential arguments made in favour of difference, one need look no further than the history of women or native peoples for examples of how difference can be, was, and is used to justify exclusion and oppression.[11] Indeed, it is significant that the so-called first-wave feminists spent a great deal of their time downplaying women's differences – arguing for 'androgyny,' as Alison Jaggar puts it – in an effort to sustain their claims for the rights of full citizenship.[12]

In fact, overlooking differences created by condition, as the rule of law insists we do, does not necessarily result in a miscarriage of justice. By juxtaposing socially constructed differences against legally constructed similarities, the Bute

Inlet episode suggested the possibilities for justice that could result from overlooking differences and treating people equally before the law. While the discourse of savagery constructed the Chilcotin as savages worthy of savage treatment, the discourse of the law deemed the differences created by condition to be irrelevant. The law's requirement that differences be ignored, that Indians be accorded equal rather than savage treatment, opened up the possibility for justice. The liberal notion of justice as equal treatment regardless of condition thus contained in it an opportunity – a 'discursive space' – that could be exploited strategically in the name of social justice and liberation as well as oppression. It is because of this that the rule of law, to quote E.P. Thompson's conclusion to *Whigs and Hunters*, is 'something a good deal more than sham' and not simply 'humbug.'[13]

While that space was not large enough to allow the Chilcotin to slip through it – they were hanged – it was nonetheless significant, for though its potential was not realized on that occasion, it has been on others, both historically and, most obviously, in the present land claims litigation.[14] By framing land claims in terms of ownership, aboriginal peoples make an effective argument that relies on the rhetorical power of 'property' in a liberal political order rather than one that rests on a claim of special status or difference. More broadly, their use of 'rights' discourse has the same result. Like 'property,' a claim of 'rights' is evocative and powerful because of its resonance in a liberal framework: rights, as defined by the liberal state, belong to everyone, regardless of their condition. Rights are resources that can empower the weak because they are fundamental and inherent to all, and are denied only at great political cost. Naming something a right, then, invokes all of these larger connotations and denies the relevance of the status of the individuals who make the claim.[15] However, in calling for a recognition of '*aboriginal* rights,' native peoples are actually doing something quite radical and subversive of liberalism: they are exploiting the rhetorical power of 'rights,' which, in a liberal universe, accrue to all *individuals*, in the name of a particular *collectivity*. In a sense, 'aboriginal rights' should be an oxymoron: for not only does it shift the locus of rights from the individual to a collectivity, but it also makes status matter in their allocation. In essence, a claim of aboriginal rights is an attempt to entrench difference (in this case, 'aboriginal') with a tool that has historically denied its importance (in this case, 'rights'), and in doing so makes it intelligible and palatable within the existing political discourse provided by liberalism.

While events of Grouse Creek illustrated the limitations of a particular kind of law in achieving justice, those of Bute Inlet suggested the possibilities for doing so – if not their realization – that were made available by exploiting the law's universality.

Despite Caribooites' experience otherwise, inherent in the law is room for the recognition of differences. For in addition to achieving like results in like cases, the law recognizes that each case must be taken on its own merits; that each case is different and cannot be resolved through the law by treating the rules as first principles that need only be applied. This principle is as much a part of the common law as is its universality; and it is, of course, why we have trials – why disputes are not simply decided by fitting them into a variety of different fact patterns. The 'legal method' – the manner in which cases are decided – may be resistant to change and hence to justice, but it is not so totalizing and self-referential as to determine the outcome of cases completely.[16] Every time a case is heard, then, there is the possibility, however slight, that something different, something unexpected, something against the grain will happen. Not only can justice come from exploiting the law's universality, it can also emerge from its particularistic nature, its requirement that each case be treated separately.

My point here is not to argue that the rule of law is perfect or even that 'things work out.' Nor is it to deny the injustices that are perpetuated under the name of law or the possibility of alternative visions of justice. My argument is simply this: despite the shortcomings of law and the liberal notion of justice, oppression is not automatic and the reproduction of relations of domination is not straightforward because the power of the law is not totalizing. There are opportunities within the rule of law and the larger discourse from which it is derived that can be exploited and turned to radical and subversive ends. This is why a historical approach is so important. The power of history lies in its particularity; in taking each case on its own merits, as it were, and making visible the opportunities for subversion and people's ongoing efforts at exploiting them, as well as highlighting the contradictions and ambiguities inherent in the exercise of power. In doing so we not only come to understand how change comes about and the terms under which it is possible, but we also keep historical agents – people – in the foreground of making it.

Appendix

HUDSON'S BAY COMPANY CONTRACTS OF ENGAGEMENT

Below is an example of a contract used by the Hudson's Bay Company to engage their servants. This particular contract belonged to Charles LaFleur, and is dated 1840 (HBCA-NAC, MG 20 A./32/37, folio 52). The standard form appears to have been used to the 1880s with few modifications.

AN AGREEMENT made this ____ day of ____ in the year one thousand eight hundred and ____ between ____ aged ____ years, formerly of the Parish of ____ in the County of ____ of the one part, and the Governor and Company of Adventurers of England, trading into Hudson Bay, represented by _____ of the other part as follows. The said ____ hereby contracts and agrees to serve the said Company in North America in the capacity of ____ for the term of years to be computed from ____

and for such further term as hereinafter mentioned,

and devote the whole of his time and labour in their service and for their sole benefit and that he will do his duty as such and perform all such work and service, by day or by night, for the said Company as he shall be required to do, and obey all orders, which he shall receive from the Governors of the Company in North America, or other their Officers or Agents for the time being; and that he will with courage and fidelity in his said station, in the said service, defend the property of the said Company and their Factories and settlements; and will not absent himself from the said service, nor engage, or be concerned in any trade or employment whatsoever, except for the benefit of the said Company and according to their orders. And that all goods obtained by barter with the Indians or otherwise, which shall come to the hands or possession of the said ____ shall be held by him for the said Company only, and shall be duly delivered up to the said

Governors or their Officers or Agents for the time being, without any waste, spoil or injury thereto, and in case of any wilful neglect or default herein, he shall make good to the said Company all such loss or damage as they shall sustain thereby, to be deducted out of his wages. And that the said ____ will faithfully obey all laws, orders and regulations established or made by the said Company for the good government of their settlements and territories; and all times during the residence of the said _____ in North America, he will defend the rights and privileges of the said Company and aid and support their Officers and Agents in the utmost of his power; and the said _____ _____ further engages and agrees that in case he shall omit to give notice to the Governor or Officers of the said Company in North America, one year or upwards before the expiration of the said term of ____ years, of his intention to quit their service and return to _____ then that he hereby promises and engages to remain one year longer upon the like terms as are contained in this contract; And the said ____ on behalf of the said Company hereby engages, That upon in like manner as aforesaid, but not otherwise; the said shall receive from the said Company after the rate of ____

per annum, to commence on and be computed from ____

aforesaid and provided always, and it is hereby expressly agreed between the said parties hereto, that it shall be lawful for the Governor or other Officers or Agents of the said Company in North America, at any time during the said term of ____ years or such additional term as aforesaid, to dismiss the said ____ from their service and direct his return to ____ in such case his wages are to cease from the day of [his dismissal] and further that in case the said ____ shall at any time desert the service of the said Company, or otherwise neglect or refuse duly to discharge his duty as such hired Servant as aforesaid, then he shall forfeit and lose all his wages, for the recovery whereof, there shall be no relief either in law or in equity. In witness whereof the said parties have hereto set their hands at ____

Signed in the presence of _____

Notes

Archival Abbreviations

BCARS British Columbia Archives and Records Service
DIA Department of Indian Affairs
HBAC Hudson's Bay Company Archives
NAC National Archives of Canada

INTRODUCTION

1 Crease to Seymour, Attorney General's Office, 14 March 1868. NAC, MG 11, CO 60/32, 169.
2 For the most recent formulation of this, see Lipset, *Continental Divide*, particularly chapter 6.
3 For two recent overviews of the Mountie and the Cowboy, see Walden, *Visions of Order*, and Slatta, *Cowboys of the Americas*, especially chapter 12.
4 For various theories about Canada's political culture, see Hartz, *Founding of New Societies*, introduction and chapter 7; Horowitz, 'Conservatism, Liberalism, and Socialism'; S.F. Wise, 'Upper Canada and the Conservative Tradition,' in Firth, ed., *Profiles of a Province*; Stewart, *Origins of Canadian Politics*; Errington, *The Lion, the Eagle*; Mills, *Loyalty in Upper Canada*.
5 Hardin, *A Nation Unaware*, chapter 8; Lipset, *Continental Divide*; and Morton, 'Cavalry or Police?'
6 On vigilantism in America, see Brown, *Strain of Violence*, McGrath, *Gunfighters*.
7 On violence and crime in Canada, see Judy Torrance, *Public Violence in Canada, 1867–1982* (Montreal and Kingston, 1986); Thomas Thorner, 'The Not So Peaceable

Kingdom'; Thorner, 'Crime and Criminal Justice in Frontier Calgary,' in Rasporich and Klassen, eds., *Frontier Calgary*; Thorner, 'The Incidence of Crime in Southern Alberta, 1878–1905,' in Bercuson and Knafla, eds., *Law and Society in Canada*; and Thorner and N. Watson, 'Patterns of Prairie Crime: Calgary, 1875–1939,' in Knafla, ed., *Crime and Criminal Justice*. On the Mounties, see Brown and Brown, *Unauthorised History*, and Walden, *Visions of Order*.

8 Shearing, 'Decriminalizing Criminology,' discusses this in relation to criminology, arguing that criminologists need to relocate their theoretical problematic from crime to the broader phenomenon of 'ordering.'

9 As the literature is fairly large, this is a selective listing. On women and the law, see Backhouse, *Petticoats and Prejudice*; Backhouse, 'Married Women's Property Law'; Coombe, 'Action for Breach of Promise'; and McCallum, 'Keeping Women in Their Place.' On class, see Chunn, 'Regulating the Poor'; Chunn, 'Rehabilitating Deviant Families'; and Tucker, 'Making the Workplace "Safe." On law and race, see Li, *Chinese in Canada*, chapter 2, and Roy, *White Man's Province*, chapter 2. On law, politics, and economic development, see Risk, 'Law and the Economy'; Hibbitts, 'Progress and Principle'; Howes, 'Property, God, and Nature'; and Wright, 'Ideological Dimensions of the Law.'

10 See, for instance, Dubinsky and Iacovetta, 'Murder'; Carolyn Strange, 'From Modern Babylon to City upon a Hill: The Toronto Social Survey Commission of 1915 and the Search for Sexual Order in the City,' in Hall, Westfall, and McDowell, eds., *Patterns of the Past*; and Iacovetta and Valverde, eds., *Gender Conflicts*. On the dangers of using 'master categories' of analysis, see Carol Smart, 'Feminist Jurisprudence,' in Fitzpatrick, ed., *Dangerous Supplements*.

11 For a lucid overview of post-structuralism and discourse analysis, see Eagleton, *Literary Theory*, chapter 4, and Eagleton, *Ideology*, chapter 7.

12 This paragraph is taken from my review of Anderson, *Vancouver's Chinatown*, in (1992) 25 *British Columbia Historical News*: 39–40.

13 The notion of the 'ideological work' of language is developed in Poovey, *Uneven Developments*, chapter 1. Poovey shows how the discourse of separate spheres constituted women, empowering them even as it limited their options. This is also the theme of a piece by Carol Smart, which deals directly with the law: see 'Disruptive Bodies and Unruly Sex: The Regulation of Reproduction and Sexuality in the Nineteenth Century,' in Smart, ed., *Regulating Womanhood*.

14 Chris Baldick, *The Concise Oxford Dictionary of Literary Terms* (Oxford: Oxford University Press, 1990), 59.

15 Dworkin, *Law's Empire*, 1.

16 Smart, *Feminism and the Power of Law*, chapter 1, and Mossman, 'Feminism and the Legal Method' both make this point.

17 This is Mossman's term. See 'Feminism and the Legal Method.'

18 I have relied on the following overviews of liberalism: Gray, *Liberalism*; Jaggar, *Feminist Politics*; Kymlicka, *Liberalism, Community, and Culture*.
19 As Terry Eagleton points out, 'it is one of the functions of ideology to "naturalize" social reality, to make it seem as unchangeable as Nature itself.' Eagleton, *Literary Theory*, 135.
20 Gray, *Liberalism*, x.
21 Taylor, *Laissez-Faire*, 18-26.
22 Ibid., 24–6. This, albeit in simplified form, is the theme of Burchell, Gordon, and Miller, eds., *The Foucault Effect*. Foucault argues that liberalism represented a transformation of monumental significance in the way government is thought about, practised, and rationalized.
23 Palmer, *Descent into Discourse*.
24 Clifford and Marcus, eds., *Writing Culture*; White, *Heracles' Bow*; : *Essays in the Rhetoric and Poetics of Law (Madison, 1985):* and Zukin, *Landscapes of Power*.
25 McDonald, review of Anderson, *Vancouver's Chinatown*.
26 Burke, *History and Social Theory*. Also see the debate in *Past and Present* sparked by Lawrence Stone's reaction to a piece published by Gabrielle M. Speigel ('History, Historicism') Stone, 'History and Post-Modernism' (1991); Joyce, 'History and Post-Modernism'; Kelly, 'History and Post-Modernism'; Stone, 'History and Post-Modernism' (1992); Speigel, 'History and Post-Modernism.'
27 Cynthia Ozick, 'Innovation and Redemption: What Literature Means,' in Ozick, *Art and Ardor: Essays* (New York 1983), 238, 244. Cited in Harris, 'Race and Essentialism,' 583.
28 Nowhere, I think, is post-structuralism's power to do this more apparent than in feminist theory and politics. This literature reveals how women's 'nature' has been and continues to be used as a rationale for their regulation. The literature is enormous, but for a good introduction to the way the law has been implicated in this process, see Smart, 'Disruptive Bodies,' and Judith Walkowitz, 'Male Vice and Female Virtue: Feminism and the Politics of Prostitution in Nineteenth-Century Britain,' in Snitow, Stansell, and Thompson, eds., *Powers of Desire*. More generally on the possibilities (rather than the dangers) opened by recognizing our own and the law's artifice, see White, *Heracles' Bow*. A less optimistic and quite thoughtful view can be found in Handler, 'Postmodernism.'
29 Barman, *The West beyond the West*.
30 An exception being Harold Innis's staples theory. However, as Cole Harris has observed, Innis's theory, for all its insights on the pattern of settlement in Canada, does not go very far in explaining the dynamics of the communities whose formation he charted. See Harris, 'Industry and the Good Life.'
31 Gough, 'Character of the British Columbia Frontier.'
32 Greer and Radforth, eds., *Colonial Leviathan*, introduction.

CHAPTER 1 'Club Law' and Order

1 Beaver to Benjamin Harrison, Fort Vancouver, 15 November 1836, in Thomas E. Jessett, ed., *Reports and Letters, 1836–1838, of Herbert Beaver, Chaplain to the Hudson's Bay Company and Missionary to the Indians at Fort Vancouver* (Portland 1959), 20.
2 Simpson to Manson, Norway House, 18 June 1853. Cited in Morice, *History of the Northern Interior*, 281–2.
3 43 Geo. III, c. 138, An Act for extending the Jurisdiction of the Courts of Justice in the Provinces of Upper and Lower Canada, to the Trial and Punishment of Crimes, and Offences within certain parts of North America adjoining the said Provinces (1803), and 1 & 2 Geo. IV, c. 66, An Act for Regulating the Fur Trade and establishing a Criminal and Civil Jurisdiction within certain parts of North America (1821). For more on these two acts see Foster, 'Long-Distance Justice,' and Foster, 'Sins against the Great Spirit.'
4 It should be noted that the company that was granted the monopoly – the HBC – was the result of a second merger, this time between the NWC and the old HBC.
5 See section 6 of the Act. Also see Foster, 'Long Distance Justice,' 32–7.
6 Foster, 'Long Distance Justice,' 14–48. Also see Foster, 'Mutiny on the *Beaver*.'
7 Though the two are not unrelated, the company expressed more concern about protecting its economic interests by limiting its employees' opportunities to trade on their own accounts.
8 Hamar Foster, 'Theoretical Justice,' paper presented to the 1986 BC Studies Conference, Victoria, BC.
9 See the appendix for an example of a contract of engagement.
10 Ibid.
11 Ibid. Servants' wages would be deducted for any damages.
12 Emphasis added. Simpson to McLoughlin, York Factory, 9 July 1827. HBCA-NAC, MG 20, D4/90, fo. 102.
13 Ibid.
14 Ibid.
15 Simpson to the Governor and Committee, Fort Vancouver, 1 March 1829. HBCA-NAC, MG 20, D4/94, fo. 10.
16 Simpson to Connolly, York Factory, 9 July 1827. HBCA-NAC, MG 20, D4/90, fo. 106.
17 John Tod, *History of New Caledonia and the Northwest Coast* (Victoria, 1878). H.H. Bancroft Collection, TS, NAC, MG 29, C15, v. 3, C-27, 40.
18 Simpson to the Governor and Committee, York Factory, 9 July 1827. HBCA-NAC, MG 20, D4/90, fo. 106.
19 Simpson to the Governor and Committee, Fort Vancouver, 1 March 1829. Ibid., fo. 7.

20 W. Stewart Wallace, ed., *John McLean's Notes of a Twenty-Five Years' Service in the Hudson's Bay Territory* (Toronto, 1932), 144.
21 Lamb, 'Five Letters of Charles Ross.'
22 Simpson to the Governor and Committee, Fort Vancouver, 1 March 1829. HBCA-NAC, MG 20, D4/94, fo. 9.
23 Ibid., fo. 7.
24 Wallace, ed., *John McLean's Notes*, 141.
25 Simpson to the Governor and Committee, York Factory, 10 August 1824. HBCA-NAC, MG 20, D4/87, fo. 45-6; Simpson to the Governor and Committee, York Factory, 1 September 1825, MG 20, D4/88, fo. 59; Minutes of Council held at York Factory Northern Department of Rupert's Land, 2 July 1825, MG 20, D4/88, fo. 104; and Morice, *History of the Northern Interior*, 138.
26 Simpson to the Governor and Committee, Fort Vancouver, 1 March 1829. HBCA-NAC, MG 20, D4/94, fo. 11.
27 Morice, *History of the Northern Interior*, 262-71.
28 Ibid., 181; Archibald McKinlay, *Narrative of a Chief Factor of the Hudson's Bay Company* (Victoria, 1878). TS, NAC, MG 29, C15. H.H. Bancroft Collection, v. 3, C-25, 11-18; Sir George Simpson, *Narrative of a Journey Round the World, During the Years 1841 and 1842*, v. 1 (London, 1847), 155-7; and Todd, *History of New Caledonia and the Northwest Coast*, 7-13.
29 Morice, *History of the Northern Interior*, 212-7.
30 Ibid., 185.
31 Merk, ed., *Fur Trade and Empire*, 338-9.
32 Simpson to the Governor and Committee, Fort George, 10 March 1829. HBCA-NAC, MG 20, D4/88, fo. 17.
33 Yale to Simpson, 22 October 1852; cited in Mackie, 'Colonial Land,' 89.
34 'Bye-Laws.' HBCA-NAC, MG 20, A37/41, fo. 7.
35 Fort Kilmaurs Journal, March-June 1826. Entry for 10 March 1826. NAC, MG 19, D8.
36 Joseph William McKay, *Recollections of a Chief Trader in the Hudson's Bay Company* (Fort Simpson, 1878), TS, H.H. Bancroft Collection, NAC, MG 29, C15, v. 3, C-24, 14.
37 Columbia Mission, *Fifth Report of the Columbia Mission, 1863*. 'Extracts from the Bishop's Speeches,' 21-2.
38 McKay, *Recollections*, 14.
39 The other was the use of liquor: Simpson to the Governor and Committee, York Factory, 1 September 1825, NAC, MG 20, D4/88, fo. 60.
40 Archibald McDonald. *Journal of the Hudson's Bay Company kept at Fort Langley*, 103-4.

41 Servants' Character and Staff Records, 1832, HBCA-NAC, MG 20, A34/2, fo. 26.
42 McLoughlin to Simpson, Fort Vancouver, 16 March 1832. Rich, ed., *Letters of John McLoughlin, First Series*, 227.
43 The themes touched on in this paragraph are dealt with more extensively in Van Kirk, '*Many Tender Ties*,' chapter 6.
44 As Van Kirk notes in *'Many Tender Ties'*, Simpson was unsympathetic to the alliances fur-trade men formed with Native women, and lamented that 'his Council were nearly "*all Family men*" and too much influenced by the "Sapient Councils of their Squaws" [123].' He also complained that conveying fur trade families around the country caused the company unnecessary delay and expense: 'We must really put a stop to the practise of Gentlemen bringing their Women & Children from the East to the West side of the mountain, it is attended with much expense and inconvenience on the Voyage, business itself must give way to domestick consideration, the Gentlemen became drones and are not disposable in short the evil is more serious than I am well able to describe [130].'
45 Beaver to Harrison, 10 March 1837. *Reports and Letters of Herbert Beaver*, 36–7. There was another side to the story, however. See Foster, 'Mutiny on the *Beaver*,' 36–7.
46 Servants' Character and Staff Records, 1832. HBCA-NAC, MG 20, A34/1, fo. 106.
47 Simpson to McLoughlin, York Factory, 9 July 1827. Ibid., fo. 87.
48 Simpson to the Governor and Committee, York Factory, 16 July 1822. Ibid., D4/85, fo. 5.
49 McLoughlin to the Governor and Committee, Fort Vancouver, 6 July 1827. Rich, ed., Letters of *John McLoughlin, First Series*, 40.
50 Beaver to Harrison, Fort Vancouver, 15 November 1836. *Reports and Letters of Herbert Beaver*, 20. The company's officers, not surprisingly, had rather different views. After joining the HBC, Chief Factor William McNeill noted that in his twenty-four years of shipboard experience he had never seen 'men more indulged in that in the Hon. H.B.Co.'s service.' Cited in Foster, 'Mutiny on the *Beaver*,' 36.
51 McLoughlin to the Governor and Committee, Fort Vancouver, 28 October 1832. Rich, ed., Letters of *John McLoughlin First Series*, 107–8.
52 Douglas to Barclay, Fort Victoria, 16 November 1850. In Bowsfield, ed., *Fort Victoria Letters*, 130–1.
53 Innis, *The Fur Trade in Canada*, 313.
54 Douglas to Barclay, Fort Victoria, 23 November 1851. Bowsfield, ed., *Fort Victoria Letters*, 230–1.
55 1824 resolution passed by the Council of the Northern Department, cited in Van Kirk, '*Many Tender Ties*,' 130.
56 Ibid., 129. A policy that acknowledged the company's responsibility was soon estab-

lished, however. See regulation 42 of the Standing Rules and Regulations (1835) referred to in Foster, 'Mutiny on the *Beaver,*' 36–7.
57 Merk, ed., *Fur Trade and Empire,* 'Introduction to the First Edition,' xxxviii-xli. For more information on Simpson see John S. Galbraith's biography in the *Dictionary of Canadian Biography,* v. 8 (Toronto, 1985), 812–19.
58 On the occupational hierarchy see Van Kirk, '*Many Tender Ties*', 10; Brown, *Strangers in Blood,* chapter 2; and Chalmers, 'Social Stratification in the Fur Trade.'
59 Morice, *History of the Northern Interior,* 104.
60 Ibid. see note 62, chapter 1.
61 Clerks received £20 in their first year, £5 more in the two subsequent years of service, and £10 more in the last two years of their apprenticeship. 'If they behaved satisfactorily then £75 was given for a term of three years. This again was increased to £100 per year.' See Roderick Finlayson, *The History of Vancouver Island and the Northwest Coast* (Victoria, 1878). H.H. Bancroft Collection, NAC, MG 29, C15, v. 2, C-15, 36. Salaries of clerks ranged from £50 to £100 in the mid-1830s. See Morice, *History of the Northern Interior,* 105.
62 After their apprenticeship clerks were graded into four classes 'according to the Education and abilities.' In 1822 clerks' wages were set as follows: first class £100; second class, £75; third class, £60; fourth class, £40. See Simpson to the Governor and Committee, 31 July 1822, in Fleming, ed., *Minutes of Council,* 346–7.
63 Morice, *History of the Northern Interior,* 104, 106.
64 Ibid., 106.
65 Wallace, ed., *John McLean's Notes,* 4–5.
66 Innis, *The Fur Trade in Canada,* 410–13.
67 Ibid., 318.
68 Cited in Morice, *History of the Northern Interior,* 107. J.W. McKay was employed in the HBC's Vancouver Island posts of Fort Nanaimo and Victoria. There is no date given for his description of the chief factor (who, given the tartan, was probably John Stuart, the head of the New Caledonia district [see Shirlee Ann Smith, 'John Stuart,' *Dictionary of Canadian Biography* v. 7, 907–8]). McKay's description certainly fits with the assessment of Stuart given by Governor George Simpson, who wrote in 1832 that although Stuart 'had not the advantage of a good Education, but being studious improved himself very much and having a very retentive Memory is superficially conversant with many subjects. Is exceedingly vain, a great Egoist, swallowing the grossest flattery, is easily cajoled, rarely speaks the truth, indeed I would not beleive [sic] him on Oath; lavish of his own Means, extravagant and irregular in business and his honesty is always questionable.' Servants' Character and Staff Records, 1832. HBCA-NAC, MG 20, A34/2, fo. 3.
69 Simpson to Governor and Committee, 31 July 1822. Fleming, ed., *Minutes of Council, Northern Department,* 346–7.

172 Notes to pages 28–34

70 Simpson to the Governor and Committee, York Factory, 1 September 1825. HBCA-NAC, MG 20, D4/88, fo. 94–5.
71 Cullen, *History of Fort Langley*, 100–1.
72 See Van Kirk, '*Many Tender Ties*,' 125, for a description of the living accommodations at Fort Vermillion on the Saskatchewan River that shows the same apportioning of social space in terms of social and occupational class.
73 Thomas Jefferson Farnham, *Travels in the Great Western Prairies, the Anahuac and Rocky Mountains, and in the Oregon Territory* (New York, 1843), cited in John Warren Dease Papers, Burpee MS, 'The Columbia Journal of J.W. Dease, 1829, edited with notes by Lawrence J. Burpee,' n.d., note 'A' to the entry for 1 November 1829. NAC, MG 19, A22.
74 McLeod, ed., *Peace River*, 24.
75 Cited in Morice, *History of the Northern Interior*, 110.
76 Simpson to the Governor and Committee, York Factory, 1 September 1822. HBCA-NAC, MG 20, D4/85, fo. 90.
77 Douglas to Barclay, Fort Victoria, 16 November 1850. Bowsfield, ed., *Fort Victoria Letters*, 130–1.
78 Douglas to the Governor and Committee, 18 October 1838. Rich, ed., Letters of *John McLoughlin, First Series*, 247.
79 'Hard usage' from McLoughlin to the Governor and Committee, 20 November 1845, in Rich, ed., Letters of *John McLoughlin, Third Series*, 100. 'Autocratic officers' from Morice, *History of the Northern Interior*, 112–13.
80 Peter Skene Ogden, cited in Morice, *History of the Northern Interior*, 200–7.
81 Simpson to the Governor and Committee, York Factory, 10 August 1824. HBCA-NAC, MG 20, D4/87, fo. 24–5.
82 Simpson to the Governor and Council, 23 June 1853. Fleming, ed., *Minutes of Council, Northern Department*, xxiv.
83 Simpson to Manson, Norway House, 18 June 1853. Cited in Morice, *History of the Northern Interior*, 281–2.

CHAPTER 2 'A Squatocracy of Skin Traders'

1 Angelo, *Idaho*, 8–9. Though Angelo's views represented what many felt about the company, the HBC never claimed Vancouver Island under the Charter of 1660.
2 Royal Charter issued 13 January 1849. See James E. Hendrickson, 'The Constitutional Development of Colonial Vancouver Island and British Columbia,' in Ward and McDonald, eds., *British Columbia*, 245–74.
3 On laissez-faire and public policy in Great Britain in general, see Taylor, *Laissez-Faire*. On the influence of laissez-faire ideas in the law, see Atiyah, *Rise and Fall of Freedom of Contract*.

Notes to pages 36–7   173

4 As W. Kaye Lamb pointed out, 'The price scale at which an individual could purchase goods depended on his relationship to the company. For this purpose, Blanshard was considered completely independent and was therefore charged the highest tariff. In 1850 this was high indeed, as it was based upon the peak prices prevailing during the gold rush in California. The consequence was that Blanshard found the cost of living ruinous, and it would seem that Douglas and the company might well have made a generous concession under the circumstances.' Lamb, 'Governorship of Richard Blanshard,' On Blanshard generally, see James E. Hendrickson, 'Richard Blanshard,' *Dictionary of Canadian Biography*, v. 12, 113–14.
5 Lamb, 'Governorship of Richard Blanshard,' 2.
6 Barclay to Douglas, 3 August 1849, cited ibid., 23.
7 Testimony of Richard Blanshard given to the Select Committee on the Hudson's Bay Company, 15 June 1857. Great Britain, House of Commons, *Report from the Select Committee on the Hudson's Bay Company, together with the proceedings of the committee* ... 289.
8 On the Fort Rupert affair, see Gough, *Gunboat Frontier*, 32–9. The phrase 'miserable affair' is J.S. Helmcken's, an HBC surgeon who was commissioned as magistrate to investigate the incidents at Fort Rupert. See his 'Fort Rupert in 1850...' *Colonist*, 1 January 1890.
9 See H. Keith Ralston, 'Miners and Managers: The Organization of Coal Production on Vancouver's Island by the Hudson's Bay Company, 1848-1862,' in Norcross, ed., *Company on the Coast*, 45–6.
10 Blanshard to Helmcken, Victoria, 22 June 1850. Great Britain, Colonial Office, Vancouver Island Original Correspondence. NAC, MG 11, CO 305/2, reel B-233, 71.
11 Blanshard to Grey, Victoria, Vancouver Island, 18 August 1850. Vancouver Island, *Despatches: Governor Blanshard to the Secretary of State, 26 December 1849 to 30 August 1851* (New Westminster, n.d.), 5.
12 Blanshard to Grey, Fort Rupert, 19 October 1850. NAC, MG 11, CO 305/2, reel B-233, 85.
13 Blanshard to Grey, Victoria, Vancouver Island, 18 August 1850. In Vancouver Island, *Despatches: Governor Blanshard to the Secretary of State, 26 December 1849 to 30 August 1851*, 5.
14 Less so for the Newitty, whose village was shelled by HMS *Daphne*, 'with the happiest effects, so filling their minds with terror, that they made no attempts at reprisals.' Douglas to Grey, Fort Victoria, Vancouver's Island, 31 October 1851. In Bowsfield, ed. *Fort Victoria Letters*, 227.
15 Blanshard to Grey, Victoria, Vancouver Island, 29 March 1851. NAC, MG 11, CO 305/3, reel B-233, 13.
16 Testimony of Richard Blanshard, 15 June 1857. Great Britain, House of Commons,

Report from the Select Committee on the Hudson's Bay Company, together with the proceedings of the committee ... (London, 1857), 289.
17 Petition to His Excellency Richard Blanshard, n.d., received 28 September 1851. NAC, MG 11, CO 305/3, reel B-233, 58-9.
18 Ibid.
19 Ogden to Simpson, 10 August 1851 (private), MS. BCARS. Cited in Lamb, 'Governorship of Richard Blanshard,' *British* 35.
20 On the discussion over who should be granted the proprietorship of Vancouver Island as well as the colony's settlement pattern and the debate over its land laws, see Mackie, 'Colonization of Vancouver Island.'
21 Although colonists referred to the regulations that governed land alienation as 'laws,' they were not statutes passed by a colonial legislature (in fact, Vancouver Island did not get one until 1854), but were part of a policy framed by the Colonial Office and the Governor and Committee of the Hudson's Bay Company.
22 On land policy on Vancouver Island, see Wrinch, 'Land Policy.' Also see Mackie, 'Colonial Land.'
23 Ormsby, 'Introduction,' in Bowsfield, ed. *Fort Victoria Letters*, lv.
24 Wakefield presented his scheme of systematic colonization as a solution to the dual problems of unemployment and poverty in England and the underdevelopment and sluggish commerce of English colonies. 'In Great Britain all classes suffer from the want of room,' he wrote in *The Art of Colonization* (1849). 'By a want of room I mean a want of the means of a comfortable subsistence according to the respective standards of living established among the classes, and obviously rising from the competition of the members of one class with another. Whatever the fund for the maintenance of any of the classes, it is divided amongst too few people; there are too many competitors for a limited fund of enjoyment.' Competition among the country's excessive numbers of labourers held out the threat of 'political disturbance.' Wakefield did not have to go far to find real examples. He considered English 'Chartism and socialism representatives of discontent,' and cited the example of the French Revolution as a warning to those who did not take him seriously. Given the historical precedent and developments at home, he concluded that 'it is well worthwhile to try colonization, or anything that affords a chance of reducing that competition amongst the working classes that is the cause of their political discontent.'
25 Wakefield's ideas were taken up eagerly by Herman Merivale, a senior member of the British Colonial Office, whose tenure coincided with the formation of the colonies of Vancouver Island and British Columbia. Merivale stated the principles of systematic colonization succinctly:

1 That the prosperity of new colonies mainly depends upon the abundance of available labour at the command of capitalists, in proportion to the extent of territory occupied.

2 That this abundance is to be secured by introducing labourers from the mother-country, and other well peopled regions, and taking measures to keep them in the condition of labourers living by wages for some considerable time; at least two or three years ...
3 That the revenue derived from the sale of new land is the fund out of which the cost of introducing them is best defrayed.
4 That the most convenient way of preventing them from rising too rapidly from the condition of labourers is to sell the land at a sufficiently high price.
5 That the entire proceeds of land sales ought to be devoted to purpose of obtaining emigrants; and that only by devoting the whole, and not any portion, will the exact equilibrium between land, labour, and capital be secured ...
See Merivale, *Lectures on Colonization*, 387–8.
26 Barclay to Douglas, 17 December 1849, HBCA-NAC A6/28, fo. 91. Cited in Ormsby, 'Introduction,' *Fort Victoria Letters*, lii–liii. The HBC colonization plan was as follows:
'Colonization of Vancouver's Island.'

1st, – That no grant of land shall contain less than twenty acres.

2nd, – That purchasers of land shall pay to the Hudson's Bay Company, at their House in London, the sum of One Pound per acre for the land sold to them to be held in free and common soccage.

3rd, – That purchasers of land shall provide a passage to Vancouver's Island for themselves and their families, if they have any; or be provided with a passage (if they prefer it) on paying for the same at a reasonable rate.

4th, – That purchasers of larger quantities of land shall pay the same price per acre, namely one pound, and shall take out with them five single men, or three married couples, for every hundred acres.

5th, – That all minerals, wherever found, shall belong to the Company, who shall have the right of digging for the same, compensation being made to the owner of the soil, for any injury done to the surface; but that the said owner shall have the privilege of working for his own benefit any good mine that may be on his land, on payment of a royalty of two shillings and sixpence per ton.

6th, – That, the right of fishing proposed to be given to the Hudson's Bay Company in the grant as printed in the Parliamentary Papers relative to Vancouver's Island having been relinquished, every freeholder will enjoy the right of fishing all sorts of fish on the seas, bays, and inlets of, or surrounding, the said Island; and that all the ports and harbours shall be open and free to them, and to all nations, either trading or seeking shelter therein.

HBCA-NAC, MG 20, A37/42, 'Deeds and Agreements, etc., Relating to Vancouver Island, 1849–1896,' reel HBC 436, fo. 13.

27 Douglas to Barclay, Fort Victoria, 3 September 1849; in Bowsfield, ed., *Fort Victoria Letters*, 42-4.
28 Mackie, 'Colonial Land,' 232.
29 Ibid., 233-42.
30 The population of Vancouver Island was as follows:

1848	32	1853	679
1849	104	1854	797
1850	255	1855	774
1851	295	1862	2,884
1852	464	1865	5,000-6,000

31 *Olympic Columbian*, 29 October 1853.
32 Ibid.
33 Ibid.
34 This is somewhat ironic, given that the Colonial Office was as responsible for the colony's land laws as the Hudson's Bay Company. Nevertheless, the colonists identified the company as the source of their problems, and they turned to Colonial Office and the imperial government for relief.
35 As James Hendrickson notes, the colony was constitutionally required to have an elected assembly. See Hendrickson, 'The Constitutional Development of Colonial Vancouver Island and British Columbia,' in Ward and McDonald, eds., *British Columbia*, 247.
36 J.D. Pemberton to Colvile, Fort Victoria, 22 January 1854. HBCA-NAC, MG 20, A11/75, reel HBC 167, fo. 20.
37 'Vancouver's Island,' *Olympic Columbian*, 29 October 1853.
38 They were Rev. Robert John Staines; Peter Skene Ogden; James Douglas; John Work; Archibald McKinlay; William Fraser Tolmie; James Murray Yale; Alexander Caulfield Anderson; Richard Grant; John Tod; Donald Manson; George Traill Allan; John Kennedy; and Dugald McTavish. Pelly to Grey, Hudson's Bay House, 13 September 1848. NAC, MG 11, CO 305/1, reel B-233, 263.
39 Blanshard to Grey, Victoria, 10 July 1850. Ibid., 67.
40 Blanshard to Grey, Victoria, VI, 10 July 1850. Vancouver Island, *Despatches*, 4.
41 Douglas to Newcastle, Victoria, Vancouver's Island, 11 April 1852. NAC, MG 11, CO 305/4, reel B-234, 20-1. Also see Farr, 'Origin of the Judicial Systems,' 9-12; and Verchere, *Progression of Judges*, introduction and 12-19. For more on the Puget's Sound Agricultural Company (the HBC's agricultural subsidiary which employed the bailiffs) see Coyle, 'Problems of the Puget's Sound Agricultural Company'; Gough, 'Corporate Farming'; and, for its origins in Washington and Oregon, see Gibson, *Farming the Frontier*, chapters 4, 5, and 6.
42 On Blinkhorn, see Dorothy Blakey Smith, 'Thomas Blinkhorn,' *Dictionary of Canadian Biography*, v. 8, 97.

43 Douglas to Newcastle, Victoria, Vancouver Island, 28 July 1853. NAC, MG 11, CO 305/4, reel B-234, 75–6. Also see Nesbitt, 'Diary of Martha Cheney Ella, Part I,' 106. On 6 October she noted a 'Court day, which happens to be the first Thursday in every month.'
44 Blanshard testified to the 1857 Select Committee on the Hudson's Bay Company that as governor he had 'very little indeed [to do] except to regulate the disputes between the Hudson's Bay Company's officers and their servants.' Testimony of Richard Blanshard given to the Select Committee on the Hudson's Bay Company, 15 June 1857. Great Britain, House of Commons, *Report from the Select Committee on the Hudson's Bay Company, together with the proceedings of the committee* ... (London, 1857), 289.
45 Vancouver Island, Notes of Proceedings, 3 October 1853-20 April 1857. BCARS, MS.
46 English law relating to justices of the peace was not amended except with respect to that touching on the property qualification. This was waived. Douglas and his executive council also authorized the island's magistrates to charge twenty shillings per day for their services because of 'the absence of a wealthy class, who might afford to devote their time gratuitously to the public office.' Douglas to Newcastle, Victoria, Vancouver's Island, 11 April 1852. NAC, MG 11, CO 305/4, reel B-234, 21.
47 See Lamb, 'Early Lumbering.'
48 Ibid.
49 Ibid., 49.
50 Douglas to Newcastle, Victoria, Vancouver's Island, 7 January 1854. NAC, MG 11, CO 305/5, reel B-235, 15.
51 The Law Officers of the Crown disallowed this ordinance and put into question the validity of those that preceded it, because 'according to the Instructions under the Sign Manual accompanying the Patent and by those Instructions the power of legislation is vested (as by Law it must be) in the Governor, Council and *General Assembly* [my italics], we do not therefore think that the ordinance or the Act in question can be properly assented to by the Crown or that it would have the force of Law.' See Bethell to Grey, Temple, 20 December 1853. NAC, MG 11, CO 305/5, reel B-235, 186.

The Colonial Office reassured Douglas that though the position of the colony's laws and superior court was serious, 'there will be no permanent difficulty, in as much as the Act "to Provide for the administration of Justice in Vancouver's Island" 12th and 13th Vict: ch:48, reserves powers to the Crown to take all necessary steps for the administration of justice I have therefore directed the preparation of an Order-in-Council, embracing the important provisions to the invalid Act, and giving power to the Court to make necessary rules and regulations for its own conduct.' See Newcastle to Douglas [confidential], 5 April 1854. NAC, MG 11. CO 305/5, reel B-235, 193–5. The order in Council was passed in February 1857.

52 Up to that time the Supreme Court of Civil Justice sat as a Court of Oyer and Terminer and General Gaol Delivery by virtue of commissions issued by the governor. In England, assize judges heard criminal cases not by virtue of the letters patent naming them judges, but by virtue of commissions of oyer and terminer and general gaol delivery. These allowed them to 'hear and deliver' (oyer and terminer) all assize criminal cases and to 'deliver the jails' (general gaol delivery) of all other prisoners awaiting trial for minor criminal offences. These commissions were granted on Vancouver Island until 1860, when the Supreme Court of Civil Justice was granted permanent jurisdiction in criminal matters. A Colonial Office opinion written on Douglas's letter to Newcastle, Victoria, Vancouver's Island, 13 March 1854 (NAC, MG 11, CO 305/5, reel B-235, 42) noted that the Governor of Vancouver Island was empowered through his commission to appoint judges and issue commissions of oyer and terminer. Granting the Supreme Court criminal jurisdiction did not mean that commissions were no longer issued. A commission was still required to allow someone else to try a case, or even to authorize a Supreme Court judge to do so if his court was not a court of assize or oyer and terminer. This became an issue on the mainland in the 1880s. See Hamar Foster, 'The Kamloops Outlaws and Commissions of Assize in Nineteenth Century British Columbia,' in Flaherty, ed., *History of Canadian Law*, v. 2, 342–7.
53 Cameron to Douglas, Belmont, Vancouver's Island, 30 May 1857. NAC, MG 11, CO 305/9, reel B-237, 32–3.
54 9 & 10 Vict., c. 95.
55 'An Act for Rendering the Administration of Justice in Minor Criminal Cases more Speedy and Certain [the Minor Offences Act, 1860],' 19 December 1860; 'An Act to amend the Manner of taking the Verdict of a Jury in Civil Cases [the Vancouver Island Jury Act, 1865],' 16 June 1865.
56 T.L. Wood to the Colonial Secretary, Attorney General's Office, Victoria, 14 September 1865. British Columbia, Colonial Correspondence, BCARS, GR 1372, box 147, file 56/13a. Also see Wood to the Colonial Secretary, Attorney-General's Office, Victoria, 15 May 1865, box 147, file 55/21.
57 'Another Chief Justice Wanted,' *British Colonist*, 26 April 1860.
58 Written on the back of Labouchere to Douglas, 8 July 1856. NAC, MG 11, CO 305/7, reel B-236, 439–40.
59 Ormsby, *British Columbia*. Also see Madge Wolfenden, 'Robert John Staines,' *Dictionary of Canadian Biography*, v. 8, 835–6.
60 James Cooper, E.E. Langford, T.J. Skinner, William Banfield, and James Yates to Newcastle, Victoria, Vancouver Island, 20 April 1854. NAC, MG 11, CO 305/5, reel B-235, 272–3. Petition addressed to The Queen's Most Excellent Majesty, [1 March 1854]. Ibid., 276–80.
61 Petition to the Queen's Most Excellent Majesty, dated 1 March 1854. Ibid., 276–80.

62 Petition to the Duke of Newcastle, dated 1 March 1854. Ibid., 281–8.
63 The following account is taken from Vancouver Island, Supreme Court, Notes of Proceedings, 3 October, 1853–20 April, 1857, BCARS, MS.
64 James Cooper, Maritime Matters on the Northwest Coast of America, cited in Slater, 'Rev. Robert John Staines,' 221n.
65 Douglas to Barclay, 3 November 1854, cited in Slater, 'Rev. Robert John Staines,' 221.
66 Ibid.
67 Unless otherwise noted, the information in this paragraph is taken from Vancouver Island, Attorney General, Notes of Proceedings, 3 October, 1853–20 April, 1857. BCARS, MS.
68 Douglas to Barclay, 3 November 1854, cited in Slater, 'Rev. Robert John Staines,' 221.
69 Ibid.
70 Petition to His Excellency James Douglas, December 1853, enclosed in Labouchere to Douglas, 8 July 1856. NAC, MG 11, CO 305/7, reel B-236, 438–9.
71 Petition to James Douglas, 11 January 1854. Ibid., CO 305/5, reel B-235, 136–8.
72 Ibid.
73 Wolfenden, 'Robert John Staines,' *Dictionary of Canadian Biography*, v. 8, 836.
74 Great Britain, House of Commons, *Report from the Select Committee on the Hudson's Bay Company, together with the proceedings of the committee ...* (London, 1857), copy of a petition addressed to Richard Blanshard, Governor of Vancouver's Island, [1852], 293. It was signed by James Yates, Robert John Staines, James Cooper, Thomas Munroe, James Sangster, John Muir, sen., William Fraser, Andrew Muir, John Muir, jun., Michael Muir, Robert Muir, Archibald Muir, and Thomas Blinkhorn.
75 Coyle, 'Problems of the Puget's Sound Agricultural Company,' chapters 2 and 3.
76 Jean Baptiste Jollibois was born in Laprairie (Lower Canada) in 1796, and joined the HBC in 1813, at the age of seventeen. He first appears on the Fort Vancouver servants' accounts in 1827. In 1831 he is listed as being employed as a boute at FortVancouver. He was transferred to Fort Simpson in 1837, where he remained until 1846, when he was moved to Fort Victoria. At the time of the Staines case Jollibois had been in the company's employ for forty years. The principal in the case, Emanuel Douillet (also Douillette or Douilet) first appears in the Fort Vancouver accounts in 1841, where he was listed as being eighteen years of age, from 'Canada,' and posted in the Thompson River district of New Caledonia, where he was a middleman. He had joined the company in 1839, at the age of fifteen. He remained in the Thompson district until he was transferred to Victoria in 1846. At the time of his involvement with the Staines case he had been with the HBC for fourteen years. We know much less about Adolpus Fearon (also Ferron), who is

listed in the Fort Victoria account book as having been previously employed in the Montreal Department. Jacob Low is also listed in this account book, but no indication of service prior to 1846 is given. See Fort Vancouver, Abstracts of Servants' Accounts, 1827–1844, B223/g71-8, HBCA-NAC, MG 20, reels HBC 1M796, 1M797; and Fort Victoria Account Book, 1846–1853, B226/d/3a. NAC, MG 20, reel 1M628.
77 Mouat, 'Notes on the "Norman Morison," ' 213–14.
78 Petition to the Queen's Most Excellent Majesty [1 March 1854]. NAC, MG 11, CO 305/5, reel B-235; Petition to the Duke of Newcastle, [1 March 1854], ibid., 281–8; Petition to James Douglas, 11 January 1854, ibid., 136–8.
79 See Mouat, 'Notes on the 'Norman Morison',' 204, and Coyle, 'Problems of the Puget's Sound Agricultural Company,' 13.
80 Pemberton to Colvile, Fort Victoria, 22 January 1854. HBCA-NAC, MG 20, A11/75, fo. 20.
81 Angelo, *Idaho*, 8–9.
82 Petition to James Douglas, 11 January 1854. NAC, MG 11, CO 305/5, reel B-235, 136–8.
83 Petition to His Excellency Richard Blanshard, n.d. Received 28 September 1851. NAC, MG 11, Co 305/3, reel B-233, 58–9.
84 *Olympic Columbian*, 29 October 1853.
85 Langford to Newcastle, 49 St Paul's Road, Camden Square, NW, 21 May 1862. NAC, MG 11, CO 305/19, reel B-244, 654–5, 664ff. On Langford's turbulent career, see Sydney Pettit, 'Trials and Tribulations.'

CHAPTER 3 Property, Geography, and British Columbia's Courts

1 Douglas to Labouchere, Victoria, Vancouver's Island, 8 May 1858. Great Britain, Colonial Office. British Columbia Original Correspondence, NAC, MG 11, CO 60/1, reel B-77, 12.
2 Ormsby, *British Columbia*, 140. Prior to its becoming a separate colony, British Columbia was a fur-trade preserve of the HBC.
3 The following account is taken from Edward McGowan (a.k.a. Ned McGowan), 'Reminiscences: Unpublished Incidents in the Life of the "Ubiquitous," ' *Argonaut* (San Francisco), 4, 11, 16, 25 May; 1, 8 June; 13 July 1878; his *Narrative of Edward McGowan* (San Francisco 1887), v. 1, 647; v. 2, 244–66; the original correspondence regarding the incident reprinted, with some commentary, in Howay, *Fraser River Mines*; Myers, *San Francisco's Reign of Terror*; and Underwood, 'Governor Douglas and the Miners.'
4 McGowan, 'Reminiscences,': 1 June 1878, 10. Whannell arrived in Victoria in the fall of 1858, with letters of introduction in which he was identified as 'Captain

Whannell formerly of the Nizam's serice in India.' After his appointment as JP at Fort Yale, the Victoria *Gazette* described him as 'of the Victoria Yeomanry Cavalry in Australia, late of the Nigarris [sic] Cavalry in the East Indies.' In response to an inquiry made by James Douglas, the Australian authorities told him that Whannell had merely been a trooper in the Yeomanry Corps. After his Hill's Bar adventure and his dismissal, Whannell tried his hand at hotelkeeping, and opened 'Clifton House' on Broad Street in Victoria. When that failed, he pre-empted 160 acres of land on the San Juan Islands and tried farming. That too proved unsuccessful, and by 1861 Whannell was broke. He applied to his brother Masons for relief – money for passage to England – and by 1862, when he was last heard from, he had gotten as far as San Francisco. The foregoing is from Smith, ed., 'Journal of Arthur Thomas Bushby,' 195.

5 Farr, 'Origin of the Judicial Systems,' 50.
6 Whannell to Douglas, Fort Yale, 31 December 1858. Colonial Correspondence, BCARS, GR 1372, f. 1854, reel B-1373. Though McGowan asserted that he had acted to release his friends, Whannell reported that he broke into the jail and released Hickson, a constable whom Whannell had arrested and committed for contempt of court and insubordination. He also alleged that McGowan did so in his capacity as a special constable sworn in by a rival magistrate (George Perrier), who had had a longstanding feud with Whannell and whose patience had finally been exceeded when Whannell arrested Hickson, Perrier's constable. Though Perrier never admitted to swearing in McGowan and his band as specials, he told Douglas that he considered Whannell's arrest of Hickson 'an insult to me as a Magistrate and likewise a contempt of court and as I considered it my duty to preserve the dignity of the Court I issued a warrant for the arrest of Captain Whannel [sic], and also an order for the release of Constable Hickson.' See Perrier to Douglas, Hill's Bar, 4 January 1859. Great Britain, Colonial Office, British Columbia Original Correspondence, NAC, NG 11, CO 60/4, reel B-80, 75-6.
7 McGowan, 'Reminiscences,' 1 June 1878, 10. On the feud between Perrier and Whannell, see the enclosures in Brew to Moody, Fort Yale, 30 January 1859. BCARS, GR 1372, reel B-1310, f. 186/3 and 186/6.
8 On vigilantes in the American west, see H.H. Bancroft, *The Works of Hubert Howe Bancroft*, v. 36 and 37, *Popular Tribunals* (San Francisco, 1887); Richard Maxwell Brown, 'The American Vigilante Tradition,' in Graham and Gurr, eds., *Violence in America*, and Brown's more recent *No Duty to Retreat*, and McGrath, *Gunfighters*.
9 Howay labelled it as such in *Fraser River Mines*, xiii.
10 Douglas to Lytton, Victoria, Vancouver's Island, 8 January 1859. NAC, MG 11, CO 60/4, reel B-80, 44-5. Douglas prefaced his request for troops by noting that McGowan's gang were 'reckless desperadoes requiring the strong arm to curb

182　Notes to pages 55–8

them.' Whannell himself warned Richard Clement Moody (whom Douglas had appointed to lead the march to Hill's Bar) that 'McGowan can at any time rally around him at least from 50 to 100 desparadoes [sic] like himself ... and are one and all, the very *scum* of the creation.' But, he assured Moody, though '[t]hey are all armed to the teeth ... I am very much mistaken if 25 British Bayonets cannot rout such rabble.' See Whannell to Moody, Fort Yale, 11 January 1859. BCARS, GR 1372, f. 1854, reel B-1373.
11 *Argonaut*, 13 July 1878.
12 'A Returned Digger,' *Cariboo. The Newly Discovered Gold Fields of British Columbia Fully Described by a Returned Digger*, 8th ed. (London 1862), 54.
13 Nind to Douglas, Williams Lake, 27 March 1861. British Parliamentary Papers, v. 24 (Dublin 1969), 193.
14 Quoted in Douglas to Newcastle, Victoria, Vancouver Island, 24 October 1861, ibid., 203. Other Americans drew even stronger contrasts between British and American territory. 'Talk about Indian fighting,' reminisced Billy Ballou, a seasoned American fortune-seeker, of his Idaho experiences, 'We had hand grenades, ... and Lord bless your soul if we did not let them have it ... Idaho ... beat anything I ever saw for murder ... I went out one morning [and] saw nine men hanging in the butcher shop where he strung cattle up; nine men all labelled Horsethief, Robber, Murderer, etc ... It was done by the Vigilance Committee ... [The worst were the] Sydney Ducks [Australians] ... There were not many of that class on Fraser River. They soon cleared them out of there. Old [British Columbia Supreme Court] Judge Begbie mighty soon made them understand who was boss.' See 'Adventures of Wm. T. Ballou', Bancroft Library, P-B1, 6-10. Cited in Foster, *English Law, British Columbia*, 35–6.
15 John Bell to John Thomson Annan, San Francisco, 27 February 1859. Cited in Ireland, ed., 'Gold-Rush Days in Victoria,' 241.
16 Douglas to Labouchere, Victoria, Vancouver's Island, 29 December 1857. Great Britain, Colonial Office, Vancouver Island Original Correspondence, NAC, MG 11, CO 305/8, reel B-237, 272–5, 285–8.
17 On Begbie see Williams, '*Man for a New Country*'; regarding his appointment as puisne judge, see 14, 16–19, 28–33.
18 Court of British Columbia. Order of Court, 24 December 1858; proclamation dated 8 June 1859.
19 Proclamation to make provision for the Speedy Trial of Persons charged with Criminal Offences, 23 April 1860; An Ordinance to amend the Law relating to Bankruptcy and Insolvency in British Columbia, 10 April 1865.
20 In the wake of Ned McGowan's War, Begbie told Douglas, 'From what has come before me I feel bound to state to your Excellency that I have no confidence that anywhere else in British Columbia higher up the Fraser the office of justice of the peace

is efficiently represented.' He then went on to make some specific recommendations: 'alterations ... chiefly in consequence of the late occurrences.' See Begbie to Douglas, Victoria, Vancouver Island, 3 February 1859. BCARS, GR 1372, reel B-1307, f. 142a/11.
21 Begbie to Douglas, 18 May 1859. BCARS, GR 1372, reel B-1307, f. 142b/7.
22 The exception Andrew Charles Elliott. See Ormsby, 'Some Irish Figures.'
23 Begbie to Douglas, 18 May 1859. BCARS, GR 1372, reel B-1307, f. 142b/7.
24 *Halsbury's Laws of England*, 2d ed. (London, 1936), v. 21, 538.
25 See Ormsby, 'Some Irish Figures.'
26 Bedford to Douglas, n.d., BCARS, GR 1372, reel B-1307, f. 141/9.
27 When British Columbia's Legislative Council was created in 1864, five of its fifteen seats were reserved for the colony's magistrates. See James E. Hendrickson, 'The Constitutional Development of Colonial Vancouver Island and British Columbia,' in Ward and McDonald, eds., *British Columbia*, 265.
28 Young to O'Reilly, Government House, Victoria, Vancouver Island, 20 April 1859. O'Reilly Family Papers. BCARS, add. MSS 412, v. 1, file 2.
29 Hicks to Cary, Fort Yale, 29 August 1859. BCARS, GR 1372, reel B-1333, f. 767/28.
30 C. Brew to the Colonial Secretary, Cariboo, 22 September 1868. British Columbia, Government Agency, Cariboo, 1860–1914. Correspondence Outward, Letterbook (Richfield), 11 January 1866–18 August 1870. BCARS, GR 216, v. 11, n.p.
31 Ball to ? BCARS, GR 1372, reel B-1305, f. 96/26.
32 Ball to the Colonial Secretary, Quesnelmouth, 31 May 1865. BCARS, GR 216, v. 10, 107.
33 See Trevor to Ball, Quesnel, 27 May, 1 December 1870. BCARS, GR 216, v. 1, box 1, files 3 and 7.
34 Seymour to Cardwell, New Westminster, 31 January 1865. NAC, MG 11, CO 60/21, reel B-92, 20; and Nind to the Colonial Secretary, Lytton, 25 November 1865, BCARS, GR 1372, reel B-1351, f. 1259/50.
35 Begbie to Douglas, Fort Yale, 13 March 1859. Colonial Correspondence.BCARS, GR 1372, reel B-1307, f. 142a/22.
36 'Nisi prius': civil actions under the jurisdiction of the Supreme Court had to be tried at New Westminster, where the superior court was based, unless the judges of assize had come into the district on circuit before to hear such cases. In short, nisi prius cases were civil actions heard at the assizes. See Hamar Foster, 'The Kamloops Outlaws and Commissions of Assize in Nineteenth Century British Columbia,' in Flaherty, ed., *History of Canadian Law*, v. 2, 316–17.
37 Begbie to Young, New Westminster, 6 April 1867. BCARS, GR 1372, reel B-1308, f. 142g/14.
38 Begbie to Douglas, Victoria, Vancouver Island, 7 November 1859. BCARS, GR 1372, reel B-1308, f. 142b1/17b.

39 Petition addressed to James Douglas, dated 24 August 1859. BCARS, GR 1372, reel B-1354, f. 1343.
40 Douglas to Lytton, Victoria, Vancouver's Island, 22 December 1859. NAC, MG 11, CO 60/5, reel B-81, 270.
41 Cary to Douglas, Attorney General's Office, Victoria, 9 December 1859. NAC, MG 11, CO 60/5, reel B-81, 274.
42 'Recovery of Debts,' *Cariboo Sentinel*, 19 August 1865.
43 'Justice v. Good Nature,' *Cariboo Sentinel* [supplement], 19 August 1865.
44 See the following petitions for county courts in the Colonial Correspondence, BCARS, GR 1372: petition addressed to James Douglas, Yale, 30 December 1861, reel B-1354, f. 1348; petition to the Colonial Secretary, Quesnelle, 28 March 1864, reel B-1354, f. 1348; petition, n.d., from Fort Hope, reel B-1355, f. 1358; Nind to the Colonial Secretary, Alexandria District, Williams Lake, 17 October 1860, box 149, f. 1254/5; Nind to the Acting Colonial Secretary, Williams Lake, Alexandria District, 9 November 1860, box 149, f. 1255/1; and Nind to the Colonial Secretary, Douglas, 17 March 1864, reel B-1351, f. 1257/9.
45 Begbie to Seymour, New Westminster, 31 January 1865. BCARS, GR 1372, reel B-1308, f. 142f/17.
46 An Ordinance amending the procedure of the County Courts of the Colony of British Columbia, 5 April 1866; and An Ordinance to define the jurisdiction of the County Courts under the 'Small Debts Act, 1859,' 5 April 1866.
47 Crease was uncomfortable with placing greater power in the hands of the colonial County Court judges because they were men untrained in the law. See Crease to Birch, Attorney-General's Office, New Westminster, 18 June 1866, NAC, MG 11, CO 60/24, reel B-94, 326; Extract from the Presentment made by the Grand Jury at Yale, 4 May 1866, enclosed in Birch to Cardwell, 21 June 1866, ibid., 328.
48 The Gold Fields Act, 1859 [31 August 1859]; Trimble, *Mining Advance*, 187–214, 336–7.
49 On miners' meetings in general, see Shinn, *Mining Camps*; for the short-lived practice in British Columbia and the operation of the Gold Commissioners' Courts see David Williams, 'The Administration of Civil and Criminal Justice in the Mining Camps and Frontier Communities of British Columbia,' in Knafla, ed., *Law and Justice*.
50 Rules and Regulations for the Working of Gold Mines under the 'Gold Fields Act, 1859' [7 September 1859]; Rules and Regulations for the working of Gold Mines, issued in conformity with the 'Gold Fields Act, 1859' (Bench Diggings) [6 January 1860]; Rules and Regulations under the 'Gold Fields Act, 1859' (Ditches) [29 September 1862]; Further Rules and Regulations under the 'Gold Fields Act, 1859' [24 February 1863]; Proclamation amending the 'Gold Fields Act, 1859' [25 March

1863]; The Mining District Act, 1863 [27 May 1863]; The Mining Drains Act, 1864 [1 February 1864]; An Ordinance to extend and improve the Laws relating to Gold Mining [26 February 1864]; and An Ordinance to amend and consolidate the Gold Mining Laws [28 March 1865].
51 An Ordinance to amend the Laws relating to Gold Mining, 2 April 1867.
52 'Election of a Mining Board,' *Cariboo Sentinel*, 6 August 1866.
53 Seymour to Needham, Government House, New Westminster, 13 November 1866. NAC, MG 11, CO 60/27, reel B-96, 150-151; Memorandum for the Right Honourable the Earl of Carnarvon, one of Her Majesty's Principal Secretaries of State, respecting the Chief Justiceship in the Supreme Court of British Columbia. Submitted by Matthew Baillie Begbie, judge in this Court, New Westminster, 18 December 1866, in Lamb, 'Memoirs and Documents'; and Crease to Seymour, New Westminster, 24 June 1867, CO 60/28, reel B-97, 234-43.
54 Memorandum for the Right Honourable the Earl of Carnarvon, one of Her Majesty's Principal Secretaries of State, respecting the Chief Justiceship in the Supreme Court of British Columbia. Submitted by Matthew Baillie Begbie, judge in this Court, New Westminster, 18 December 1866, in Lamb, 'Memoirs and Documents.'
55 However, in 1867 Needham apparently changed his mind, ruling that union had indeed merged the courts. See Williams, '*Man for a New Country*,' 159.
56 Carnarvon to Seymour, Downing Street, 14 March 1867. NAC, MG 11, CO 60/27, reel B-96, 127-8.
57 Ibid.
58 An Ordinance respecting the Supreme Courts of Justice of British Columbia, 1 May 1868.
59 In fact, the situation was a source of embarrassment to British Columbians. Seymour's replacement, Anthony Musgrave, told the colonial secretary that William Seward, the American secretary of state, made British Columbia's Supreme Courts 'the subject of pointed jest, not intended to operate to the praise of British institutions.' NAC, MG 11, CO 60/36, reel B-104, 562-3.
60 See 'Nicholson's Petition,' [Victoria, 18 December 1868] in British Columbia, Attorney-General, Drafts of Bills, Ordinances, some opinions. BCARS, GR 673, box 2; Seymour to Buckingham and Chandos, New Westminster, 29 April 1868, contains papers connected with Nicholson's petition: NAC, MG 11, CO 60/32, reel B-99, 231-85.
61 Report of the Committee struck to study the jurisdictional problems brought up by Nicholson's Petition, dated 23 February 1869. BCARS, GR 673, box 2.
62 There were 155 in all. Musgrave to Granville, Government House, 22 December 1869. NAC, MG 11, CO 60/36, reel B-104, 540-1.
63 Petition from 155 merchants, n.d., enclosed ibid., 555-7.

64 Petition from the colony's lawyers, n.d., enclosed ibid., 558–9.
65 Musgrave to Granville, Government House, 22 December 1869. NAC, MG 11, CO 60/36, reel B-104, 542.
66 Taylor, *Laissez-Faire*.
67 Giddens, *Contemporary Critique*, 38
68 This is what Giddens calls 'time-space distanciation.' See *Contemporary Critique*, 65–6. On this and related themes see Donald Meinig, 'Geographical Analysis of Imperial Expansion,' in Baker, ed., *Period and Place*; Steele, *English Atlantic*, and Wolch and Dear, eds., *Power of Geography*. As people avail themselves of these common, state-defined and -mediated practices, they become self-regulating; and, as Foucault has argued, it is the creation of a self-regulating population rather than one that is regulated through direct coercion that is the key to modern governance. See Burchell, Gordon, and Miller, eds., *The Foucault Effect*.
69 On this idea see White, *Heracles' Bow*.
70 Crease to Blake, Victoria, Supreme Court, 27 November 1877, Crease Legal Papers. BCARS, add. MSS 54, v. 12/65, 8288–94.
71 The purpose of Begbie's first circuit in the spring of 1859 was to dispose of the colony's legal business and to map and gather information about the state of the interior. Though subsequent circuits lost their cartographical aspect, Begbie and his fellow magistrates continued to be important sources of non-legal information, reporting on the state of the colony (particularly its economy) in their letters to the colonial secretary. See Williams, '*Man for a New Country*,' 48–54.
72 Smith, 'Journal of Arthur Thomas Bushby,' 144.
73 Mills, *Early Court Houses*, v. 1, 8. The horse reference is from Williams, '*Man for a New Country*,' 58.
74 See MacRae and Adamson, *Cornerstones of Order*, and Isaac, *Transformation of Virginia*, 88–94. The latter discusses how a society's material culture, and particularly its architecture, reflects its social organization and political values.
75 *British Colonist*, 10 July 1863.
76 *British Columbian*, 6 May 1865, cited in Mills, *Early Court Houses*, 10. Despite its condition, New Westminster's courthouse remained in use throughout the colonial period; its poor state of repair was a constant point of comment for those forced to occupy it. 'Very great inconvenience is incurred by all parties being jumbled together in a small low room, with a canvas ceiling, in an old wooden building, without ventilation or means of warming it,' the grand jury complained to Puisne Judge Henry Crease in 1870. 'We cite as an instance the fact of a juryman, during a late trial, fainting, and also it being well known that officers of the Court have been frequently obliged to leave, owing to the extreme closeness of the room.' *Mainland Guardian*, 31 August 1870, cited in Chambers, *Court House of New Westminster*, 14.
77 'Scope' and 'intensity' of power from Giddens, *Nation-State*, 10. Here I am referring

to the courts. Other state agents and institutions, like the police, were thin on the ground.
78 Pearkes to Douglas, Victoria, 27 October 1858. NAC, MG 11, CO 60/1, reel B-77, 281-4.
79 The Justices' Act, 1859, Colonial Correspondence. BCARS, GR 1372, reel B-1307, f. 142a/12a. This must have been the piece of legislation Begbie suggested to Douglas in a letter dated 3 February 1859 (ibid., f. 142a/11). He made six suggestions (below) regarding the jurisdiction and powers of JPs in the letter, which he 'proposed to reduce into the form of a proclamation having the force of law.' I have found no evidence that this piece of legislation was ever proclaimed, but its provisions appear to have been adhered to and retrospective acknowledgment of them given in An Ordinance respecting Stipendiary Magistrates, 10 March 1869. Begbie's six suggestions were as follows: '1. the abolition of all districts wch are at present wholly undefined and seem to promote confusion and jealousies [a reference to the Perrier-Whannell feud]. 2. Empowering a single Justice to do all acts for wch by the English law two justices are required. 3. Augmenting the peculiar penalties: the English fines of 5/ and 40/ are quite inadequate in the "ounce diggings" districts. 4. Regulating the fees to be taken. At present I am not aware of any authorized table of fees. Very different amounts are demanded at different places and in some, the fees seem perfectly exorbitant. 5. Throwing the excise and customs duties proceedings into the summary jurisdiction of the justices. 6. Generally codifying & clarifying offences. This draft I have in a great measure prepared.'
80 *Halsbury's Laws of England*, v. 8, 528.
81 See Coleman, *Debtors and Creditors*, 4-5.
82 Elliott to Young, Yale, BC, 25 February 1860. BCARS, GR 1372, reel B-1327, f. 513/2.
83 Begbie to Douglas, New Westminster, 22 December 1862. Ibid., reel B-1308, f. 142e/12.
84 An Ordinance to amend the Law relating to Bankruptcy and Insolvency in British Columbia, 10 April 1865.
85 Proclamation allowing for the Speedy Trial of Prisoners charged with Criminal Offences, 23 April 1860.
86 Begbie to Douglas, 28 May 1862. BCARS, GR 1372, reel B-1308, f. 142e/6.
87 The Speedy Trials Act was disallowed in 1862. On this issue and the question of commissions of assize in British Columbia, see Foster, 'Kamloops Outlaws,' 318-19.
88 Proclamation to obviate the difficulty in procuring a sufficient number of British Subjects to sit on Grand and Petit Juries, 8 March 1860.
89 *Halsbury's Laws of England* (1907), v. 18, 603-10.
90 *British Colonist*, 25 November 1861.
91 *British Columbian*, 17 March 1863.

188 Notes to pages 71–6

92 Proclamation to enable the High Sheriff to act as a Justice of the Peace and in other respects alter the law relating to Sheriffs, 8 March 1860.
93 *Halsbury's Laws of England* (1907), v. 25, 'Sheriffs and Bailiffs,', part III, 804–7.
94 The term is associated with the work of American legal historian J. Willard Hurst. See his *Law and the Conditions of Freedom.* On using Hurst's approach in the Canadian context, see David H. Flaherty, 'Writing Canadian Legal History,' and R.C.B. Risk, 'The Law and the Economy in Mid-Nineteenth Century Ontario,' in Flaherty, ed., *History of Canadian Law*, v. 1.

CHAPTER 4 'A California Phase'

1 Robert Harkness to Sabrina Harkness, Richfield, BC, 10 June 1863, Harkness Letters. BCARS, TS.
2 Thomas McMicking's recollections describe the overland journey to British Columbia and mention Robert Harkness. See Leduc, ed., *Overland from Canada to British Columbia.*
3 'A Returned Digger,' *Cariboo. The Newly Discovered Gold Fields of British Columbia* (London, 1862), 9.
4 Biographical information on Harkness from Mary Dell Harkness Race to Isabel Kathleen Race Eddy, c. 1952, in Harkness Letters. BCARS, TS.
5 This theme is explored for another British Columbia mining community established a generation or so later in a different part of the province. See Harris, 'Industry and the Good Life.'
6 Mann, *Neighbors and Strangers.*
7 On the 'flatness' of modern society, see Taylor, *Malaise of Modernity.*
8 Douglas to Lytton, Victoria, Vancouver's Island, 18 October 1859. Great Britain, British Columbia Original Correspondence. NAC, MG 11, CO 60/5, reel B-81, 184.
9 Ibid. On land settlement policy in British Columbia, see Mikkelsen, 'Land Settlement Policy' and Cail, *Land, Man and the Law*, chapter 1. Only 1696 pre-emption claims were made by 1868 (ten years after the creation of the colony), and not more than 6,000 acres were under cultivation. In the New Westminster district (the oldest area of settlement) only 27,797 acres of land were purchased by 1868, and of this fewer than 250 acres were under cultivation. See Mikkelsen, 2, 163.
10 The small debts courts were created in 1859 to deal with the many suits for debt generated during the Fraser River gold rush. The courts sat in the principal settlements along the river and had colony-wide jurisdiction to hear cases involving sums of less than fifty pounds. A stipendiary magistrate, who was also the assistant gold commissioner, sat in judgment over the cases. The mining, or gold commissioner's, courts were also created in 1859 and sat in the primary mining settlements. They had jurisdiction to hear all mining or mining-related cases and to determine them summarily.

The assistant gold commissioner also issued mining licences and collected the associated fees.
11 McCalla, *Upper Canada Trade*, and Wynn, *Timber Colony*, especially chapter 5.
12 Sanders to Young, Yale, 11 May 1860. British Columbia, Colonial Correspondence. BCARS, GR 1372, reel B-1362, f. 1554.
13 Sanders to Young, Yale, 8 August 1860. Ibid.
14 W.G. Cox to the Colonial Secretary, New Westminster, 18 January 1867, enclosed in Seymour to Carnarvon, New Westminster, 18 March 1867. Great Britain, Colonial Office, British Columbia Original Correspondence. NAC, MG 11, CO 60/27, reel B-97, 414.
15 Brew to the Colonial Secretary, New Westminster, 21 January 1867, enclosed in Seymour to Carnarvon, New Westminster, 18 March 1867. Ibid., 401–2.
16 The Richfield County Court is the only one for which data for civil and criminal cases are strictly comparable. Because civil cases from this County Court comprise almost half (45.8 per cent) of the cases in the period from 1858 to 1871, I have assumed that it is 'typical.'
17 The information on pretrial procedure is taken from *Halsbury's Laws of England*, Hailsham edition (London, 1907), v. 8, 'County Courts.'
18 Sylvia Van Kirk, 'A Vital Presence: Women in the Cariboo Gold Rush, 1862–1875,' in Creese and Strong-Boag, eds., *British Columbia Reconsidered*.
19 Ledger, 1862. BCARS, add. MSS 2622, 232–4 and 262–3.
20 B.C. Blue Books of Statistics. NAC, MG 11, CO 64/6, reel B-199, 135.
21 'A Returned Digger,' *Cariboo*, 51.
22 Ormsby, *British Columbia*, 209.
23 Robert Harkness to Sabrina Harkness, 10 June 1863. Harkness Papers. BCARS, TS.
24 Miners were not the only people who appeared before the courts, however. More than half (53.6 per cent) of Richfield's County Court plaintiffs, who were probably miners, appeared only once. However, these 'one shot players,' to use Marc Galanter's terminology, accounted for only 18.4 per cent of the County Court cases launched in Richfield. 'Repeat players' (those appearing more than once) are responsible for the remaining four-fifths. Of the cases involving these repeat players, over one-quarter (25.4 per cent, or 20.7 per cent of the total) were initiated by ten individuals, or just 2.1 per cent of the plaintiffs; and almost half (45.5 per cent, or 37.1 per cent of all cases) were initiated by just 30 (5.9 per cent) people. These 30 individuals might be considered Richfield's 'litigious class.' Of these, 19 (63.3 per cent) were merchants and 4 (13.3 per cent) were saloonkeepers. (There was one auctioneer, one expressman [stagecoach] and four plaintiffs of unknown occupation.) The predominance of merchants is not surprising, and conforms to contemporary opinions about the extension of credit on the resource frontier. On 'repeat players,' see Galanter, 'Why the "Haves" Come Out Ahead.' The number of

190   Notes to page 80

appearances by Richfield plaintiffs between 1862 and 1870 breaks down as follows:

Appearances	Number of plaintiffs	Percentage of plaintiffs	Number of cases	Percentage of cases
1	254	53.2	254	18.4
2	93	19.5	186	13.4
3	35	7.3	105	7.6
4	23	4.8	92	6.6
5	20	4.2	100	7.2
6	14	2.9	84	6.1
7	7	1.5	49	3.5
8	7	1.5	56	4.0
9	2	0.4	18	1.3
10	1	0.2	10	0.7
11–15	5	1.0	73	5.3
16–20	6	1.3	70	5.1
21+	10	2.1	287	20.7
Total	447	100.0	1384	100.0

Source: see Note on Sources.

25 Richfield defendants comprised a larger pool of the general population (777 versus 477 people). As with the plaintiffs, however, 'one-shot' defendants made up over two-thirds of all defendants but accounted for only 37.8 per cent of all cases. Sixteen per cent of the actions involving repeat defendants are accounted for by only 12 (1.6 per cent) individuals. This 'debtor class' consisted of a surprising mix of people. Instead of miners, Richfield's most frequent debtors were doctors, lawyers, saloon-keepers, boarding-house operators, merchants, and carpenters. These people were even less mobile than the miners because of the nature of their occupations. The gold rush had brought them to the colony's interior, but when the gold claims were played out they were left with ledgers full of credit notes and debts of their own. The number of appearances by Richfield defendants breaks down as follows:

Appearances	Number of defendants	Percentage of defendants	Number of cases	Percentage of cases
1	523	67.3	523	37.8
2	125	16.1	250	18.1
3	58	7.5	174	12.6
4	21	2.7	84	6.1
5	20	2.6	100	7.2

Appearances	Number of defendants	Percentage of defendants	Number of cases	Percentage of cases
6	11	1.4	66	4.8
7	7	0.9	49	3.5
8	2	0.3	6	1.2
9	3	0.4	27	1.9
10	3	0.4	30	2.2
11+	4	0.5	65	4.7
Total	777	100.0	1,384	100.0

Source: see Note on Sources.

26 James Anderson [a.k.a. Sawney], 'The Poor but Honest Miner,' *Sawney's Letters and Cariboo Rhymes*.
27 Claudet, *'Gold,'* 12–18, and Ormsby, *British Columbia*, 183, 212.
28 Robert to Sabrina, 31 May 1864. Harkness Papers. BCARS, TS.
29 Robert to Sabrina, Richfield, 10 June 1863. Harkness Papers. Ibid.
30 Robert to Sabrina, 31 May 1864. Harkness Letters. Ibid.
31 Robert to Sabrina, Williams Creek, 28 June 1864. Ibid.
32 As was noted in the Colonial Office's Blue Books of Statistics, prices 'increase as you proceed into the Interior, and at the Mines Flour, Sugar, Tea, Coffee, Wines are as much as 2 to 5 times the ... figures [for New Westminster.' British Columbia Blue Books of Statistics. NAC, MG 11, CO 64/6, reel B-199, 135.
33 British Columbia Blue Books of Statistics, 'Average Prices of Various Produce and Merchandise, &c [including wages].' Ibid., CO 64/1-11, reels B-199 and B-200.
34 Ibid.; for 1864, CO 64/5, reel B-199, 105; for 1867–70, CO 64/8, 118, CO 64/9, 115, CO 64/10, 120, and CO 64/11, 117, all on reel B-200.
35 James Douglas, 24 May 1858, 'Diary of Gold Discovery on Fraser's River in 1858.' Private Papers of Sir James Douglas, First Series, H.H. Bancroft Collection. NAC, MG 29, C15, v. 2, c-12, 66.
36 Begbie to Douglas, New Westminster, 30 November 1861. Enclosed in Douglas to Newcastle, Victoria, Vancouver's Island, 5 February 1862. Ibid., CO 60/13, reel B-86, 78–79.
37 Bescoby, 'Aspects of Society in the Cariboo,' 58. For the cost of provisions, see the British Columbia Blue Books of Statistics, 'Average Prices of various Produce and Merchandise, &c.' NAC, MG 11, CO 64/1, 113, CO 64/2, 113, CO 64/3, 161, CO 64/4, 97, CO 64/5, 107, and CO 64/6, 135, all on reel B-199; CO 64/7, 112, CO 64/8, 120, CO 64/9, 117, CO 64/10, 122, and CO 64/11, 119, all on reel B-200.
38 On the criminal side of the law, difficulties in enforcement were a constant source of worry to Begbie and his fellow magistrates. These difficulties were different from those encountered in enforcing civil law, however, and included problems of detec-

tion and prosecution (securing witnesses, for instance). However, as with the civil law, few persons other than legal officials voiced complaints.
39 'A Voice from the Dungeon!' *British Columbian*, 3 December 1862.
40 'The Late Judicial Murder.' *British Columbian*, 26 November 1862; 'The Inquest.' ibid., 22 November 1862; 'A History of the Wrongs of the Cranfords ...' ibid., 7 January 1863; and ibid., 14 February 1863.
41 An Ordinance respecting Arrest and Imprisonment for Debt, 11 April 1863 [Imprisonment Exemption Ordinance, 1865]. G.R. Rubin argues that despite statutory amendments abolishing imprisonment for debt, it continued in Britain in the nineteenth century. See Rubin, 'Law, Poverty and Imprisonment for Debt, 1869–1914,' in Rubin and Sugarman, eds., *Law, Economy, and Society*, 241–9.
42 Legal anthropologists proceed from the assumption that law should be defined by function rather than form, and hence that the absence of the familiar formal institutions of dispute settlement associated with centralized states in small-scale, pre-modern or pre-industrial societies does not mean that those societies lack law. All societies have culturally based forms of dispute resolution, and to interpret the absence of western-style legal institutions as indicating the absence of law is ethnocentric. For an introduction, see Roberts, *Order and Dispute*. On formal law as a cultural convention, see John Phillip Reid's book on the Overland Trail pioneers, *Law for the Elephant*.
43 The 'litigation-as-social-breakdown' theme has been developed in the literature dealing with the pre-modern settler societies of New England. See Mann, *Neighbors and Strangers*, introduction; Konig, *Law and Society*; Lockridge, *A New England Town*, 145, 159; and Nelson, *Dispute and Conflict Resolution*. New Zealand, a British colony settled at about the same time as British Columbia, is perhaps a better point of comparison. There, according to Miles Fairburn, the high levels of civil litigation that characterized the colony were symptomatic of 'the inadequacy of the "middle range" or informal social mechanisms of control,' and hence evidence of the lack of community. See Fairburn, *Ideal Society*, 327.
44 Indeed, some sociologists have argued that, ironically, social conflict has an 'integrative' function. See Coser, *Function of Social Conflict*, 72–85.
45 As Douglas's successor, Frederick Seymour noted, 'Where on the Fraser 12,000 or 13,000 white men washed up Gold, a solitary Chinaman working his "rocker" represents the population for the mile of river.' 'Hope is "played out." Lytton languishes. Princeton contains one occupied house ... My great grievance with the colony is this determination of people to leave it. Let them set themselves in opposition to the Government. That is fair in an unprospering colony. But the opposition shewn by selling off furniture and nailing up doors and windows and leaving the Colony is one, I confess, to which I cannot be indifferent.' Seymour to Buckingham and Chandos, New Westminster, 17 March 1868. NAC, MG 11, CO 60/32, reel B-99, 111, 119–20.

The Colonial Office called the letter 'a protracted groan' that 'requires no answer.'
46 Some sociologists have drawn this distinction by calling the former (that is, societies in which people have a variety of ties with a limited number of people) 'multiplex' and the latter (societies in which people have limited kinds of ties with a number of different people) 'simplex.' See Kidder, *Connecting Law and Society*, 70–3.
47 W.A. Baillie-Grohmann. *Fifteen Years' Sport and Life in Western America and British Columbia* (London, 1900), 316; cited in Roy, ed., *History of British Columbia*, 3.
48 John Dickinson, writing on New France, noted that 'les litiges civils constituent 90 à 95 pour 100 de l'activité globale des officiers de justice ... A l'encontre de la criminalité qui met en évidence les aberrations, donc les comportments, l'une minorité, la justice civile s'attache un normatif et aux transactions de la vie quotidienne qui touchent l'ensemble d'une population.' Dickinson reported that cases for debt comprised the largest proportion (20 to 30 per cent) of all civil suits. See Dickinson, *Justice et justiciables*, 3, 123. Evelyn Kolish looked at the civil courts in Lower Canada and found that actions to recover debts accounted for 80 to 90 per cent of all civil litigation from 1785 to 1840. See Kolish, 'Some Aspects of Civil Litigation,' 351. Clinton Francis's study of the English common law courts from 1740 to 1840 revealed that debt collection accounted for 90 per cent of actions. See Francis 'Practice, Strategy and Institution,' 810. John Wunder's monograph on law in Washington Territory noted that actions for debt made up almost 93 per cent of all civil cases that came before the lower courts. See Wunder, *Inferior Courts*, 149.

CHAPTER 5 Cranford v. Wright

1 Nind to the Acting Colonial Secretary, Alexandria District, Williams Lake, 27 April 1861. British Columbia. Government Agency. Cariboo, 1860–1914. BCARS, GR 216, Correspondence Outward, Letterbook (Alexandria), 17 October 1860–21 January 1863, v. 9, 84–5.
2 Begbie to Douglas, 18 May 1859. BCARS, GR 1372, reel B-1307, f. 142b/7.
3 There is some debate as to whether a distinction should be made between legitimate and illegitimate authority. Authority, because it rests on consent, is inherently legitimate. Put another way, illegitimate authority, according to this line of argument, is not authority at all. On this, see Green, *Authority of the State*, 59–62, and Wrong, *Power*, chapter 3, especially 49–52. I will maintain (and have maintained) the distinction between legitimate and illegitimate authority, because it is often the case that those who occupy positions of power can claim authority and indeed be possessed of the institutions and resources necessary to produce intended effects, but cannot command the consent of those over whom they rule. Such was the case on Vancouver Island under the HBC's proprietorship. In short, there can be a disjuncture between

the *claim* and assertion of authority and its *recognition*; and it is the latter that makes authority legitimate.
4 'Cranford vs. Wright,' *British Columbian*, 13 December 1862, and 'Cranford vs. Wright,' *British Colonist*, 24 December 1862.
5 Value of suit taken from the *British Colonist*, 23 December 1862.
6 'A History of the Wrongs of the Cranfords, Including an Account of the Two Celebrated Suits, – Wright vs Cranford and Cranford vs Wright,' part 1 *British Columbian*, 27 December 1862.
7 'A History of the Wrongs of the Cranfords,' part 2, ibid., 31 December 1862.
8 'A History of the Wrongs of the Cranfords,' part 3, ibid., 7 January 1863.
9 'A History of the Wrongs of the Cranfords,' part 2, ibid., 31 December 1862.
10 Ibid. The *British Columbian* reproduced the contract as follows: 'The following is the agreement as it was when first written.

April 25
Agreed with R. Cranford, Jr.,
to carry goods for him from Douglas
to Lillooet at nine cents per pound, to
wait sixty days after delivery at Lillooet for pay.
If freight falls, to come down in price.

'Recollecting this most positively they gladly accepted Mr. Wright's proposition that his memorandum of agreement should be shown; what was their astonishment to find it garbled as follows:

April 25
Agreed with R. Cranford, Jr., &
Brother to carry goods for them from Douglas
to Lillooet at nine cents per pound, to
wait sixty days after delivery at Lillooet for pay.
If freight falls, to come down in price.'

11 'Cranford vs Wright.' *British Columbian*, 10 December 1862.
12 *Taylor on Evidence* was the work of John Pitt Taylor (1811–88); the full title was *A Treatise on the Law of Evidence as Administered in England and Ireland: with illustrations from America and other foreign laws* (London, 1855).
13 'Cranford vs Wright,' *British Colonist*, 25 December 1862.
14 Ibid., 31 December 1862.
15 Ibid.
16 Ibid.
17 'Cranford vs Wright,' letter to the editor from eight of the jurors, *British Columbian*, 21 January 1863.

18 *Linaker v. Ballou.*
19 'The Assizes,' *British Columbian*, 20 December 1862.
20 'Cranford vs. Wright,' *British Colonist*, 1 January 1863.
21 *British Columbian*, 4 April 1863; *British Colonist*, 15 April 1863.
22 'A Complimentary Address,' *British Columbian*, 20 December 1862.
23 Great Britain. Colonial Office, British Columbia Blue Books. NAC, MG 11, CO 64/3, reel B-199, 4. In 1862–3 the colony's population was 7,738, with 5,525 in the Cariboo.
24 As will become apparent, John Robson, the editor of the *British Columbian* and a future premier of the province, took a special interest in the case. Robson emigrated from Canada West in 1859 as a gold-seeker. Almost from his arrival he took an interest in colonial politics, aligning himself with other 'reformers' who took issue with the lack of representative institutions in the colony and its absentee governor. After serving as the editor of the *New Westminster Times* for a year, Robson founded the *British Columbian* in 1861 as an organ dedicated to 'a resident governor, responsible government and representative institutions.' Some of his reform sentiments were aimed directly at the colony's legal administration. In giving them voice he quickly ran afoul of British Columbia's Supreme Court judge. The first broadside in what was to be a long and vitriolic exchange was fired in November 1862, when Robson wrote an editorial charging the colony's law officers with speculation in gold claims. He followed these allegations by printing an anonymous letter which further charged that Matthew Begbie had accepted twenty acres in the Cottonwood district near Quesnel in exchange for issuing a certificate of improvement on a parcel of land owned by one Dud Moreland. Begbie charged Robson with contempt of court for printing the letter and precipitating what became known as the 'Cottonwood Scandal.' *R. v. John Robson* came before the New Westminster assizes in December 1862, in the same session that featured the Cranford case. The coincidence of the two cases and his anti-government stance explain Robson's readiness to allow his newspaper to be used as a platform for the Cranfords' grievances. See Antak, 'John Robson, especially chapter 1; Pettit, 'Matthew Baillie Begbie,' chapter 4; and Williams, '*The Man for a New Country*,' 190–1.
25 'A History of the Wrongs of the Cranfords,' parts 1, 2, and 3, *British Columbian* 27 and 31 December 1862, 7 January 1863.
26 Atiyah, *Rise and Fall of Freedom of Contract.*
27 Atiyah, *Law of Contract*, 9.
28 'Cranford vs Wright,' *British Columbian*, 10 December 1862.
29 'A History of the Wrongs of the Cranfords,' part 3, *British Columbian*, 7 January 1863.
30 This interpretation of agency is taken from Treitel, *Law of Contract*, chapter 17. Also see *Halsbury's Laws of England*, 2d ed., v. 1 (London, 1931), 202ff.

31 This is what some scholars have labelled liberalism's notion of the 'pre-social' individual. See Jaggar, *Feminist Politics*, 40–7.
32 For a brief overview of changing attitudes towards debt and debtor–creditor legislation, see Zainaldin, *Law in Antebellum Society*, 39–41. For a more thorough treatment see Coleman, *Debtors and Creditors in America*.
33 For a piece that argues for the persistence of attitudes towards indebtedness in this so-called age of reform, see G.R. Rubin, 'Law, Poverty and Imprisonment for Debt, 1869–1914,' in Rubin and Sugarman, eds., *Law, Economy and Society*, 241–99.
34 Cited in Zainaldin, *Law in Antebellum Society*, 41.
35 James Willard Hurst. *Law and the Conditions of Freedom*, 26–7, cited in Zainaldin, *Law in Antebellum Society*, 41.
36 Beattie, *Crime and the Courts in England*, and generally chapter 7.
37 British Columbia, Supreme Court, Notes on Proceedings, 1 December 1862–16 April 1863, 23. BCARS, MS.
38 *Cariboo Sentinel*, 26 July 1865.
39 'Sawmill Company v. Ericson Company,' ibid., 12 August 1865.
40 'Grouse Creek Bed Rock Flume Company v. Black Hawk Company,' ibid., 30 May 1867.
41 *Cariboo Sentinel*, 24 June 1865.
42 Ibid., 18 June 1865.
43 In criminal cases, jury deliberation was usually a brief affair. Rather than retire to a separate room, jurors 'huddled around their foreman,' taking only two or three minutes to come to a decision. In this brief interval the jurors could not possibly review the evidence and come to a common decision. The character of the accused must have weighed heavily in determining a verdict. 'Most often,' noted Beattie, 'the majority must simply have acquiesced in a verdict arrived at by one or two dominant figures on the jury.' See Beattie, *Crime and the Courts in England*, 397. Such a process, however, may not have been not common to British Columbia's civil trial juries.
44 Ibid.
45 Letter from 'One of the Jurors,' 10 January 1863; Letter from Robert McCleese and 3 Others, 17 January 1863; Letter from William Grieve and 7 Others, 21 January 1863; and Letter from William Grieve, 21 January 1863.
46 Letter from William Grieve and 7 Others, *British Columbian*, 21 January 1863.
47 Letter from 'One of the Jurors,' *British Columbian*, 10 January 1863.
48 Ibid.
49 Emphasis added. 'Cranford v. Wright,' *British Colonist*, 31 December 1862.
50 Landsman, *Adversary System*.
51 Beattie, 'Scales of Justice.'
52 Ibid., and Beattie, *Crime and the Courts*, chapter 7; Landsman, 'Contentious Spirit';

and Langbein, 'Criminal Trial.' All of these works are on criminal trials. In those trials, defence counsel did not appear until the 1780s, and full right to counsel was not granted until 1832. Civil trials, however, had long featured lawyers (which makes Begbie's objection curious). On that, see Baker, *Introduction to English Legal History*, chapter 10. In British Columbia, only those lawyers who were trained in Great Britain were allowed to plead in the colony's courts. This was not changed until 1863, with the passage of the 'Proclamation to regulate the admission of persons who shall be allowed or entitled to practice in the Superior Courts of the Colony ...,' 18 June 1863' (The Legal Professions Act, 1863). Under pressure from the American government, however, Douglas convinced Begbie to allow American lawyers to plead in British Columbia's courts as a temporary measure in 1858 because of the gold rush. See Reid, 'John Nugent,' 62–3.
53 Begbie to Douglas, Victoria, 15 August 1858. BCARSm GR 1372, reel B-1307, f. 142a/4.
54 'He who acts through another acts himself.' In short, the acts of an agent are the acts of the principal. Ring wanted to get the invoices made out to *Robert* Cranford entered as evidence because they showed that he and not J.P. was the principal, and J.P. was not his agent.
55 'Cranford vs Wright,' *British Colonist*, 29 December 1862.
56 'A History of the Wrongs of the Cranfords,' part 3, *British Columbian*, 7 January 1863.
57 'Cranford vs Wright,' *British Colonist*, 29 December 1862.
58 Beattie makes this point regarding the resistance to the introduction of defence counsel in criminal trials in the eighteenth century. See his 'Scales of Justice,' 231–2.
59 Goodrich, *Reading the Law*, 22, and chapter 2 generally. Also see Clanchy, *Memory to Written Record*; Clanchy discusses the transition from an oral to a written, or literate, mentality, and suggests some of its wider implications. Michel Foucault argued that writing opened up the possibilities for new regimes of control. Record-keeping, or the 'codification' of various aspects of peoples' lives, represented a new and more extensive form of surveillance that came to characterize modernity. See Foucault, *Discipline and Punish*.
60 Douglas Hay has written about the importance of the law's theatricality in accomplishing the same thing. See his 'Property, Authority and the Criminal Law,' in Hay et. al., eds., *Albion's Fatal Tree*.
61 For other examples of the collasping of the real and the symbolic, see Valverde, *Light, Soap, and Water*, chapter 2. The signified and signifier are the two components of a sign, the basic element of linguistic communication (such as words or letters) and non-linguistic communication (such as a picture or dress). The signifier is the concrete or material part of the sign (the word or thing), while the signified refers to its conceptual or symbolic aspect. Take, for instance, a rose: the signifier is

the actual flower, but that flower signifies, or stands for, the larger and abstract concept of love.
62 Goodrich, *Reading the Law*, 45.
63 McCreight frequently used *Burn's Justice of the Peace, Dicken's Quarter Sessions, Bailey on Convictions, Russell on Crime, Grimsby on Confessions* and *Maxwell on Statutes*. See Johnson, 'McCreight and the Law,' and 'McCreight and the Bench,' as well as the MA thesis from which they were drawn, 'John Foster McCreight.'
64 Remarks in *R. v. Stroebel* (1893), *Daily Columbian*, 18 November 1893. Cited in Johnson, 'John Foster McCreight,' 73.
65 As evidence of the nineteenth-century preference for regulation by mechanical means as a solution to a fundamental tension in liberal democratic states between order and freedom, which parallels McCreight's metaphor of law as a machine, I offer this example: During the nineteenth century the British were very concerned with figuring out how to police a liberal society – that is, a society committed to laissez-faire and individual freedom. Considerations of public safety aside, people had to be able to act as they chose and without interference. A perfect emblem of policing in this era and of the tension in liberalism between order and freedom was London's first traffic signal, designed by Sir Richard Mayne (of Metropolitan Police fame). Mayne was committed to non-interference and to the neutrality of the police – so much so that he could not bring himself to allow his constables to direct traffic: even that was too much intervention. Of course, traffic flows had to be controlled; the question was how to do so. Mayne's solution was a mechanical traffic signal. Whereas liberal sensibilities were not offended by a mechanical device that imposed order, they would have recoiled at the sight of a traffic policeman (an actual person) doing the same thing because that person, by the very nature of human nature, was not neutral – but a machine was. Technology allowed the state to regulate by masking its invasiveness behind its alleged neutrality, its efficiency, and its association with progressiveness. I owe this example to J.H. Winter.
66 Goodrich, *Reading the Law*, 85ff.
67 For an introduction to English legal literature, see Baker, *Introduction to English Legal History*, chapter 11.
68 Ibid., 87.
69 Baker argues that '[t]reatises were not accorded the same authority in English jurisprudence as decisions of the courts ... A remarkable feature of the history of English legal literature, however, is the paucity of works deserving to be called literature. With an handful of notable exceptions, law books until recent times were devised not as original contributions to jurisprudence but as ancillary aids to practice or keys to source material.' *Introduction to English Legal History*, 161.
70 See David Ricardo Williams, 'Matthew Baillie Begbie,' *Dictionary of Canadian Biography*, v. 12, 77.

71 *British Colonist*, 1 February 1862. The phrase was used in reference to the skills of John Foster McCreight, who attempted to get his client off by arguing that he had been improperly charged.
72 The anthropologist Claude Lévi-Strauss provides a good example of the possibility of divorcing form from content in the law. In discussing the discovery of writing among the Nambikwara, Lévi-Strauss noted that the tribal leader began imitating his (Lévi-Strauss's) note-taking, scribbling a series of lines on pads of paper. Having produced a number of these pieces of paper so inscribed, he began to read from them when adjudicating disputes among his people. Lévi-Strauss concludes that the tribal leader's actions demonstrated the possibility of understanding the form of authority without having a clue (or needing to have a clue) of its content. The chief recognized the real symbolic power of the written word in buttressing his authority. Cited in Goodrich, *Reading the Law*, 22–3. In the case of British Columbia, people understood the form of legal argumentation (reference to textual authority) and its power, but did not have to understand its content. Indeed, Peter Goodrich and Yifat Hachamovitch argue that because 'the language of English law is in many aspects a foreign dialect ... [and is] unlikely to be read outside the profession ... [t]he texts of law are ... likely to have a symbolic rather than an immediately semantic – that is linguistic – content.' In short, though most people are unfamiliar with the intricacies of meaning in the law, they still defer to it (and indeed, have a certain amount of reverence for it), thus proving that '[l]aw is in that sense nothing other than its image, its textuality and its rhetoric.' See Goodrich and Hachamovitch, 'Time out of Mind: An Introduction to the Semiotics of Common Law,' in Fitzpatrick, ed., *Dangerous Supplements*, 159–60.
73 On the textbook tradition in legal education, see David Sugarman, ' "A Hatred of Disorder": Legal Science, Liberalism and Imperialism,' in Fitzpatrick, ed., *Dangerous Supplements*. On legal argument, see White, *Legal Imagination*. Cranford demonstrated that British Columbians appreciated a legal argument based on 'technicalities' (to use Nind's term). Clearly, reference to written authority was an important component of legal rhetoric – of the lawyer's ability to persuade. On legal rhetoric, see Goodrich, *Reading the Law*, chapter 6, and White, *Heracles' Bow*.
74 The acceptance and utility of treatises and texts – of partially systematized and digested common law – that was born of frontier exigencies may go a small distance to explaining why Canada was the first common law jurisdiction to codify its laws. For a political history of codification, see Brown, *Criminal Code of 1892*. Also see Kasirer, 'Canada's Criminal Law Codificiation. David Sugarman has identified the period from 1850 to 1907 – and the 1880s as particularly crucial – as being central to this transition to textbook authority. See Sugarman, ' "A Hatred of Disorder." '
75 On 'black Letter' law and the textbook tradition, see Sugarman, ' "A Hatred of Disorder." '

200   Notes to pages 113-19

CHAPTER 6 The Meaning of Law and the Limits of Authority

1 'On Dit,' *Cariboo Sentinel*, 15 October 1866.
2 Petition to Governor Frederick Seymour, Williams Creek, 3 November 1866 Colonial Correspondence. BCARS, GR 1372, reel B-1355, f. 1352.
3 See the *Cariboo Sentinel*, 22 October, 15 November, and 15 December 1866. On Cox's subsequent fate, see Smith, 'Journal of Arthur Thomas Bushby,' 169–70.
4 Sophie Cox Correspondence. BCARS, GR 1372, reel B-1310, f. 373; and Seymour to Cardwell, New Westminster, 31 January 1865. Great Britain, Colonial Office, British Columbia Original Correspondence. NAC, MG 11, CO 60/21, reel B-92.
5 David Williams discusses them in *'Man for a New Country'* 68–80.
6 Ibid.
7 Letter from 'Miner,' *Cariboo Sentinel*, 31 May 1866.
8 'The British Columbia Judiciary,' from the *British Colonist*, reprinted in *Cariboo Sentinel*, 2 July 1866.
9 'Irresponsible Deputies,' *Cariboo Sentinel*, 31 May 1866.
10 Ibid.
11 'Supreme Court,' *Cariboo Sentinel*, 18 June 1866.
12 Ibid.
13 *Cariboo Sentinel*, 21 June 1866.
14 Ibid.
15 'Mass Meeting,' *Cariboo Sentinel*, 25 June 1866.
16 Ibid. Also see 'The Tyrant Judge,' *British Colonist*, 28 June 1866, and 'Another Verdict Set Aside,' and 'From Cariboo,' *British Columbian*, 27 June and 4 July 1866.
17 An Ordinance to amend the Laws relating to Gold Mining 2 April 1867.
18 Crease to Seymour, New Westminster, 28 August 1867. NAC, MG 11, CO 60/28, reel B-97, 380.
19 Nind to O'Reilly, Yahwalpa, Pimpama, Brisbane, Queensland, 11 April 1868, O'Reilly Family Papers. BCARS, add. MSS, 412, v. 1, f. 6a.
20 *Canadian Company v. Grouse Creek Flume Co., Ltd.*, 27 September 1867. Archer Martin, *Reports of Mining Cases decided by the Courts of British Columbia and the Courts of Appeal therefrom to the 1st of October, 1902* ... (Toronto, 1903), 3–8.
21 'Magistrate's Court,' *Cariboo Sentinel*, 3 June 1867. Spalding heard the case on 22 April 1867, and the order ejecting the Canadian Company was issued on 24 April.
22 Ibid.
23 'Trespassing on Grouse Creek Bed Rock Flume Co.'s Ground,' *Cariboo Sentinel*, 3 June 1867.
24 Bench Books, vol. 5, 4 July 1867. Cited in Williams, *'Man for a New Country,'* 77.
25 'Grouse Creek Difficulty,' *Cariboo Sentinel*, 15 July 1867.

Notes to pages 119-23   201

26 Letter to the Editor from C. Booth, dated 13 July 1867, *Cariboo Sentinel*, 15 July 1867.
27 'Public Meeting,' *Cariboo Sentinel*, 15 July 1989.
28 'Grouse Creek Troubles – Great Excitement,' *Cariboo Sentinel*, 18 July 1867.
29 Seymour to Buckingham and Chandos, New Westminster, 16 August 1867. NAC, MG 11, CO 60/28. reel B-97, 333.
30 Ibid.
31 'The Situation,' *British Columbian*, 27 July 1867.
32 'The Grouse Creek Difficulty,' *British Colonist*, 24 July 1867.
33 'The Governor and the Grouse Creek Difficulty,' *Cariboo Sentinel*, 12 August 1867.
34 Anonymous letter to the Editor, dated Williams Creek, 21 August 1867, *British Colonist*, 2 September 1867.
35 Letter to the Editor from 'Crimea,' dated Richfield, 20 August 1867, *British Colonist*, 9 September 1867.
36 Anonymous letter to the Editor, dated Williams Creek, 21 August 1867, *British Colonist*, 2 September 1867.
37 Letter to the Editor from 'Crimea,' dated Richfield, 20 August 1867, *British Colonist*, 9 September 1867.
38 'The Grouse Creek War,' *British Colonist*, 29 July 1867; also see 'The Grouse Creek Imbroglio,' 19 August 1867, and 'The Patched Up Peace on Grouse Creek,' 23 August 1867.
39 Resolution passed by the Canadian Company, at Booth's Saloon, Grouse Creek, 30 August 1867. Reprinted in 'Grouse Creek Dispute Again,' *Cariboo Sentinel*, 2 September 1867.
40 Letter to the Editor from Cornelius Booth, dated Grouse Creek, 31 August 1867, *Cariboo Sentinel*, 2 September 1867.
41 *Cariboo Sentinel*, 16 September 1867.
42 *Canadian Company v. Grouse Creek Flume Co., Ltd.*, 27 September 1867. Archer Martin, *Reports of Mining Cases*, 8.
43 'Tyrant Judge' from 'The Tyrant Judge,' *British Colonist*, 28 June 1866. For Begbie and mining cases after 1867, see Williams, 'Man for a New Country,' 80.
44 Williams, 'Man for a New Country,' 68.
45 'The Grouse Creek "War,"' *British Colonist*, 29 July 1867.
46 'Public Meeting,' *Cariboo Sentinel*, 15 July 1867.
47 'Mass Meeting,' *Cariboo Sentinel*, 25 June 1866. Similar sentiments were expressed in a letter from 'Miner' to the *Cariboo Sentinel*, 14 June 1866, which argued that Begbie's maladministration of the law 'is calculated to upset all confidence in the future of the colony, to drive out every honest man and prevent others from coming in; capitalists will not invest their means, nor prospectors their time and labor while they have no security that the laws, which are set before them as their guide will be administered as they read.'

48 Emphasis added. Resolution passed at a meeting of the members of the Canadian Mining Company, convened at Booth's Saloon, Grouse Creek, on the evening of the 30th August 1867. 'Grouse Creek Dispute Again,' *Cariboo Sentinel*, 2 September 1867.
49 Williams, *'Man for a New Country,'* 76.
50 Letter to the Editor from Cornelius Booth, dated 31 August 1867, *Cariboo Sentinel*, 2 September 1867.
51 See Greg Marquis, 'Doing Justice to British Justice: Law, Ideology and Canadian Historiography,' in Pue and Wright, eds., *Canadian Perspectives*.
52 The usual legal phrase is 'from time immemorial.' Peter Goodrich and Yitfat Hachamovitch discuss this usage in 'Time out of Mind: An Introduction to the Semiotics of Common Law,' in Fitzpatrick, ed., *Dangerous Supplements*. It is interesting that such powerful language, evocative of ancient use rights and custom, was used to buttress claims to property that were just a few days or months old.
53 ' "A Daniel Come to Judgement, Yea a Daniel!!" ' *Cariboo Sentinel,* 14 June 1866, and 'The Administration of Justice,' *Cariboo Sentinel*, 30 November 1866. Judge Jeffreys was George Jeffreys (Lord Jeffreys of Wem), a lawyer of considerable ability who went on to become chief justice of the Court of King's Bench and chancellor. Jeffreys was notorious for his coarse and bullying conduct, and used his position to promote his own interests. He presided over the 'Bloody Assizes' of 1685, which became emblematic of injustice and tyranny. See Walker, *Oxford Companion to the Law*, 661. The Court of Star Chamber was the legal body used by the Tudors to control the lawlessness that plagued England after 1485. Its proceedings were in camera, and influenced by politics. Though it was abolished in 1641, the Star Chamber has become synonymous with arbitrariness and tyranny. See *Oxford Companion to the Law*, 1174. 'Baron Garrow' was William Garrow, one of the most celebrated English lawyers of the eighteenth century; he was associated with the development of the prisoner's right to counsel. Garrow established himself first through his work as defence counsel in criminal trials, and went on to become king's counsel, solicitor-general and attorney-general. See Beattie, 'Scales of Justice,' 236–46.
54 'British Columbia's Judiciary,' from the *British Colonist*, reprinted in the *Cariboo Sentinel*, 2 July 1866.
55 'The Grouse Creek Dispute Again,' *Cariboo Sentinel*, 2 September 1867. The rest of the quote reads as follows: 'Had either of the judges of the Supreme Court, or even a barrister of good standing, been selected as the arbitrators ... no reasonable objection could have been urged against the arrangement; but to entrust the settlement of an important case like the present, which requires the exercise of no small amount of legal skill in the hands of a gentleman who has no pretensions to that knowledge, is simply preposterous.'

56 'Litigation Amongst the Miners,' *British Columbian*, 22 November 1865.
57 *Cariboo Sentinel*, 25 June 1866.
58 Letter to the Editor, *Cariboo Sentinel*, 1 October 1866. Anti-lawyer sentiment was common in colonial contexts and usually emerged in association with discussions of law reform. See Marquis, 'Anti-Lawyer Sentiment.'
59 'The Administration of the Mining Laws,' *Cariboo Sentinel*, 15 December 1866.
60 The following account is drawn from Baker, *Introduction to English Legal History*, chapter 6.
61 Walker, *Oxford Companion to the Law*, 424.
62 Ibid., 204.
63 Chancery's reputation for arbitrary, protracted and unnecessarily complex proceedings was given full expression in Charles Dickens's *Bleak House*, which was published in 1859, not long before the *Aurora* case. British Columbians were familiar with the Dickens novel and used it when petitioning the colonial government for relief: 'no mining case should go into Chancery ... there should be no Jarndyce & Jarndyce trials between miners.' See *Cariboo Sentinel*, 17 May 1866. Also see 'Petition from the Miners of Cariboo,' *British Columbian*, 16 December 1865, signed by 313 people, on the same issue.
64 Clifford Geertz, 'Local Knowledge: Fact and Law in Comparative Perspective,' in his *Local Knowledge*.
65 Petition dated Williams Creek, 3 November 1866, Colonial Correspondence. BCARS, GR 1372, reel B-1355, f. 1352.
66 The first two examples are from Ormsby, *British Columbia*, 181. The last example is from G.R. Newell, 'William George Cox,' *Dictionary of Canadian Biography*, v. 10, 198. The chicken oath was a recognized form of oath in colonies were Chinese lived. There are reported cases from British Columbia in which it was administered. See, for instance, *Rex v. Ah Wooey* (1902), 8 CCC 25 (BCSC).
67 Confidential Report upon the characters and qualifications of Public Servants, 1863. Enclosed in Douglas to Newcastle, Victoria, Vancouver Island, 18 February 1863. NAC, MG 11, CO 60/15, reel B-88.
68 Seymour to Buckingham and Chandos, New Westminster, 12 May 1868. Ibid., CO 60/32, reel B-100, 368.
69 Seymour to Buckingham and Chandos, Victoria, 4 September 1867. Ibid., CO 60/29, reel B-97, 5.
70 'From Cariboo,' *British Colonist*, 4 July 1866.
71 'The Administration of Justice,' *Cariboo Sentinel*, 30 November 1866.
72 'Judge Begbie and his Judges,' *Cariboo Sentinel*, 4 June 1866.
73 ' "A Daniel Come to Judgement, Yea A Daniel!!" ' *Cariboo Sentinel*, 14 June 1866; Letter to the Editor, *Cariboo Sentinel*, 11 June 1866; and 'The Administration of Justice,' *Cariboo Sentinel*, 30 November 1866.

74 Selim Franklin was the president of the Grouse Creek Flume Company and none other than J.P. Cranford was its treasurer.
75 Van Holthoon and Olson, eds., *Common Sense*, 3–4.
76 Geertz, 'Local Knowledge.' On 'common sense' see the introduction to van Holthoon and Olson's *Common Sense* as well as the following essays in that volume: Thomas Luckmann, 'Some Thoughts on Common Sense and Science,' and Siegwart Lindenberg, 'Common Sense and Social Structure: a Sociological View.'
77 On law as a social activity, see White, *Heracles' Bow*. The importance of local voices and sensibilities in the construction of justice and social order has also been explored by historians. See Thompson, 'Moral Economy'; Thompson, ' "Rough Music"; Davis, 'The Rites of Violence,' in her *Society and Culture*; Nicholas K. Blomley, 'Interpretive Practices, the State and the Locale,' in Wolch and Dear, eds., *Power of Geography*; and Blomley, 'Business of Mobility.'
78 Gaggin to the Colonial Secretary, Douglas, 2 July 1862. BCARS, GR 1372, reel B-1330, f. 621/14. For more on this episode and Gaggin see Smith, ' "Poor Gaggin." '
79 Cited in Smith, ' "Poor Gaggin," ' 45.
80 Ibid., 47.
81 The paradox between the elaboration of formal rights and the simultaneous contraction of informal freedoms is a theme that has been explored in the context of the transition from a pre-modern to a modern capitalist economy. This economic transformation resulted in the creation of a number of 'social crimes': acts that had been sanctioned by custom, but were criminalized with the rise of capitalism and the reification of property. For instance, see Thompson, *Whigs and Hunters*; Hay, et al., eds., *Albion's Fatal Tree*; Linebaugh, 'Karl Marx' and *The London Hanged*; Ditton, 'Perks'; and Innes and Styles, 'Crime Wave.'
82 Alison Jaggar discusses this aspect of liberalism in the context of the problems it poses for feminism in *Feminist Politics*, 42–4.
83 Alan Trachtenberg calls this phenomenon – the homogenization of local cultures as both a prerequisite and a byproduct of capitalist enterprise – 'incorporation,' and discusses it in the context of the evolution of American culture. See his *Incorporation of America*.

CHAPTER 7 Bute Inlet Stories

1 'Things are not as they were,' *British Columbian*, 27 August 1864.
2 Miles, *Racism*, 11. Also see Mason, *Deconstructing America*. Echoing Miles, Mason notes (at 44) that Europeans 'defined themselves and the culture they defended in a way resembling that of the photographic negative: by portraying everything that they were *not*, they created – by antithesis – an implicit image of what they in fact *were* – or rather, thought themselves to be.'

3 Faller, *Turned to Account*, xi; and Wiener, *Reconstructing the Criminal*, 11.
4 Daniel Francis argues that images of the Indian have been (and continue to be) fundamental to Canadian culture, and in particular to Euro-Canadians' self-identification. See his *Imaginary Indian*, as well as 'The Image of the Indian,' in Fisher, *Contact and Conflict*. Anthony Pagden has examined European perceptions of the 'incommensurability' of their own culture with that of the indigenous inhabitants of the Americas. See his *European Encounters* and *Fall of Natural Man*, as well as Mason, *Deconstructing America*, from whom the term 'alterity' comes. Marianna Torgovnick explores the place, value, and changing content of 'the primitive' in North American popular and high culture in *Gone Primitive*. Natives have not been the only Others studied as such in the Canadian context. Both W. Peter Ward and Kay J. Anderson discuss the otherness of the Chinese in Canada. See *White Canada Forever* and *Vancouver's Chinatown* respectively. The theoretical basis for all this work was laid in great part by Edward Said in *Orientalism*.
5 Cited in W. Kaye Lamb, 'Alfred Penderell Waddington,' *Dictionary of Canadian Biography*, v. 10, 698.
6 Unless otherwise noted, all biographical information on Waddington is taken from Lamb's entry in volume 10 of the *Dictionary of Canadian Biography*; Kershaw and Spittle, *Bute Inlet Route*, 4-8; and Shanks, *Waddington*.
7 Richard Carr (the father of Emily) was one of the most notable, and certainly one of the most vocal, expatriate Britons to voice his distaste for California and to migrate to Victoria with the discovery of gold in British Columbia. See Tippett, *Emily Carr*, 2–9. Matthew Begbie claimed that a California sojourn rendered an otherwise respectable Englishman unfit for colonial service, and told James Douglas so. (Douglas himself was not enamoured of his Yankee neighbours after his experience at Fort Vancouver during a time when British sovereignty in the Oregon Territories was contested by the Americans, and as governor of Vancouver Island, where he again had to fight off American incursions in the San Juan Islands.) 'I am afraid,' he told Douglas, 'that English sentiments are less prevalent than could be wished in Englishmen who have long resided in California. I do not mean to insinuate that such a residence diminishes – on the contrary, I believe, it often even augments – their natural loyalty & good affection to Her Majesty. But there is usually to be remarked among such persons an alteration in voice, in tone and manner, and an accretion of prejudices, which, I think, render them less fit, and contrast unfavorably with the tone[,] manner and prejudices of Englishmen habitually resident in the United Kingdom.' See Begbie to Douglas, Victoria, Vancouver Island, 18 May 1859. BCARS, GR 1372, reel B-1307, f. 142b1/7.
8 'Fraser River fever' and 'Fraser River humbug' are both terms used by Waddington himself, in *The Fraser mines vindicated, or the history of four months* (Victoria, 1858), a defence of the economic prospects of the new colony.

9 See W. Champness, *To Cariboo and Back: An Emigrant's Journey to the Gold Fields of British Columbia* (from 'The Leisure Hour,' 1862); M. Claudet, *The Handbook of British Columbia and Emigrant's Guide to the Gold Fields* (London [1862]); Jules H. Féry, *Map and Guide to the Cariboo Gold Mines of British Columbia* (San Francisco, 1862); and William Carew Hazlitt, *The Great Gold Fields of Cariboo* ... (London, 1862).
10 Chartres Brew, Remarks on Mr. Waddington's Petition, Undated. BCARS, MS.
11 Ibid.
12 Figure from 'Alfred Pendrell Waddington,' *Dictionary of Canadian Biography*, v. 10, 697.
13 It was 363 miles from New Westminster to Williams Lake via the Brigade Trail and 329 via the River Trail. See Jo. Lindley, *Three Years in Cariboo: Being the Experience and Observations of a Packer* (San Francisco, 1862), 3–14.
14 Hewlett, 'Chilcotin Uprising,' 91.
15 'Waggish distortion' from 'The Bute Route,' *Daily Evening Press*, 16 June 1861, cited ibid. The £100,000 figure is from Brew, 'Remarks on Mr. Waddington's Petition.' Brew was probably mistaken, for the Bute Inlet Waggon Road Company's prospectus estimated the profits to be on the order of $100,000. See Bute Inlet Wagon Road Company Limited [Prospectus] (Victoria, 1863).
16 In return for building the road, the Bute Inlet Wagon Road Company was granted the right to levy and collect a toll for ten years: ibid. Waddington also hoped to profit from the sale of town lots in 'Waddington,' the settlement he envisioned at the head of Bute Inlet as a provisioning-point for the journey overland.
17 Frederick Seymour told the Colonial Office that he 'never saw so difficult a country. The mountains in many cases rise simply at right angles to the plains. Glaciers are poised over narrow valleys of almost tropical heat, and the cascades fall from the summit of the precipice scarcely wetting the perpendicular wall of rock.' Seymour to Cardwell, New Westminster, 9 September 1864. NAC, MG 11, CO 60/19, 150.
18 In refuting Waddington's claim that he had spent $63,000 on the Bute Inlet road, Brew argued that '[t]here is not work done to be seen [and] besides the cost of what work [was] done did not all come out of Mr. Waddington's pocket. I know persons who subscribed towards the outlay and a company was formed in Victoria to support Mr. Waddington's scheme. When the trail did not progress as rapidly or as easily as Mr. Waddington promised, faith in his representations was very much shaken, and the shareholders were satisfied to let Mr. Waddington buy them out for a trifle.' See Brew, 'Remarks on Mr. Waddington's Petition' and 'Alfred Penderell Waddington,' *Dictionary of Canadian Biography*, v. 10, 697.
19 Brew to the Colonial Secretary, Waddington, 23 May 1864. BCARS, GR 1372, reel B-1310, f. 193/14.
20 Ibid.

21 Fisher, *Contact and Conflict*, 107–9, and Hewlett, 'Chilcotin Uprising,' chapters 2 and 3.
22 Fisher, *Contact and Conflict*, 107–9; Hewlett, 'Chilcotin Uprising,' chapter 5.
23 Seymour to Cardwell, New Westminster, 31 August 1864. Great Britain, Colonial Office, British Columbia Original Correspondence. NAC, MG 11, CO 60/19, 95ff. As Seymour noted, 'on the departure of Sir James Douglas, who had been known by the Indians as a great Chief, the principal authority in this territory, for upwards of forty years, an impression was allowed to arise among them [the Indians] that their protector was withdrawn and would have no successor. The Fraser River Indians uttered many lamentations over their deserted condition and it became desirable for me to make myself known to the natives and show them that I had succeeded to all the power of my successor and to his solicitude for their welfare.' In an earlier letter to Cardwell discussing the causes of the 'massacre,' Seymour noted that '[o]thers throw out the conjecture that the proceedings previous to Sir James Douglas's departure [that is, the ceremonies surrounding his retirement] may have induced the Indians to believe that the white men are without a head. Possibly so. We know that the more civilized tribes on the Fraser have been allowed to believe that they are now without a protector or a friend.' See Seymour to Cardwell, New Westminster, 20 May 1864. NAC, MG 11, CO 60/18, 283.
24 Hewlett, 'Chilcotin Uprising,' 123.
25 Seymour to Cardwell, New Westminster, 20 May 1864. NAC, MG 11, CO 60/18, 276.
26 Ibid.
27 For a detailed account of the killings, see Hewlett, 'Chilcotin Uprising,' chapter 5, and 'The Chilcotin Uprising of 1864.'
28 Hewlett, 'Chilcotin Uprising,' 130–4; Rev. R.C. Lundin Brown, *Klatsassan, and other Reminiscences of Missionary Life in British Columbia* (London 1873), 17–36.
29 For a breakdown of the expenses, see the ledger sheets enclosed in BCARS, GR 1372, reel B-1321, f. 380/6.
30 Hewlett, 'Chilcotin Uprising,' 165–76.
31 Birch to Cox, Colonial Secretary's Office, 14 May 1864, BCARS, GR 1372, f. 379/22, noted that 'the Governor regrets that he cannot furnish you with the names or description of the offenders, but he is advised that their own tribe would easily identify them should they think fit. You are at liberty to offer such rewards as you may think fit to the Indians for the apprehension of the murderers.'
32 Only six were tried. Cheeloot and Tnanaki were freed, and Chedekki, whom no witnesses recognized, but who it was said would be recognized by one of the survivors, was taken to New Westminster for identification and, if identified, to stand trial. Chedekki escaped while en route to New Westminster, and was never captured. See Hewlett, 'The Chilcotin Uprising of 1864,' 71.

33 Seymour to Cardwell, New Westminster, 9 September 1864. NAC, MG 11, CO 60/19, 180.
34 'The Last Indian Atrocity.' *British Colonist*, 12 May 1864.
35 Emphasis added.
36 On the importance of melodrama as a literary form in the Victorian period, and particularly in crime stories, see Poovey, *Uneven Developments*, 66–7; Paul Craven, 'Law and Ideology: the Toronto Police Court, 1850-80,' in Flaherty, ed., *History of Canadian Law*, v. 2; and Wiener, *Reconstructing the Criminal*, 21.
37 'Horrible Massacre,' *Daily Chronicle*, 12 May 1864.
38 'The Bute Tragedy,' *British Columbian*, 27 May 1864.
39 Lundin Brown, *Klatsassan*, 16.
40 This reaction also underlay European British Columbians' opposition to the potlatch. See Loo, 'Dan Cranmer's Potlatch.'
41 'The Bute Tragedy,' *British Columbian*, 27 May 1864. The Chilcotin had even left money strewn on the ground, further testimony to their profligacy.
42 Seymour to Cardwell, New Westminster, 9 September 1864. NAC, MG 11, CO 60/19, 154.
43 Lundin Brown, *Klatsassan*, 13–14. Brown described the evening before the attack on the packers as follows, again emphasizing the Europeans' work ethic: 'they [the packers] had had a long day of it, and were glad enough ... to reach the place of bivouac. No one can realize, who has not felt it, the delight to the worn-out miner or packer of gaining a nightly resting place ... Sweet indeed is rest after labour' [20]. And, I would add, how unjust it was that these hard-working men be killed in the course of doing an honest day's work.
44 Brown emphasized (at 36) the progress represented by Manning's presence and actions: 'as the years rolled on, Manning replaced his tent by a good substantial log house; he extended his garden, and cleared more land; he procured a plough, and turned up the rich virgin soil, and the yellow corn waved by the bank of that far-off lake.'
45 Lundin Brown, *Klatsassan*, 36.
46 'Dreadful Massacre,' *British Colonist*, 12 May 1864.
47 Seymour to Cardwell, New Westminster, 20 May 1864. NAC, MG 11, CO 60/18, 276.
48 Frederick Whymper, *Travel and Adventure in the Territory of Alaska* ... (London, 1868), 36. Mariana Valverde discusses the use of the volcanic metaphor in the nineteenth-century discourse of moral reform. See *Light, Soap, and Water*, 132.
49 Francis, *Imaginary Indian*, 120–2.
50 Lundin Brown, *Klatsassan*, 21–6. On Pocahontas and the image of Indian women, see Francis, *Imaginary Indian*, 120–2, and Green, 'The Pocahontas Perplex.'
51 Lundin Brown, *Klatsassan*, 34–5.

52 Fisher, *Contact and Conflict*, 87.
53 Ibid, 38–9. Still later, during the trial, Nancy once again demonstrated what Brown and others would describe as female fickleness when she testified against her native compatriots, and asked for government support afterwards, for she was fearful of returning to her village. Seymour complied, but Nancy eventually returned home, to an unknown fate. See Cox to the Colonial Secretary, Quesnelmouth, 2 October 1864. BCARS, GR 1372, reel B-1321, f. 380/1; Colonial Secretary to Cox, New Westminster, 8 October 1864, ibid.; and Cox to Colonial Secretary, Richfield, B.C., 8 November 1864, ibid., f. 380/9.
54 Lundin Brown, *Klatsassan*, 9.
55 Brew to the Colonial Secretary, Waddington, 23 May 1864. BCARS, GR 1372, reel B-1310, f. 193/14. Also see Whymper, *Travel and Adventure*, 36. Whymper contended that the killings were motivated out of 'a strong desire for plunder.'
56 Seymour to Cardwell, New Westminster, 20 May 1864. NAC, MG 11, CO 60/18, 282.
57 For a provocative overview and a critique of anthropologists' work on anthropophagy, see Arens, *Man-Eating Myth*. Looking at reports of anthropophagy over time, Arens contends (at 166) that 'anthropology [through its uncritical treatment of reports of cannibalism] has often served as a reviver and reinventor of the notion of savagery.' For a piece that deals with the alleged cannibalism of Canadian native peoples, see Christon Archer, 'Cannibalism.'
58 Arens, *Man-Eating Myth*, chapter 1.
59 Pagden, *Fall of Natural Man*, 80–7.
60 Ibid.
61 Ibid., 16, and chapter 2 generally.
62 Lundin Brown, *Klatsassan*, 4.
63 Whymper, 36. The 'half child-half animal' description is very similar to that used by Rudyard Kipling's description of the Hindu population of India ('half child-half devil') in 'The White Man's Burden.' See Hutchins, *Illusion of Permanence*, 77.
64 Wiener, *Reconstructing the Criminal*, 33.
65 Nicholas Canny discusses the similarities between the language used by the English to describe the Irish and that used to describe the natives of North America, arguing that both were part of a discourse of colonization. See 'The Ideology of English Colonization: From Ireland to America,' in Katz and Murrin, eds., *Colonial America*. Also see Mason, *Deconstructing America*, chapter 2.
66 Henry Mayhew, *London Labour and the London Poor* (London 1862), v. 1, 2–3; cited in Emsley, *Crime and Society*, 61.
67 Fisher, *Contact and Conflict*, chapter 5. Sylvia Van Kirk, in her study of Native women in the fur trade, also points to the mid-nineteenth century as a time when attitudes towards Native and mixed blood peoples were hardening. See her *'Many Tender Ties.'*

68 Francis Jennings argues that phrases like 'trackless wilderness' and 'virgin land' are part of a 'cant of conquest' – a language that disqualifies Native peoples' claim to the land by denying their existence. See Jennings, *Invasion of America*.
69 See Bolt, *Victorian Attitudes to Race*, 201ff; Hutchins, *Illusion of Permanence*, chapter 4; and Williams, *India Office*, 336. Thanks to my colleague, Edward Ingram, for guiding me through the relevant literature on the mutiny.
70 'The Bute Tragedy,' *British Columbian*, 27 May 1864.
71 'Horrible Massacre,' *Daily Chronicle*, 12 May 1864.
72 'Additional Particulars,' *Daily Chronicle*, 12 May 1864.
73 Lundin Brown, *Klatsassan*, 7, 98–9.
74 Ibid., 98–9; emphasis added.
75 Ibid., 102.
76 'Emergency Meeting,' *British Colonist*, 2 June 1864.
77 Jennings describes how the Puritan settlers of New England constructed Natives as savages so as to legitimate their own savage treatment of them. See *Invasion of America*.
78 'The Bute Massacre,' *British Columbian*, 14 May 1864. There was some question as to the number of Chilcotin attackers: this report identifies sixteen, while others say eighteen.
79 'The Bute Massacre,' *Weekly Colonist*, 24 May 1864.
80 'The Indian Murders,' *Weekly British Colonist*, 7 June 1864.
81 'The Bute Massacre,' *British Columbian*, 18 May 1864.
82 On this theme in colonial America, see James Axtell, 'The Unkindest Cut, or Who Invented Scalping?: A case study,' 'The White Indians of Colonial America,' and 'Scalping: The Ethnohistory of a Moral Question,' all in Axtell, *The European and the Indian*.
83 Begbie to Douglas, Victoria, Vancouver's Island, 18 May 1859. BCARS, GR 1372, reel B-1307, f. 142b1/7.
84 Recall Charles Aubrey Angelo's observations (quoted at the beginning of chapter 2), for instance.
85 'Extracts from Bishop's Journal, 1861,' in Columbia Mission, *Third Report of the Columbia Mission* (1861?), 19.
86 Seymour to Cardwell, New Westminster, 30 August 1864. NAC, MG 11, CO 60/19, 167.
87 'An Indian Policy,' *British Columbian*, 14 May 1864. The same article criticized James Douglas's administration with respect to its Indian policy, and to call for the colonial government to formulate a more effective one.
88 Matthew Baillie Begbie, Memorandum on Indian relief legislation and Indian Chiefs' jurisdiction, Cache Creek, 11 September 1876. Canada, DIA, Black Series. NAC, RG 10, reel C-10112, volume 3638, file 7271.

89 As Seymour told Cardwell, 'this was a war – merciless on their side – in which we were engaged with the Chilcoaten nation and must be carried on as a war by us.' Seymour to Cardwell, New Westminster, 9 September 1864. NAC, MG 11, CO 60/19, 178–9.
90 Seymour to Cardwell, New Westminster, 20 May 1864. Ibid., CO 60/18, 290 (emphasis added).
91 Ibid., 179.
92 Ibid. (emphasis added). However, from E.A. Atkins's recollection, it is apparent that the distinction drawn by Seymour between the less restrained Americans and the decorous Britons was not complete. The following incident indicated that the New Westminster party was not completely imbued with the dour discipline one might expect. Atkins recalled that on locating the road party's camp, they 'found nothing but some Kegs of Black blasting powder and they were all busted and spilt on the ground. There was a laughable thing happened there[.] Mr. Bonson got a sun glas [sic] (it was a hot day) and though he had drawn a piece of the powder far enough away and was sitting on his Haunches holding the glass over it. I saw him so did Mr. Brough and we went to see what he was doing and got nicly [sic] sitting on our Haunches when the whole thing went up in a big Blase [sic] knocked us over on our backs and burnt some of Broughs whiskers... See E.A. Atkins, 'History of the Chilcotin War.' BCARS, MS.
93 Ibid., 291.
94 'The Indian Expedition,' *British Columbian*, 24 August 1864.
95 'Things are not as they were,' *British Columbian*, 27 August 1864.
96 Begbie to Seymour, Quesnellemouth, 30 September 1864. BCARS, GR 1372, reel B-1309, f. 142f/16.
97 Hanging often raised moral doubts, and authorities were always concerned that the prisoner make a good death. Even so, some observers failed to see the difference between capital punishment and homicide. One of these, interestingly enough, was Alfred Waddington. Shortly after his arrival in Victoria, he wrote and published a pamphlet entitled 'Judicial Murder,' in which he condemned the execution of Allache, a Native found guilty of killing a Black man who had made advances on his wife. Allache was tried without the benefit of counsel or an interpreter, convicted, and hanged. See 'Judicial Murder, signed and dated August 27, 1860, Victoria, V.I.' [n.p.]. More generally on the questionable morality of hanging and the need to make a good death, see Peter Linebaugh, 'The Tyburn Riot Against the Surgeons,' in Hay et al., eds., *Albion's Fatal Tree*, and Linebaugh, *The London Hanged*.
98 'The Chilcoaten Expedition. Diary of a Volunteer,' *British Colonist*, 17 October 1864.
99 Ibid.
100 'Terror' and 'Justice' are elements identified as part of the ideology of the law by

Douglas Hay. See his 'Property, Authority, and the Criminal Law,' in Hay et al., eds., *Albion's Fatal Tree*.

101 Lundin Brown, *Klatsassan*, 118–21.
102 Angela Harris made this point in her critique of feminist legal theory. See Harris, 'Racism and Essentialism,' 584ff.
103 Growing body of historical work illustrates this tension. For instance, Constance Backhouse, Karen Dubinsky and Franca Iacovetta, and Carolyn Strange all point out how the legal recognition of difference, whether based on gender, class, or ethnicity, can work to temper as well as exacerbate the effect of the law. Women accused of infanticide were often treated leniently by the courts because judges recognized their desperate straits and because infant life – particularly the infants of poor or working-class people – was not highly valued. Women who killed, like Angelina Napolitano, Clara Ford, and Carrie Davies, also could benefit from stereotypes about their ethnicity, race, or class: as a 'hot-blooded' Italian, Napolitano was presumed to be naturally predisposed to committing a crime of passion. The same was true of Clara Ford, who, though not Italian, was of African descent and therefore also considered somewhat unpredictable and childlike – and ultimately not quite responsible for her actions. Carrie Davies, by contrast, was portrayed as the epitome of the chaste woman, who was driven to kill in defence of her feminine honour. See Backhouse, *Petticoats and Prejudice*, chapter 4; Dubinsky and Iacovetta, 'Murder'; and Strange, 'Wounded Womanhood and Dead Men: chivalry and the trials of Clara Ford and Carrie Davies,' in Iacovetta and Valverde, eds., *Gender Conflicts*. Feminist jurisprudence is also divided over the relative costs and benefits of recognizing difference. At one end of the spectrum are people like Carol Gilligan and Robin West, who, in critiquing liberal jurisprudence, argue that the 'different voice' in which women speak must be heard in both making and enforcing the law. At the other are people like Catharine MacKinnon, who contend that recognizing women's difference is tantamount to recognizing and reinforcing male dominance. See Gilligan, *In a Different Voice*; West, 'Jurisprudence and Gender'; and Catharine A. MacKinnon, 'Difference and Dominance: on sex discrimination,' in her *Feminism Unmodified*.

CONCLUSION

1 Much of the literature on 'social crime' certainly implies, if not overtly makes, this point. See, for instance, Thompson, *Whigs and Hunters*, and the essays in Hay et al., eds., *Albion's Fatal Tree*. The homogenization of culture with the expansion of the American state in the nineteenth century and the razing of local knowledges and practices – what Alan Trachtenberg calls 'the incorporation of America' – is explored in his book of the same name. The conflict that emerged from this process of incorporation is explored by Richard Maxwell Brown, who argues that the gun-

fighting that characterized much of the American west was not the manifestation of frontier individualism, but a result of the clash of two communities of interest: the forces of incorporation – big business – and the people whose way of life and communities they threatened to destroy. See his essay in McLaren, Foster, and Orloff, eds., *Law for the Elephant*. Finally, on the 'creative destruction' of place that accompanies capitalist expansion, see the geographer Sharon Zukin's book, *Landscapes of Power*.

2 Blomley, 'Business of Mobility,' 238.
3 Miners' meetings were established in British Columbia, but did not have a chance to entrench themselves. See David Ricardo Williams, 'The Administration of Civil and Criminal Justice in the Mining Camps and Frontier Communities of British Columbia,' in Knafla, ed., *Law and Justice in a New Land*.
4 Burchell, Gordon, and Miller, eds., *The Foucault Effect*.
5 These themes are explored in a contemporary context in Blomley, 'Business of Mobility.'
6 'The Administration of Justice,' *Cariboo Sentinel*, 30 November 1866.
7 Though feminists are not alone in calling for the recognition of differences. Like Robin West, whose work is discussed below, Rupert Ross, in commenting on native systems of justice, argues that non-native society has much to learn and stands to benefit from both recognizing and adopting native ways of seeing and dealing with conflict. See Ross, *Dancing with a Ghost*.
8 Gilligan, *In a Different Voice*.
9 West, 'Jurisprudence and Gender,' 2
10 MacKinnon, 'Difference and Dominance: on sex discrimination,' in her *Feminism Unmodified*.
11 See, for instance, Tobias, 'Protection,' and Carol Smart, 'Disruptive Bodies and Unruly Sex: The Regulation of Reproduction and Sexuality in the Nineteenth Century,' in Smart, ed., *Regulating Womanhood*.
12 Jaggar, *Feminist Politics*, 35–9. Also see Smart, *Feminism and the Power of Law*, 139.
13 Thompson, *Whigs and Hunters*, 265 and more generally, 258–69.
14 See Loo, 'Dan Cranmer's Potlatch.' Land claims, of course, are not a new phenomenon, but have their roots in the early part of the century. As Paul Tennant's book reveals, many native people at the forefront of claims activity used the rhetoric of the law to their own ends. See his *Aboriginal Peoples*.
15 On the attraction and strength of rights discourse, see Smart, *Feminism and the Power of Law*, 141–4.
16 Mossman, 'Feminism and the Legal Method,' argues that the self-referential nature of legal reasoning (the legal method) – its reliance on precedence, its rules of evidence especially, and its tendency to make decisions on the narrowest possible basis – has the effect of reproducing the status quo. As a result, social justice cannot be effected through the law, but rather must be sought outside it.

Bibliography

NOTE ON SOURCES

The primary material on which this book is based comes from four major sources: the correspondence to and from the colonial secretaries of Vancouver Island and British Columbia (referred to as 'Colonial Correspondence') comprises the most substantive record of the internal communication between the colonial governments of the island and mainland colonies and their officers in the field, as well as letters and petitions from other 'ordinary' colonists; the British Colonial Office's correspondence with the governors of Vancouver Island and British Columbia (CO 305 and CO 60 respectively); contemporary newspapers, particularly the *British Colonist* (Victoria), the *British Columbian* (New Westminster), and the *Cariboo Sentinel* (Barkerville); and the court records and correspondence in the voluminous attorney-general's collection at the British Columbia Archives and Records Service.

The quantitative analysis of civil litigation presented in chapter 4 is based on a complete analysis of all the existing county court records contained in the 'plaint' or 'plaint and procedure' books for the mainland colony. These recorded the names of the plaintiff and defendant, the nature and monetary value of the suit, court costs, the presence or absence of lawyers, and the disposal of the case. Mining Court records for the colonial period are extant for the Richfield District only and contain the same information as the plaint and procedure books, though in prose rather than ledger form. The gold production figures that are the basis of the figure in chapter 4 were taken from Isabel Bescoby, 'Some Aspects of Society in the Cariboo' (see bibliography).

NEWSPAPERS

The British Colonist (Victoria)
The British Columbian (New Westminster)
The Cariboo Sentinel (Barkerville)

Bibliography

PRIMARY UNPUBLISHED SOURCES

Allan, Alexander. 'Cariboo and the Mines of British Columbia.' Victoria, 1878. H.H. Bancroft Collection. NAC, TS.
– 'History of the Northwest Coast.' Victoria, 1878. H.H. Bancroft Collection. NAC, TS.
Bayley, C.A. 'Early Life on Vancouver Island.' H.H. Bancroft Collection. NAC, TS.
British Columbia. Attorney General. Bills, draft ordinances, orders of the day and other working papers, 1867–1868. BCARS, GR 556.
– County Court. Cariboo (Alexandria). Plaint and Procedure Books, 1862–1864. BCARS, GR 572.
– County Court. Cariboo (Clinton). Plaint and Procedure Books, 1867-1871. BCARS, GR 568.
– County Court. Cariboo (Lillooet). Plaint and Procedure Books, 1861–1871. BCARS, GR 569.
– County Court. Cariboo (Quesnel). Plaint and Procedure Books, 1864–1871. BCARS, GR 570.
– County Court. Cariboo (Richfield). Plaint and Procedure Books, 1862–1870. BCARS, GR 584.
– County Court. New Westminster (Fort Hope). Plaint and Procedure Books, 1858–1871. BCARS, GR 574.
– County Court. New Westminster (Lytton). Plaint and Procedure Books, 1866–1871. BCARS, GR 576.
– County Court. New Westminster (New Westminster). Plaint and Procedure Books, 1865–1873. BCARS, GR 712.
– Drafts of bills, ordinances, some opinions, 1858-1910. BCARS, GR 673.
– Letters and copies of letters from the Attorney General to the Governor, forwarding ordinances and commenting on bills and ordinances, 1864–1870. BCARS, GR 752.
– Provincial Court. Fort Hope. Police Book, 1858–1862. BCARS, GR 592.
– Provincial Court. Lillooet. Charge and Sentence Books, 1862–1867. BCARS, GR 593.
– Provincial Court. Lytton. Plaint and Procedure Books, 1860–1864. BCARS, GR 594.
– Provincial Court. Richfield. Police Court Case Book, 1863–1874. BCARS, GR 598.
– Registrar-General. Registry of Companies. BCARS, GR 1438.
– Supreme Court of Vancouver Island. Cause Books, 1858-1871. BCARS, GR 657.
– Supreme Court. Record of Cases Heard, 1861–1863. BCARS, GR 714.
– Colonial Secretary. Colonial Correspondence. BCARS, GR 1372.
– Government Agency. Cariboo, 1860–1934. BCARS, GR 216.
– Supreme Court. Notes of Proceedings as a Court of Assize, 18 February, 1867–10 June, 1870. BCARS, MS.
– Supreme Court. Notes of Proceedings. 2 May 1864–5 May 1865. BCARS, MS.

Bibliography 217

- Supreme Court. Notes of Proceedings. 8 May 1865–15 January 1867. BCARS, MS.
- Supreme Court. Notes of Proceedings. 15 January 1867–16 February 1870. BCARS, MS.
- Supreme Court. Notes of Proceedings. 25 March 1870–18 April 1871. BCARS, MS.
- Supreme Court. Notes of Proceedings. 24 April 1871–16 January 1873. BCARS, MS.
- Supreme Court. Notes of Proceedings. 16 September 1867–4 October 1867. BCARS, MS.
- Supreme Court. Notes of Proceedings. 1 July 1871–23 November 1871. BCARS, MS.
- [Brown, William.] Fort Kilmaurs Journal, March–June 1826. NAC, MS.

Compton, P.N. 'Forts and Fort Life in New Caledonia Under the Hudson's Bay Company Regime.' Victoria, 1878. H.H. Bancroft Collection. NAC, TS.

Cooper, James. 'Maritime Matters in the Northwest Coast and Affairs of the Hudson's Bay Company in Early Times.' Victoria, 1878. H.H. Bancroft Collection. NAC, TS.

Courtery, H.C. 'The Mines and Miners of British Columbia.' Victoria, 1878. H.H. Bancroft Collection. NAC, TS.

Crease, Henry Pering Pellew. Legal Papers, 1853–1895. BCARS, MS.
- Crease Family Papers. BCARS, MS.

Cridge, Edward. 'Characteristics of James Douglas.' Victoria, 1878. H.H. Bancroft Collection. NAC, TS.

Deans, James. 'Settlement of Vancouver Island.' Victoria, 1878. H.H. Bancroft Collection. NAC, TS.

Dease, John Warren. 'The Columbia Journal of John Warren Dease,' 1829. NAC, MS.

DeCosmos, Amor. 'The Governments of Vancouver Island and British Columbia.' Victoria, 1878. H.H. Bancroft Collection. NAC, TS.

Douglas, James. 'Journal of Sir James Douglas, 1840–1841: Fort Vancouver and the Northwest Coast.' H.H. Bancroft Collection. NAC, TS.
- Private Papers of Sir James Douglas. First and Second Series. H.H. Bancroft Collection. NAC, TS.

Duncan, William. Papers. NAC, MS.

Finlayson, Roderick. 'The History of Vancouver Island and the Northwest Coast.' Victoria, 1878. H.H. Bancroft Collection. NAC, TS.

Good, John B. 'British Columbia.' Victoria, 1878. H.H. Bancroft Collection. NAC, TS.

Great Britain. Colonial Office. British Columbia Original Correspondence. NAC, MG 11, CO 60.
- Colonial Office. Vancouver Island Original Correspondence. NAC, MG 11, CO 305.

Great Britain. Parliament. House of Commons Select Committee on the Hudson's Bay Company. *Report from the Select Committee on the Hudson's Bay Company: together with the proceedings of the committee, minutes of evidence, appendix, and index.* Ordered by the House of Commons to be printed 31 July and 11 August 1857.

Hudson's Bay Company Archives. Bye Laws. NAC, MG 20, A37/41.

218 Bibliography

- Deeds and Agreements, etc., relating to Vancouver Island, 1849–1896. NAC, MG 20, A37/42.
- Governor George Simpson, Official Reports to the Governor and Committee in London. NAC, MG 20, D4.
- London Correspondence Inward from Sir George Simpson. NAC, MG 20, A34/1.
- Servants' Character and Staff Records. NAC, MG 20, A34/1.
- Western Department Land Records. NAC, MG 20, H1/9.

Lewis, Herbert George. 'British Columbia Sketches.' Victoria, 1878. H.H. Bancroft Collection. NAC, TS.

McDonald, Archibald. Journal of the Hudson's Bay Company kept at Fort Langley during the years 1827–9. H.H. Bancroft Collection. NAC, TS.

Macdonald, William John. 'British Columbia Sketches.' Victoria, 1878. H.H. Bancroft Collection. NAC, TS.

McKay, Joseph William. 'Recollections of a Chief Trader in the Hudson's Bay Company,' Fort Simpson, 1878. H.H. Bancroft Collection. NAC, TS.

McKinlay, Archibald. 'Narrative of a Chief Factor of the Hudson's Bay Company.' Victoria, 1878. H.H. Bancroft Collection. NAC, TS.

McLeod, John. Papers. NAC, MS.

Muir, Michael. 'British Columbia Sketches.' Victoria, 1878. H.H. Bancroft Collection. NAC, TS.

O'Reilly Family Papers. BCARS, MS.

Strathcona and Mount Royal, Sir Donald Alexander Smith, First Baron. Strathcona Collection of Fur Trade Papers. NAC, MS.

Tarbell, Frank. 'Life and Trade in Victoria during the Fraser River Excitement.' Victoria, 1878. H.H. Bancroft Collection. NAC, TS.

Tod, John. 'History of New Caledonia and the Northwest Coast.' Victoria, 1878. H.H. Bancroft Collection. NAC, TS.

Vancouver Island. Attorney General. Letterbooks, v. 1–3. BCARS, MS.
- Police and Prisons Department. Victoria. Charge Books, 1858–1860, 1862–1871. BCARS, MS.
- Notes of Proceedings. 6 October, 1853–20 20 1857. BCARS, MS.
- Notes of Proceedings: civil cases. 19 October 1863–9 May 1864; 13 October 1865–24 August 1866. BCARS, MS.
- Notes of Proceedings: chancery cases. 8 January, 1863–9 August 1865; 7 December 1865–15 November 1866. BCARS, MS.
- Notes of Proceedings: bankruptcy. 19 October 1863–1 November 1865; 8 November 1865–7 November 1866; 6 January 1866–1 November 1866. BCARS, MS.
- Notes of Proceedings: criminal cases. 23 November 1865–16 August 1866. BCARS, MS.

- Notes of Proceedings as a Court of Assize. 21 January 1862–16 August 1866. BCARS, MS.
- Supreme Court: outward correspondence, 12 April 1861–26 October 1866; 29 December 1866–4 October 1870. BCARS, MS.
- Inferior Court of Civil Justice. Notes of Proceedings, 31 October 1865–2 February 1870. BCARS, MS.

Vowell, Arthur Wellesley, and Thomas Spence. 'Mining Districts of British Columbia.' Victoria, 1878. H.H. Bancroft Collection. NAC, TS.

PRIMARY PUBLISHED SOURCES

Addresses and Memorials together with Articles, Reports, etc., etc., from the Public Journals upon the Occasion of the Retirement of Sir James Douglas, K.C.B. from the Governorship of Vancouver Island and British Columbia. Deal: E. Hayward, 1864.

Anderson, Alexander Caulfield. *The Dominion of the West: A Brief Description of the Province of British Columbia, Its Climate and Resources.* Victoria: R. Wolfenden, 1872.

Anderson, James. *Sawney's Letters and Cariboo Rhymes.* Toronto: W.S. Johnston & Company, 1895.

Angelo, Charles Aubrey (Chaos). *Idaho: A Descriptive Tour and Review of Its Resources and Route, Prefaced by a Sketch of British Misrule in Victoria, V.I..* San Francisco: H.H. Bancroft and Company, 1865.

Begbie, Matthew Baillie. 'Journey into the Interior of British Columbia.' *Royal Geographical Society Proceedings* 1860: 33–7.

Bowsfield, Hartwell, ed. *Fort Victoria Letters, 1843–1851.* Winnipeg: Hudson's Bay Record Society, 1978.

British Columbia. *Statutes,* 1859–1871. Micromedia Collection of Pre-Confederation Statutes.

Champness, W. *To Cariboo and Back: an Emigrant's Journey to the Gold Fields of British Columbia.* [London: n.p., 1865?].

[Church Missionary Society]. *Ten Years' Work among the Tsimpshean Indians.* London: Church Missionary Society, 1869.

Claudet, F.G. *'Gold', Its Properties, Modes of Extraction, Value, &c., &c.* New Westminster: Mainland Guardian, 1871.

Claudet, M. *The Handbook of British Columbia and Emigrant's Guide to the Gold Fields ...* London: W. Oliver [1862].

Cox, Ross. *Adventures on the Columbia River ...* New York: J. & J. Harper, 1832.

DeGroot, Henry. *British Columbia: Its Condition and Prospects, Soil, Climate and Mineral Resources Considered.* San Francisco: Alta California Job Office, 1859.

Downie, W. *Hunting for Gold.* San Francisco: California Publishing Company, 1893.

Féry, Jules H. *Map and Guide to the Gold Fields.* San Francisco: F. Truette, 1862.
Finlayson, Roderick. *Biography of Roderick Finlayson.* Victoria, 1913.
Fitzgerald, James Edward. *An Examination of the Charter and Proceedings of the Hudson's Bay Company, with Reference to the Grant of Vancouver Island.* London: T. Saunders, 1849.
Fleming, R. Harvey, ed. *Minutes of Council, Northern Department of Rupert's Land, 1821–1831.* Toronto: Champlain Society, 1940.
Ireland, Willard E. 'First Impressions: Letter of Col. Richard Moody to Arthur Blackwood, 1859.' *British Columbia Historical Quarterly* 15(1951): 85–107.
Knaplund, Paul. 'Letters from James Edward Fitzgerald to W.E. Gladstone concerning Vancouver Island and the Hudson's Bay Company.' *British Columbia Historical Quarterly* 13(1949): 1–22.
Lamb, W. Kaye. 'British Columbia Official Records: The Crown Colony Period.' *Pacific Northwest Quarterly* 29(1938): 17–25.
– 'The Census of Vancouver Island, 1855.' *British Columbia Historical Quarterly* 8(1940): 51–8.
– 'Memoirs and Documents Relating to Judge Begbie.' *British Columbia Historical Quarterly* 5(1941): 125–220.
– 'The Diary of Robert Melrose: Part I, 1851–1853; Part II, 1854–55; Part III, 1856–57.' *British Columbia Historical Quarterly* 7(1943): 119–34; 199–218; 283–95.
– 'Five Letters of Charles Ross, 1842–4.' *British Columbia Historical Quarterly* 7(1943):103–18.
– *Sixteen Years in Indian Country: The Journal of Daniel Williams Harmon, 1800–1816.* Toronto: Champlain Society, 1957.
Leduc, Joanne, ed. *Overland from Canada to British Columbia.* Vancouver: University of British Columbia Press, 1981.
Lundin Brown, Rev. R.C. *Klatsassan, and other Reminiscences of Missionary Life in British Columbia.* London: Society for Promoting Christian Knowledge, 1873.
Macdonald, Duncan. *British Columbia and Vancouver Island ...* London: Longman, Green, Longman, Roberts and Green, 1862.
McDonald, Lois Halliday. *Fur Trade Letters of Francis Ermatinger Written to His Brother Edward during His Service with the Hudson's Bay Company, 1818–1853.* Glendale: The Arthur H. Clark Company, 1980.
McLeod, Malcolm, ed. *Peace River: A Canoe Voyage from Hudson's Bay to the Pacific by the Late Sir George Simpson ... .* Ottawa: J. Durie, 1872.
Martin, Archer. *Reports of Mining Cases, 1853–1902*, volume 1. Toronto: The Carswell Company, 1903.
Martin, R. Montgomery. *The Hudson's Bay Company Territories and Vancouver's Island, with an Exposition of the Chartered Rights, Conduct and Policy of the Honble. Hudson's Bay Corporation.* London: T. and W. Boone, 1849.

Merivale, Herman. *Lectures on Colonization and Colonies Delivered Before the University of Oxford in 1839, 1840 & 1841.* London: Longman, Green, Longman and Roberts, 1861.

Merk, Frederick, ed. *Fur Trade and Empire: George Simpson's Journal Entitled Remarks Connected with the Fur Trade in the Course of a Voyage from York Factory to Fort George and Back to York Factory 1824–25.* Cambridge: The Belknap Press, 1968.

Nesbitt, James K. 'The Diary of Martha Cheney Ella, 1853–1856,' parts 1 and 2. *British Columbia Historical Quarterly* 13(1949): 91–112, 257–70.

Oliver, E.H., ed. *The Canadian North-West: Its Early Development and Legislative Records.* In two volumes. Ottawa: Government Printing Bureau, 1914.

Rich, E.E., ed. *The Letters of John McLoughlin from Fort Vancouver to the Governor and Committee, First Series, 1825–1838.* London: Hudson's Bay Record Society, 1941.

– *The Letters of John McLoughlin from Fort Vancouver to the Governor and Committee, Second Series, 1839–1844.* London: Hudson's Bay Record Society, 1943.

– *The Letters of John McLoughlin from Fort Vancouver to the Governor and Committee, Third Series, 1844–1846.* London: Hudson's Bay Record Society, 1944.

– *Part of a Despatch from George Simpson, Esqr. Governor of Rupert's Land to the Governor & Committee of the Hudson's Bay Company London March 1, 1829. Continued and Completed March 24 and June 5, 1829.* London: Hudson's Bay Record Society, 1947.

– *London Correspondence Inward from Eden Colvile, 1849-1852.* London: Hudson's Bay Record Society, 1956.

Sage, Walter N. 'Peter Skene Ogden's Notes on Western Caledonia.' *British Columbia Historical Quarterly* 1(1937): 45–56.

Smith, Dorothy Blakey, ed. *The Reminiscences of Doctor John Sebastian Helmcken.* Vancouver: University of British Columbia Press, 1975.

Voorhis, Ernest. *Historic Forts and Trading Posts of the French Regime and of the English Fur Trading Companies.* Ottawa: Department of the Interior, 1930.

Waddington. Alfred. *The Fraser River Mines Vindicated.* Victoria: P. DeGarro, 1858.

– *Judicial Murder.* Victoria: Alfred Waddington, 1860.

Wallace, W. Stewart, ed. *John McLean's Notes of Twenty-five Years Service in Hudson's Bay Territory.* Toronto: Champlain Society, 1932.

Whymper, Frederick. *Travel and Adventure in the Territory of Alaska ... .* New York: Harper, 1871.

Wolfenden, Madge, ed. '[Gilbert Malcolm Sproat's] John Tod: "Career of a Scotch Boy."' *British Columbia Historical Quarterly* 18(1954): 133–238.

SECONDARY SOURCES: ARTICLES

Archer, Christon. 'Cannibalism in the Early History of the Northwest Coast: Endur-

ing Myths and Neglected Realities.' *Canadian Historical Review*, 61(1980): 453–479.
Backhouse, Constance B. 'Desperate Women and Compassionate Courts: Infanticide in Nineteenth-Century Canada.' *University of Toronto Law Journal* 34(1984): 447–478.
- '"Pure Patriarchy": Nineteenth-Century Canadian Marriage.' *McGill Law Journal* 31(1986): 264–312.
- Married Women's Property Law in Nineteenth-Century Canada.' *Law and History Review* 6(1988): 211–57.
Beattie, J.M. 'Scales of Justice: Defense Counsel and the English Criminal Trial in the Eighteenth and Nineteenth Centuries.' *Law and History Review* 9(1991): 221–67.
Blomley, Nicholas K. 'The Business of Mobility: Geography, Liberalism, and the Charter of Rights.' *Canadian Geographer* 36(1992): 236–56.
Chalmers, John. 'Social Stratification in the Fur Trade.' *Alberta Historical Review*, (Winter 1969): 10–20.
Chunn, Dorothy. 'Regulating the Poor in Ontario: From Police Courts to Family Courts.' *Canadian Journal of Family Law* 6(1987): 85–102.
'Rehabilitating Deviant Families through Family Courts: the Birth of "Socialized" Justice in Ontario, 1920–1940.' *International Journal of the Sociology of Law* 16(1988): 137–58.
Coombe, Rosemary J. '"The Most Disgusting, Disgraceful and Inequitous Proceeding in Our Law": the Action for Breach of Promise in Marriage.' *University of Toronto Law Journal* 38(1988): 64–116.
Ditton, Jason. 'Perks, Pilferage, and the Fiddle: The Historical Structure of Invisible Wages.' *Historical Journal* 22(1979): 825–60.
Dubinsky, Karen, and Franca Iacovetta. 'Murder, Womanly Virtue, and Motherhood: The Case of Angelina Napolitano.' *Canadian Historical Review* 72(1991): 505–31.
Foster, Hamar. 'Long-Distance Justice: The Criminal Jurisdiction of the Canadian Courts West of the Canadas.' *American Journal of Legal History* 34(1990): 1–48.
- 'Sins against the Great Spirit: The Law, the Hudson's Bay Company and the Mackenzie's River Murders.' *Criminal Justice History* 11(1990): 23–76.
- 'Mutiny on the *Beaver*: Law and Authority in the Fur Trade "Navy," 1835–1840.' *Manitoba Law Journal* 20(1991): 15–45.
Francis, Clinton. 'Practice, Strategy, and Institution: Debt Collection in the English Common Law Courts.' *Northwestern University Law Review* 80(1986): 807–955.
Galanter, Marc. 'Why the "Haves" Come Out Ahead: Speculations on the Limits of Legal Change.' *Law and Society Review* 9(1974): 95–160.
Galbraith, John S. 'James Edward Fitzgerald versus the Hudson's Bay Company: The Founding of Vancouver Island.' *British Columbia Historical Quarterly* 16(1952): 191–207.

Gough, Barry M. 'Keeping British Columbia British: The Law and Order Question on the Gold Mining Frontier.' *Huntington Library Quarterly* 38(1974–75): 269–80.
- 'The Character of the British Columbia Frontier.' *BC Studies* 32(1976–7): 28–40.
- 'Send a Gunboat! Checking Slavery and Controlling Liquor Traffic among the Coast Indians of British Columbia in the 1860s.' *Pacific Northwest Quarterly* 69(1978): 159–68.
- 'Corporate Farming on Vancouver Island, 1846-1857.' *Canadian Papers in Rural History* 4(1984): 72–82.
Green, Rayna. 'The Pochahontas Perplex: The Image of Indian Women in American Culture.' *Massachusetts Review* 16 (1975): 698–714.
Handler, Joel F. 'Postmodernism, Protest, and the New Social Movements.' *Law and Society Review* 26(1992): 697–731.
Harris, Angela P. 'Race and Essentialism in Feminist Legal Theory.' *Stanford Law Review* 42(1990):581–616.
Harris, Cole. 'Industry and the Good Life around Idaho Peak.' *Canadian Historical Review* 66(1985): 315–43.
Hewlett, Edward S. 'The Chilcotin Uprising of 1864.' *BC Studies* 19(1973): 50–72.
Hibbitts, Bernard J. 'Progress and Principle: The Legal Thought of Sir John Beverley Robinson.' *McGill Law Journal* 34(1989): 454–529.
Horowitz, Gad. 'Conservatism, Liberalism and Socialism in Canada: An Interpretation.' *Canadian Journal of Economics and Political Science* 32(1966): 147–71.
Howes, David. 'Property, God, and Nature in the Thought of Sir John Beverley Robinson.' *McGill Law Journal* 30(1985): 365–13.
Innes, Joanna, and John Styles. 'The Crime Wave: Recent Writing on Crime and Criminal Justice in Eighteenth-Century Britain.' *Journal of British Studies* 25(1986): 395–9.
Ireland, Willard E. 'The Appointment of Governor Blanshard.' *British Columbia Historical Quarterly* 8(1944): 213–26.
- 'Gold Rush Days in Victoria, 1858–1859.' *British Columbia Historical Quarterly* 12 (1948): 231–46.
Johnson, Patricia M. 'McCreight and the Bench.' *British Columbia Historical Quarterly* 12 (1948): 211–29.
- 'McCreight and the Law.' *British Columbia Historical Quarterly* 12(1948): 127–49.
Joyce, Patrick. 'History and Post-Modernism.' *Past and Present* 133(1991): 204–209.
Kasirer, Nicholas. 'Canada's Criminal Law Codificiation Viewed and Reviewed.' *McGill Law Journal* 35(1990): 841–79.
Kelly, Catriona. 'History and Post-Modernism.' *Past and Present* 133(1991): 209–13.
Kolish, Evelyn. 'Some Aspects of Civil Litigation in Lower Canada, 1785–1825: Towards the Use of Court Records for Canadian Social History.' *Canadian Historical Review* 70(1989): 337–65.

- 'Imprisonment for Debt in Lower Canada, 1791–1840.' *McGill Law Journal* 32(1987): 602–35.
Lamb, W. Kaye. 'Early Lumbering on Vancouver Island, part I, 1844–1855.' *British Columbia Historical Quarterly* 2(1938): 31–53.
- 'The Governorship of Richard Blanshard.' *British Columbia Historical Quarterly* 14(1950): 1–40.
Landsman, Stephan. 'The Rise of the Contentious Spirit: Adversary Procedure in Eighteenth-Century England.' *Cornell Law Review* 75(1990): 498–609.
Langbein, John. 'The Criminal Trial before the Lawyers.' *University of Chicago Law Review* 50(1983): 1–136.
Linebaugh, Peter, 'Karl Marx, the Theft of Wood, and Working Class Composition: A Contribution to the Current Debate.' *Crime and Social Justice* 6 (1976): 5–16.
- '(Marxist) Social History and (Conservative) Legal History: A Reply to Professor Langbein.' *New York University Law Review* 60(1985): 212–43.
Loo, Tina. 'Dan Cranmer's Potlatch: Law as Coercion, Symbol, and Rhetoric, 1884–1951.' *Canadian Historical Review* 73(1992): 125–65.
McCallum, Margaret E. 'Keeping Women in Their Place: The Minimum Wage in Canada, 1910–25.' *Labour/le travail* 17(1986): 29–56.
McDonald, R.A.J. Review of Kay J. Anderson, *Vancouver's Chinatown. Labour/Le Travail* 30 (1982): 279–82.
McKelvie, B.A., and Willard E. Ireland. 'The Victoria Voltigeurs.' *British Columbia Historical Quarterly* 20(1956): 221–39.
Mackie, Richard, 'The Colonization of Vancouver Island, 1849–1858.' *BC Studies* 96 (1992–3): 3–40.
Marquis, Greg. 'Anti-Lawyer Sentiment in Mid-Victorian New Brunswick.' *University of New Brunswick Law Journal* 36 (1987): 163–74.
Morton, Desmond. 'Cavalary or Police? Keeping the Peace on Two Adjacent Frontiers.' *Journal of Canadian Studies* 12(1977): 27–37.
Mossman, Mary Jane. 'Feminism and the Legal Method: The Difference It Makes.' *Australian Journal of Law and Society* 3(1986): 30–52.
Mouat, A.N. 'Notes on the "Norman Morison."' *British Columbia Historical Quarterly* 3(1939): 203–14.
Ormsby, Margaret. 'Some Irish Figures of Colonial Days.' *British Columbia Historical Quarterly* 14(1951): 61–82.
Pettit, Sydney. 'The Trials and Tribulations of Edward Edwards Langford.' *British Columbia Historical Quarterly* 17(1953): 5–40.
Reid, Robie L. 'John Nugent: The Impertinent Envoy.' *British Columbia Historical Quarterly* 8(1944): 53–71.
Risk, R.C.B. 'The Law and the Economy in Mid-Nineteenth-Century Ontario.' *University of Toronto Law Journal* 27(1977): 403–38.

Shearing, Clifford D. 'Decriminalizing Criminology: Reflections on the Literal and Tropological Meaning of the Term.' *Canadian Journal of Criminology* 31(1989): 169–78.
Slater, G. Hollis. 'Rev. Robert John Staines: Pioneer, Priest, Pedagogue and Political Agitator.' *British Columbia Historical Quarterly* 14(1950): 187–240.
Smith, Dorothy Blakey. '"Poor Gaggin": Irish Misfit in the Colonial Service.' *BC Studies* 32(1976–7): 41–63.
– 'The Journal of Arthur Thomas Bushby, 1858–1859.' *British Columbia Historical Quarterly* 21 (1957–8): 83–198.
Spiegel, Gabrielle M. 'History, Historicism, and the Social Logic of the Text.' *Speculum* 65(1990): 59–86.
– 'History and Post-Modernism.' *Past and Present* 135(1992): 194–208.
Stone, Lawrence. 'History and Post-Modernism.' *Past and Present* 131(1991): 217–18.
'History and Post-Modernism.' *Past and Present* 135(1992): 184–94.
Thompson, E.P. 'The Moral Economy of the English Crowd in the Eighteenth Century.' *Past and Present* 50(1971): 76–136.
'"Rough Music": Le Charivari anglais.' *Annales E.S.C.* 27(1972): 285–312.
Tobias, John L. 'Protection, Civilization, Assimilation: An Outline History of Canada's Indian Policy.' *Western Canadian Journal of Anthropology* 6(1976): 13–30.
Tucker, Eric. 'Making the Workplace "Safe" in Capitalism: The Enforcement of Factory Legislation in Nineteenth-Century Ontario.' *Labour/le Travail* 21(1988): 45–85.
West, Robin. 'Jurisprudence and Gender.' *University of Chicago Law Review* 55(1988): 1–72.
Wheat, Carl I. 'Ned the Ubiquitous: The Further Narrative of Edward McGowan.' *California Historical Society Quarterly* 6(1927): 3–36.
White, Hester E. 'John Carmichael Haynes: Pioneer of the Okanagan and Kootenay.' *British Columbia Historical Quarterly* 4(1940): 183–201.
Wright, Barry. 'The Ideological Dimensions of the Law in Upper Canada: The Treason Proceedings of 1838.' *Criminal Justice History* 10(1989): 131–78.

SECONDARY SOURCES: BOOKS

Anderson, Kay J. *Vancouver's Chinatown: Racial Discourse in Canada, 1875-1980.* Montreal and Kingston: McGill-Queen's University Press, 1990.
Arens, W. *The Man-Eating Myth: Anthropology and Anthropophagi.* New York: Oxford University Press, 1979.
Atiyah, P.S. *The Rise and Fall of Freedom of Contract*, Oxford: Clarendon Press, 1979.
– *An Introduction to the Law of Contract*, 4th ed. Oxford: Clarendon Press, 1989.
Axtell, James. *The European and the Indian: Essays in the Ethnohistory of Colonial North America.* New York: Oxford University Press, 1981.

Backhouse, Constance B. *Petticoats and Prejudice: Women and the Law in Nineteenth-Century Canada.* Toronto: The Osgoode Society 1991.
Baker, A.R.H., and Mark Billinge, eds. *Period and Place: Research Methods in Historical Geography.* Cambridge: Cambridge University Press, 1982.
Baker, J.H. *An Introduction to English Legal History,* 2d ed. London: Butterworths, 1983.
Bakken, Gordon M. *The Development of Law on the Rocky Mountain Frontier: Civil Law and Society.* Westport: Greenwood Press, 1983.
Bancroft, Hubert Howe. *Popular Tribunals.* San Francisco: The History Company, 1887.
Banwell, Selwyn. *A Frontier Judge.* Toronto: Rous and Mann, 1938.
Barman, Jean. *The West beyond the West: A History of British Columbia.* Toronto: University of Toronto Press, 1991.
Beattie, J.M. *Crime and the Courts in England, 1660–1800.* New Jersey: Princeton University Press, 1986.
Bercuson David J., and Louis A. Knafla, eds. *Law and Society in Canada in Historical Perspective.* Calgary: University of Calgary Press, 1979.
Bolt, Christine. *Victorian Attitudes to Race.* London: Routledge, 1971.
Bowen, Lynne. *Three-Dollar Dreams.* Lantzville, BC: Oolichan Books, 1987.
Brown, Desmond H. *The Canadian Criminal Code of 1892.* Toronto: University of Toronto Press, 1989.
Brown, Jennifer S.H. *Strangers in Blood: Fur Trade Families in Indian Country.* Vancouver: University of British Columbia Press, 1980.
Brown, Lorne, and C. Brown. *An Unauthorized History of the RCMP.* Toronto: James Lorimer, 1973.
Brown, Richard Maxwell. *Strain of Violence: Historical Studies of American Violence and Vigilantism.* New York: Oxford University Press, 1975.
– *No Duty to Retreat: Violence and Values in American Society.* New York: Oxford University Press, 1992.
Burchell, Graham, Colin Gordon, and Peter Miller, eds. *The Foucault Effect: Studies in Governmentality with Two Lectures by and an Interview with Michel Foucault.* Chicago: University of Chicago Press, 1991.
Burke, Peter. *History and Social Theory.* Ithaca: Cornell University Press, 1993.
Cail, Robert. *Land, Man, and the Law: The Disposal of Crown Lands in British Columbia, 1871–1913.* Vancouver: University of British Columbia Press, 1974.
Chambers, Lucy B. *The Court House of New Westminster.* Victoria: British Columbia Heritage Trust, 1980.
Clanchy, M.T. *From Memory to Written Record: England, 1066–1307.* London: Blackwell, 1979.
Clifford, James, and George E. Marcus, eds. *Writing Culture: The Poetics and Politics of Ethnography.* Berkeley: University of California Press, 1986.

Coleman, Peter J. *Debtors and Creditors in America: Insolvency, Imprisonment for Debt and Bankruptcy, 1607–1900*. Madison: University of Wisconsin Press, 1974.
Coser, Lewis A. *The Function of Social Conflict*. Glencoe: Free Press, 1956.
Creese, Gillian, and Veronica Strong-Boag, eds. *British Columbia Reconsidered: Essays on Women*. Vancouver: Press Gang, 1992.
Crowe, Arthur Fleming. *Mines and Mining Laws of British Columbia*. Calgary: Burrows and Company, 1930.
Cullen, Mary K. *The History of Fort Langley*. Ottawa: Parks Canada, Historic Parks and Sites Branch, 1979.
Davis, Natalie Zemon. *Society and Culture in Early Modern France*. Stanford: Stanford University Press, 1975.
Dickinson, John. *Justice et justiciables: La Procédure civile à la prévôté de Québec, 1667–1759*. Laval: Les Presses de l'Université Laval, 1982.
Dworkin, Ronald. *Law's Empire*. Cambridge: Belknap Press, 1986.
Eagleton, Terry. *Literary Theory: An Introduction*. Minneapolis: University of Minnesota Press, 1983.
– *Ideology: An Introduction*. London: Verso, 1991.
Emsley, Clive. *Crime and Society in England, 1750-1900*. London: Longmans, 1987.
Errington, Jane. *The Lion, the Eagle and Upper Canada: a Developing Colonial Ideology*. Montreal and Kingston: McGill-Queen's University Press, 1987.
Fairburn, Miles. *The Ideal Society and Its Enemies: The Foundations of Modern New Zealand Society*. Auckland: Auckand University Press, 1989.
Faller, Lincoln B. *Turned to Account: The Forms and Functions of Criminal Biography in Late Seventeenth and Early Eighteenth Century England*. Cambridge: Cambridge University Press, 1987.
Firth, Edith, ed. *Profiles of a Province*. Toronto: Ontario Historical Society, 1967.
Fisher, Robin. *Contact and Conflict: Indian-European Relations in British Columbia, 1774–1890*. Vancouver: University of British Columbia Press, 1977.
Fitzgeorge-Parker, Ann. *Gold Rush Justice*. Toronto: Burns and MacEachern, 1968.
Fitzpatrick, Peter, ed. *Dangerous Supplements: Resistance and Renewal in Jurisprudence*. London: Pluto Press, 1991.
Flaherty, David H., ed. *Essays in the History of Canadian Law*, volumes 1 and 2. Toronto: The Osgoode Society, 1981, 1983.
Foster, Hamar. *English Law, British Columbia: Establishing Legal Institutions West of the Rockies*. Winnipeg: University of Manitoba Canadian Legal History Project, Working Paper Series, 1992.
Foucault, Michel. *Discipline and Punish: The Birth of the Penitentiary*. Harmondsworth: Penguin, 1979.
Francis, Daniel. *The Imaginary Indian: The Image of the Indian in Canadian Culture*. Vancouver: Pulp Press, 1992.

Fraser, Joan M. *Judges of British Columbia to 1957: A Sourcebook*. Victoria: University of Victoria Faculty of Law, Occasional Paper no. 1, 1984.

Geertz, Clifford. *Local Knowledge: Further Essays in Interpretive Anthropology*. New York: Basic Books, 1983.

Gibson, James R. *Farming the Frontier: The Agricultural Opening of the Oregon Country*. Vancouver: University of British Columbia Press, 1985.

Giddens, Anthony. *A Contemporary Critique of Historical Materialism, Volume One: Power, Property, and the State*. London and Basingstoke: Macmillan, 1981.

– *The Nation State and Violence: Volume Two of a Contemporary Critique of Historical Materialism*. Cambridge: Polity Press, 1985.

Gilligan, Carol. *In a Different Voice: Psychological Theory and Women's Development*. Cambridge: Harvard University Press, 1982.

Goodrich, Peter. *Reading the Law: A Critical Introduction to Legal Method and Techniques*. Oxford: Blackwell, 1986.

Gough, Barry M. *Gunboat Frontier: British Maritime Authority and the Northwest Coast Indians*. Vancouver: University of British Columbia Press, 1984.

Graham, Hugh Davis, and Ted Robert Gurr. *Violence in America: Historical and Comparative Perspectives*, rev. ed. Beverly Hills: Sage, 1979.

Gray, John. *Liberalism*. Milton Keynes: Open University Press, 1986.

Green, Leslie. *The Authority of the State*. Oxford: Oxford University Press, 1988.

Greer, Allan, and Ian Radforth, ed. *Colonial Leviathan: State Formation in Mid-Nineteenth Century Canada*. Toronto: University of Toronto Press, 1991.

Hall, Roger, William Westphall, and Laurel Sefton McDowell, eds. *Patterns of the Past: Interpreting Ontario's History*. Toronto: Dundurn Press, 1988.

Halpenny, Frances G., and Jean Hamelin, eds. *Dictionary of Canadian Biography*. Toronto: University of Toronto Press, 1966–91.

Hardin, Herschel. *A Nation Unaware: A Canadian Economic History*. North Vancouver: J.J. Douglas, 1974.

Hartz, Louis. *The Founding of New Societies: Studies in the History of the United States, Latin America, Canada, and Australia*. New York: Harcourt Brace and World, 1964.

Hay, Douglas, Peter Linebaugh, John G. Rule, E.P. Thompson, and Cal Winslow, eds. *Albion's Fatal Tree: Crime and Society in Eighteenth-Century England*. London: Allen Lane, 1975.

Howay, F.W. *The Early History of the Fraser River Mines*. Victoria: Charles Banfield, 1926.

Hurst, J. Willard. *Law and the Conditions of Freedom in Nineteenth-Century United States*. Madison: University of Wisconsin Press, 1956.

Hutchins, F.G. *The Illusion of Permanence: British Imperialism in India*. Princeton: Princeton University Press, 1967.

Iacovetta, Franca, and Mariana Valverde, eds. *Gender Conflicts: New Essays in Women's History*. Toronto: University of Toronto Press, 1992.

Innis, Harold A. *The Fur Trade in Canada: An Introduction to Canadian Economic History*, rev. ed. Toronto: University of Toronto Press, 1956.

Isaac, Rhys. *The Transformation of Virginia, 1740–1790*. Chapel Hill: University of North Carolina Press, 1982.

Jaggar, Alison. *Feminist Politics and Human Nature*. Totowa: Rowman and Allanheld, 1983.

Jennings, Francis. *The Invasion of America: Indians, Colonialism, and the Cant of Conquest*. Chapel Hill: University of North Carolina Press, 1975.

Katz, Stanley, and John M. Murrin, eds. *Colonial America: Essays in Politics and Social Development*, 3d ed. Third Edition. New York: Knopf, 1983.

Kershaw, Adrian, and John Spittle. *The Bute Inlet Route: Alfred Waddington's Road, 1862–64*. Kelowna: Okanagan College, 1978.

Kidder, Robert J. *Connecting Law and Society: An Introduction to Research and Theory*. Englewood: Prentice-Hall, 1983.

Knafla, Louis A. *Crime and Criminal Justice in Europe and Canada*. Waterloo: University of Waterloo Press, 1981.

Knafla, Louis A., ed. *Law and Justice in a New Land: Essays in the Legal History of Western Canada*. Calgary: University of Calgary Press, 1985.

Konig, David Thomas. *Law and Society in Puritan Massachusetts: Essex County, 1629–1692*. Chapel Hill: University of North Carolina Press, 1979.

Kymlicka, Will. *Liberalism, Community and Culture*. New York: Oxford University Press, 1989.

Landsman, Stephan. *The Adversary System: A Description and Defense*. Washington: American Enterprise Institute for Public Policy, 1984.

Li, Peter S. *The Chinese in Canada*. New York: Oxford University Press, 1988.

Linebaugh, Peter. *The London Hanged: Crime and Civil Society in the Eighteenth Century*. London: Allen Lane, 1992.

Lipset, Seymour Martin. *Continental Divide: the Values and Institutions of the United States and Canada*. London: Routledge, 1990.

Lockridge, Kenneth. *A New England Town: The First Hundred Years: Dedham, Massachusetts, 1636–1736*, expanded ed. New York: Basic Books, 1985.

McCalla, Douglas. *The Upper Canada Trade, 1834–1872: A Study of the Buchanans' Business*. Toronto: University of Toronto Press, 1979.

McGowan, Edward. *McGowan v. the California Vigilantes*. Oakland, California: Biobooks, 1941 (first published 1857).

McGrath, Roger. *Gunfighters, Highwaymen, and Vigilantes*. Berkeley: University of California Press, 1984.

MacKinnon, Catharine A. *Feminism Unmodified: Discourses in Life and Law.* Cambridge: Harvard University Press, 1987.

McLaren, John, Hamar Foster, and Chet Orloff, eds., *Law for the Elephant, Law for the Beaver: Essays in the Legal History of the North American West.* Regina: Canadian Plains Research Center, 1992.

Macleod, R.C. *The Northwest Mounted Police and Law Enforcement, 1873–1905.* Toronto: University of Toronto Press, 1975.

MacRae, Marion, and Anthony Adamson. *Cornerstones of Order: Courthouses and Town Halls of Ontario, 1784–1914.* Toronto: University of Toronto Press, 1983.

Mann, Bruce. *Neighbors and Strangers: Law and Community in Early Connecticut.* Chapel Hill: University of North Carolina Press, 1987.

Mason, Peter. *Deconstructing America: Representations of the Other.* London: Routledge, 1990.

Miles, Robert. *Racism.* London: Routledge, 1989.

Miller, E.F. *Ned McGowan's War.* Toronto: Burns and McEachern, 1968.

Mills, David. *The Idea of Loyalty in Upper Canada, 1784–1850.* Montreal and Kingston: McGill-Queen's University Press, 1988.

Mills, Edward. *The Early Court Houses of British Columbia.* Ottawa: Parks Canada, Manuscript Report Series no. 288, 1977.

Morice, A.G. *The History of the Northern Interior of British Columbia.* London: J. Lane, 1906; reprinted Smithers: Interior Stationery, 1978.

Myers, John Myers. *San Francisco's Reign of Terror.* New York: Doubleday, 1966.

Nelson, William E. *Dispute and Conflict Resolution in Plymouth County, Massachusetts, 1725–1825.* Chapel Hill: University of North Carolina Press, 1981.

Norcross, E. Blanche. *The Company on the Coast.* Nanaimo: Nanaimo Historical Society, 1983.

Ormsby, Margaret. *British Columbia: A History.* Toronto: Macmillan, 1958.

Pagden, Anthony. *The Fall of Natural Man: The American Indian and the Origins of Comparative Ethnology.* Cambridge: Cambridge University Press, 1982.

– *European Encounters with the New World from the Renaissance to Romanticism.* New Haven: Yale University Press, 1993.

Palmer, Bryan D. *Descent into Discourse: The Reification of Language in the Writing of Social History.* Philadelphia: Temple University Press, 1990.

Poovey, Mary. *Uneven Developments: The Ideological Work of Gender in Mid-Victorian England.* Chicago: University of Chicago Press, 1988.

Pue, W. Wesley, and Barry Wright, eds. *Canadian Perspectives on Law and Society: Issues in Legal History.* Ottawa: Carleton University Press, 1988.

Rasporich, A.W., and H.C. Klassen, eds. *Frontier Calgary.* Calgary: McClelland and Stewart West, 1979.

Reid, John Phillip. *Law for the Elephant: Property and Social Behavior on the Overland Trail*. San Marino: Huntington Library, 1980.
Roberts, Simon. *Order and Dispute: An Introduction to Legal Anthropology*. New York: St Martin's Press, 1977.
Ross, Rupert. *Dancing with a Ghost: Exploring Indian Reality*. Markham: Octopus Books, 1992.
Roy, Patricia A. *A White Man's Province: British Columbia Politicians and Chinese and Japanese Immigrants, 1858–1914*. Vancouver: University of British Columbia Press, 1989.
Rubin, G.R., and David Sugarman, eds. *Law, Economy, and Society, 1750–1914: Essays in the History of English Law*. Abingdon: Professional Books, 1984.
Said, Edward. *Orientalism*. New York: Vintage Books, 1978.
Shanks, Neville. *Waddington: A Biography of Alfred Penderill [sic] Waddington*. Port Hardy: North Island Gazette, 1975.
Shinn, Charles Howard. *Mining Camps: A Study in American Frontier Government*. New York, 1965 (first published 1884).
Slatta, Richard W. *Cowboys of the Americas*. New Haven: Yale University Press, 1990.
Smart, Carol. *Feminism and the Power of Law*. London: Routledge, 1989.
– ed. *Regulating Womenhood: Historical Essays on Marriage, Motherhood, and Sexuality*. London: Routledge, 1991.
Snitow, Ann, Christine Stansell, and Sharon Thompson, eds., *Powers of Desire: The Politics of Sexuality*. New York: Monthly Review Press, 1983.
Steele, I.K. *The English Atlantic, 1675–1740: An Exploration in Communication and Community*. Oxford: Oxford University Press, 1986.
Stewart, Gordon T. *The Origins of Canadian Politics: A Comparative Approach*. Vancouver: University of British Columbia Press, 1985.
Taylor, Arthur J. *Laissez-Faire and State Intervention in Nineteenth-Century Britain*. London: Macmillan, 1972.
Taylor, Charles. *The Malaise of Modernity*. Toronto: Anansi, 1992.
Tennant, Paul. *Aboriginal Peoples and Politics: The Indian Land Question in British Columbia, 1849–1989*. Vancouver: University of British Columbia Press, 1990.
Thompson, E.P. *Whigs and Hunters: The Origins of the Black Act*. London: Allen Lane, 1975.
Tippett, Maria. *Emily Carr: A Biography*. New York: Oxford University Press, 1979.
Torgovnick, Marianna. *Gone Primitive: Savage Intellects, Modern Lives*. Chicago: University of Chicago Press, 1990.
Torrance, Judy M. *Public Violence in Canada, 1867–1982*. Montreal and Kingston: McGill-Queen's University Press, 1986.

Trachtenberg, Alan. *The Incorporation of America: Culture and Society in the Gilded Age*. New York: Hill and Wang, 1982.

Treitel, G.H. *The Law of Contract*, 7th ed. London: Stevens and Sons, 1987.

Trimble, W.J. *The Mining Advance into the Inland Empire*. Madison: Bulletin of the University of Wisconsin no. 638, 1914.

Valverde, Mariana. *The Age of Light, Soap, and Water: Moral Reform in English Canada, 1885–1925*. Toronto: McClelland and Stewart, 1990.

Van Holthoon, Frits, and David R. Olson, eds. *Common Sense: The Foundations of Social Science*. Lanham: University Press of America, 1987.

Van Kirk, Sylvia. *'Many Tender Ties': Women in Fur Trade Society, 1670–1870*. Winnipeg: Watson and Dwyer, 1980.

Verchere, David R. *A Progression of Judges: A History of the Supreme Court of British Columbia*. Vancouver: University of British Columbia Press, 1988.

Walden, Keith. *Visions of Order: The Mounties in Symbol and Myth*. Toronto: Butterworths, 1980.

Walker, David M. *The Oxford Companion to the Law*. Oxford: Clarendon Press, 1980.

Ward, W. Peter. *White Canada Forever: Popular Attitudes and Public Policy toward Orientals in British Columbia*. Montreal and Kingston: McGill-Queen's University Press, 1978.

Ward, W. Peter, and Robert A.J. McDonald, eds. *British Columbia: Historical Readings*. Vancouver: Douglas and McIntyre, 1981.

White, James Boyd. *The Legal Imagination*. Chicago: University of Chicago Press, 1973.

– *Heracles' Bow: Essays on the Rhetoric and Poetics of the Law*. Madison: University of Wisconsin Press, 1986.

Wiener, Martin J. *Reconstructing the Criminal: Culture, Law, and Policy in England, 1830–1914*. Cambridge: Cambridge University Press, 1990.

Williams, David R. *'... The Man for a New Country': Sir Matthew Baillie Begbie*. Sidney: Gray Publishers, 1977.

Williams, Donovan. *The India Office, 1858–1869*. Hoshiarpur: Vishveshvaranand Vedic Research Institute, 1983.

Wolch, Jennifer, and Michael Dear, eds. *The Power of Geography: How Territory Shapes Social Life*. Boston: Unwin Hyman, 1989.

Wright, Richard Thomas. *Discover Barkerville*. Vancouver: Maclean Hunter, 1984.

Wrong, Dennis Hume. *Power: Its Forms, Bases, and Uses*. Oxford: Basil Blackwell, 1979.

Wunder, John R. *Inferior Courts, Superior Justice: A History of the Justices of the Peace on the Northwest Frontier, 1853–1889*. Westport: Greenwood Press, 1979.

Wynn, Graeme. *Timber Colony: A Historical Geography of Early Nineteenth-Century New Brunswick*. Toronto: University of Toronto Press, 1980.

Zainaldin, Jamil. *Law in Antebellum Society: Legal Change and Economic Expansion.* New York: Borzoi Books, 1983.

Zukin, Sharon. *Landscapes of Power: From Detroit to Disneyworld.* Berkeley: University of California Press, 1991.

SECONDARY SOURCES: THESES

Antak, Ivan E. 'John Robson, British Columbian.' University of Victoria, MA thesis, 1972.

Bescoby, Isobel, M.L. 'Some Aspects of Society in the Cariboo from its Discovery Until 1877.' University of British Columbia, BA essay, 1932.

– 'Some Social Aspects of the American Mining Advance into the Cariboo and Kootenay.' University of British Columbia, MA thesis, 1935.

Coyle, Brian Charles. 'Problems of the Puget's Sound Agricultural Company on Vancouver Island, 1847–1857.' Simon Fraser University, MA thesis, 1977.

Farr, David M.L. 'The Origin of the Judicial Systems in the Colonies of Vancouver Island and British Columbia, 1849–1871.' University of British Columbia, BA essay, 1944.

Hewlett, Edward Sleigh. 'Chilcotin Uprising: A Study of Indian-White Relations in Nineteenth Century British Columbia.' University of British Columbia, MA thesis, 1972.

Johnson, Patricia Mary. 'John Foster McCreight: First Premier of British Columbia' University of British Columbia, MA thesis, 1947.

Mackie, Richard Somerset. 'Colonial Land, Indian Labour and Company Capital: The Economy of Vancouver Island, 1849–1858.' University of Victoria, MA thesis, 1984.

Mikkelsen, Phyllis Margaret. 'Land Settlement Policy on the Mainland of British Columbia, 1858–1874.' University of British Columbia, MA thesis, 1950.

Pettit, Sydney G. 'Matthew Baillie Begbie, Judge of B.C., 1858–1866.' University of British Columbia, MA thesis, 1945.

Reid, James Gordon. 'John Robson and the British Columbian.' University of British Columbia, MA thesis, 1950.

Underwood, Morley Arthur. 'Governor Douglas and the Miners, 1858–1859.' University of British Columbia, BA essay, 1974.

Wrinch, Leonard A. 'Land Policy of the Colony of Vancouver Island, 1849–1866.' University of British Columbia, MA essay, 1932.

Index

agency: law of 101–2
American: miners 54, 57; as Other 150–1; violence 56
Anderson, Kay J. 10
Atiyah, Patrick 100
Aurora v. Davis (1866) 104, 116–17
authority: conflict of 35–53, 108–9; definition 93–5; establishing 56–7; foundations of 93–112, 114, 124–5; limits of 113–33; standards of 99-100; textual 100, 109

Barman, Jean 15
Beaver, Herbert 18, 25
Begbie, Matthew: appointment 57–8; attitudes towards legal texts 107–8; on contract law 101–2; in *Cranford* 14, 94–8; and juries 71, 106, 116–17, 128; and lawyers 97, 107–8; and mining disputes 118–19, 122, 130–1; responsibilities 107; understanding of law 114
Blanshard, Richard 36–7, 41. *See also* Fort Rupert
Borealis v. Watson (1865) 104, 115–16
British Columbia: courts 54-72; economy 75, 79–80, 91; formation 54; history 15–16; settlement 75; social relations 89–90
Bute Inlet Massacre: motivations for 142; representations of 139–41; response to 139, 149; sentencing of perpetrators 153–4; significance of 146–7, 155–6; violence of 141. *See also* Chilcotin; homicides
Bute Inlet road 137
Bute Inlet Wagon Road Company 137, 138

Cameron, David 35, 41, 43–4, 46–7, 88, 99. *See also* Douillet, Emanuel; petitions; *R. v. Staines*; Vancouver Island
Canadian Company 118, 119, 120–1. *See also Canadian Company v. Grouse Creek Flume Company*; Grouse Creek Flume Company; Grouse Creek War
Canadian Company v. Grouse Creek Flume Company (1867) 14, 121–2. *See also* Canadian Company; Grouse Creek Flume Company; Grouse Creek War
cannibalism: as defining savagery 144. *See also* Bute Inlet Massacre; Chilcotin; savagery, discourse of

character: in decision-making 105, 107
Chilcotin: attack on Alexander Macdonald party 138–9; attack on Bute Inlet road party 138; relations with whites 138; representations of 139, 145–6, 148; surrender of 139, 153–4. *See also* Bute Inlet Massacre; cannibalism
civil trials 103–5
common sense: as basis of law 125–7
contract: between Cranford and Wright 95, 96–7; law 100–2
County Court (British Columbia): actions 77–80, 82–5; decisions 85–7; procedure 77–9
County Court judges: qualifications of 93–4
court houses: in British Columbia 67
court orders: execution of 87–8
courts (British Columbia): business of 75–7; Chancery 115–16, 126; County or Small Debts 60–1, 68–9; and economy 77–8; Gold Commissioner's or Mining 61; structure 54–72; Supreme 57–8, 60, 61–4, 66, 67; and union of the colonies 61–4. *See also* County Court (British Columbia); Mining Court
courts (Vancouver Island): Inferior Court of Civil Justice 43; petty sessions 41; structuring of 35; Supreme Court 41, 42–3, 61–4. *See also* justices of the peace; *Webster* case
Cox, William George 76, 104, 113, 116, 125–7, 139. *See also* petitions
Cranford, John 88, 95–6
Cranford, Robert 88, 95–7
Cranford v. Wright 14, 93–112
credit and economic development 76, 91; extent of 60–1, 76–7
Creighton, Donald 15

crime: and identity 135

debt: extent of 80; imprisonment for 88, 100, 102–3; nature of 60, 91
discourse analysis 6–8, 10, 11–12
Douglas, James: as fur trader 26, 31; as governor of British Columbia 54, 75, 84; as governor of Vancouver Island 35, 54, 57; in *R. v. Staines* 46. *See also* Cameron, David; petitions; *R. v. Staines*; Staines, Robert John
Douillet, Emanuel 45–7, 50

evidence: documentary 108

Faller, Lincoln 135
Fort Rupert 35–6
frontier 5, 16, 66–7, 114
fur trade: authority 19, 26; conditions of service 22–3; family affairs 25–6; law 18–33; sources of conflict 24–6. *See also* Hudson's Bay Company

Geertz, Clifford 127
geography: and law 57, 64, 83; and power 57, 64, 65–6
Giddens, Anthony 64
gold rush: Cariboo 80–1; formation of British Columbia 54; social relations 74–5
Gough, Barry 15
Grouse Creek Flume Company 118, 129. *See also* Canadian Company; *Canadian Company v. Grouse Creek Flume Company*; Grouse Creek War
Grouse Creek War 14, 62, 113–33. *See also* Canadian Company; *Canadian Company v. Grouse Creek Flume Company*; Grouse Creek Flume Company; Seymour, Frederick

Harkness, Robert 74, 80, 81–2
Helmcken, John Sebastian 36, 41. *See also* Fort Rupert; justices of the peace
H.M. Curry v. Forest Rose Company (1865) 104
homicides: Bute Inlet Massacre 134–56; fur trade 23
Hudson's Bay Company: role of bailiffs 41; conflict 22, 25–6, 30, 36–7; corporate organization 26–8; labour contracts 20–1; law 18–33; post life 26, 28–31; proprietorship of Vancouver Island 34–53. *See also* Vancouver Island

Indians: Bella Bella 24; Haida 24; nature of 143–4; Newitty 36; Tsimshian 24; treatment of 148–9. *See also* Chilcotin
informal law 75
Innis, Harold 26

juries 70–1, 105–6, 128. *See also* Begbie, Matthew
justice: foundations of 159–61
justices of the peace 58–9, 68; and fur trade 20; on Vancouver Island 35, 36, 41–2. *See also* stipendiary magistrates

Klatssassin 139. *See also* Bute Inlet Massacre; Chilcotin

laissez-faire: and contract law 101, 102; and courts 64; and law 57, 71; and Vancouver Island politics 51–2. *See also* liberalism
law: and authority 13–14; British Columbia 54–72; 'Club Law' 18; control of labour 41, 51; miners customary 114; and disorder 114; and economy 4, 19, 35, 51–3, 56, 60–4, 71, 73–92, 103; and extension of state power 65; fur trade 18–33; and geography 67–71, 72; and identity 3, 4–6, 134–56; imprisonment for debt 88; informal 23–5; and justice 15, 131–3, 159–62; and laissez-faire 122–3, 129; and politics 51–3; and recognition of differences 156; and security of property 123; and social relations 100; as socially constructed 130; symbolic power of 124; Vancouver Island 34–53. *See also* British Columbia; fur trade; geography; Hudson's Bay Company; justice; laissez-faire; proclamations; statutes; Vancouver Island
lawyers 14, 125
legal procedure 66–7
liberalism: and authority 99–100; and defining savagery 145; definition of 8–9; and law 3, 9, 94, 157; limits of justice 157–62
Linaker v. Ballou (1862) 104
litigation: British Columbia 73–92; meaning of 75, 82, 89–90, 91–2; nature of 59–60, 91; Vancouver Island 42

McCalla, Douglas 76
McCreight, John Foster 95, 97–9, 110
McGowan, Ned 54–5
Mann, Bruce 74
Mason, Peter 135
Miles, Robert 135
miners: American 57; attitudes towards law 114, 128–9; mobility of 89
miners' meetings 61
Mining Court (Richfield): actions 81, 83–4; decisions 87
mining laws: criticisms of 117

Ned McGowan's War 55

Needham, Joseph 62, 63, 121–2. *See also Canadian Company v. Grouse Creek Flume Company*; Grouse Creek War
Nind, Philip Henry 56, 93, 94

O'Reilly, Peter 59, 80, 118, 125–7. *See also* Grouse Creek War

Palmer, Bryan D. 11
paternalism 19, 32, 35, 56–7. *See also* authority
Perrier, George 55
petitions: anti-Cameron 38, 44–5, 47, 49–50, 51; anti-Douglas 37; anti-land laws 38, 39–41, 52; William George Cox 113–14, 127; Nicholson's 63; pro-Cameron 47–8, 49–50; Small Debts Court 60. *See also* Cameron, David; courts; Cox, William George; Vancouver Island
proclamations: gold 57; Gold Fields Act 61; Small Debts Court 60; Supreme Court 58. *See also* statutes

R. v. Robert John Staines (1854) 44–50. *See also* Douillet, Emanuel; Cameron, David; Vancouver Island
Ring, David Babington 95, 97–9, 101, 110. *See also Cranford v. Wright*; McCreight, John Foster
rule of law 151–3

Said, Edward 135
savagery, discourse of 144–5
Self and Other: relationship 135–6
Seymour, Frederick 62, 120–1. *See also* Grouse Creek War
Simpson, George 18, 22, 30
Skinner, Thomas James 41–2, 46, 47. *See also* justices of the peace; Vancouver Island; *Webster* case
Staines, Robert John 12, 44–5, 48, 88. *See also* Cameron, David; Douillet, Emanuel; *R. v. Robert John Staines*; Vancouver Island
state: and economy 57; exercise of power 65; formation 16–17; and law 16, 157; power 16–17, 159
statutes: Act for regulating the Fur Trade (1821) 20; Act of 1 & 2 George IV, c. 66, 41; Act of Union (1866) 62; bankruptcy and insolvency (1865) 69; Canada Jurisdiction Act (1803) 20; County Courts Ordinance (1866) 69–70; Courts Declaratory Ordinance (1868) 63; District Court Act (1866) 43; Gold Fields Acts 14, 88–9, 117; Jurors Act (1860) 70; Jury Act (1865) 43; Minor Offences Act (1860) 43; Sheriff's Act (1860) 71; Speedy Trials Act (1860) 70. *See also* proclamations
stipendiary magistrates 58, 68. *See also* justices of the peace
summonses, service of 77–8

Taylor on Evidence 97. *See also* texts
testimony, oral 106
texts: authority of 14; legal 110–11. *See also* authority
Trutch, Joseph 121. *See also* Grouse Creek War

Valverde, Mariana 10
Vancouver Island: colonization 38–41; courts 35; franchise 39; independent settlers 34–5, 48; justices of the peace 35; land laws 38–41; law 12, 34–53; politics 40, 48–50; social divisions 49–50. *See also* Cameron, David; courts; Douillet, Emanuel; Hudson's Bay

Company; petitions; Skinner, Thomas James; Staines, Robert John; *Webster* case
vigilantes 55
violence 55–6

Waddington, Alfred 136–7. *See also* Bute Inlet Massacre
wage labour: in gold fields 80–2
wages 84–5
Wakefield, Edward Gibbon 38–40. *See also* Vancouver Island

Webster case 42. *See also* justices of the peace; Skinner, Thomas James; Vancouver Island
Whannell, Peter Brunton 54
Wiener, Martin J. 135
women: and the gold rush 80; Native 24, 25, 142–3
Wright, Gustavus Blinn, 95–8. *See also* Begbie, Matthew; *Cranford v. Wright*
written word: as defining civility 144–5
Wynn, Graeme 76

Photo Credits

British Columbia Archives and Records Services: Cariboo Road (763, A-350), Cariboo Camel (759, A-347), Barkerville (10109, A-3786), 'Mucho Oro' Mine (1379, A-613), 'Never Sweat' Mine (761, A937), Canadian Company (13665, A-5192), Grouse Creek Expedition (63650, D-2847), Matthew Begbie (51325, C-4848), Bute Inlet Route (H-5994)